5o

Events *of the* 20th Century that Shaped
Evangelicals in America

Steve Rabey & Monte Unger

Broadman
&Holman
Publishers

Nashville, Tennessee

0–8054–2496–2

Published by Broadman & Holman Publishers, Nashville, Tennessee

Dewey Decimal Classification: 270
Subject Heading: CHURCH HISTORY

Photos courtesy of:
Billy Graham Center Museum, pp. 9, 18, 25.
University Library Basel, Switzerland, p. 13.
Christian Booksellers Association, pp. 32, 39, 47, 54, 64, 71, 82, 99, 100, 103, 109,
113, 121, 126, 129, 134, 140, 143, 145, 149, 152, 157, 160, 162, 169, 172, 173, 185, 189.
Library of Congress, pp. 52, 67, 78, 91.
Douglas Kirkland, p. 59.
World Vision, p. 63.
UPI/Corbis-Bettmann, pp. 87, 147, 156.
Focus on the Family, p. 117.
Crestwood Agency, p. 131.
National Archives, p. 150.
David Ward/World Vision, p. 164.
Promise Keepers, p. 186.

1 2 3 4 5 6 7 8 9 10   07 06 05 04 03 02

Contents

Introduction

When we were asked to shoehorn the 50 high points of 20th-century American evangelicalism between the covers of a single book, we emphatically declared that such a task was clearly impossible, and possibly even intellectually irresponsible. Then we immediately jumped at the chance to do it.

We both love history, so we welcomed the opportunity to spend time exploring this fascinating story. Even more, we both believe that history can be a vast and fascinating repository of truth and wisdom. It might be an overstatement to say that those who are ignorant of history are doomed to repeat its mistakes. But we are convinced that those who seek to live out their faith in the complex and increasingly pluralistic culture that is 21st-century America can learn much from those who attempted to do so during the previous century.

Typically, evangelicals are so pressed by the urgent demands of the present or entranced by the fantastic promises of the future that they seem oblivious to the past. If our little volume can help offset this deficit, we would be truly grateful.

Unraveling the Past

The record of the past is a rich tapestry made up of a multitude of colorful and sometimes contradictory strands. Rather than trying to detail every stitch, we have attempted to isolate and explain some of the major patterns.

The process of coming up with a list of the 50 major events, movements, personalities, and trends of the 20th century was both exciting and frustrating.

Readers will undoubtedly disagree with some of our choices, but for us, at least, there was never any question about the top 20 or 30 candidates. For example, Billy Graham, who came to national prominence in 1949, dominated the evangelical scene for the remainder of the century. And the U.S. Supreme Court's 1973 *Roe v. Wade* decision did more than anything else to inspire the evangelical activism that would become front-page news in the 1980s and 1990s.

We also found important milestones in areas some evangelical thinkers consider too far off the beaten track. A number of chapters explore the

1

powerful implications of popular culture and "material Christianity," the books, magazines, broadcasts, and musical recordings from which millions of laypeople derived not only doses of daily inspiration but also much of their theology and cultural identity. On the other hand, we don't have a single chapter about seminaries, although some of the more influential schools make cameo appearances in a number of chapters.

The primary question we asked in selecting and describing the topics covered here was a simple one: What things, for better or worse, have had the greatest impact on making evangelicals who they are today?

Writing about these matters in a way that was both reader-friendly and respectful of the complexity of the historical record was another challenge. Late-night TV show host David Letterman's "Top Ten Ways to Make Religious History More Entertaining" gave two suggestions: "Instead of parting the Red Sea, Moses drives Ford pickup into a Red Lobster"; and, "Scratch 'n' sniff plagues of Egypt." We didn't want to go that far, but we did follow a few rules of thumb that we hope will make this book accessible to laypeople and students while not driving card-carrying historians to despair.

For one, we focused on major players and events, and paid less attention to those personalities, organizations, and activities that may have been important but were less influential. We tried to summarize key developments as well as we could, but we also attempted to place these events within their broader historical and cultural contexts. And, when possible, we attempted to illustrate some lessons to be learned from the ways earlier generations of evangelicals applied their faith to the challenges of the world.

It may have been presumptuous for us to attempt all that in less than 1,400 words per chapter, but we gave it our best shot.

A Reader's Guide to This Book

Each of the following 50 chapters explores an event, personality, trend, or movement that had an important impact on the 20th century and, we believe, will continue to have a powerful impact on evangelicals in the 21st century.

Beginning with the Azusa Street revival of 1906 and continuing through the Y2K scare of January 1, 2000, the events proceed in chronological order. Reading the book from beginning to end will help you gain a sense of the flow of history, but we have written the chapters in such a way that you can pick and choose among ones that look most interesting.

Most chapters cover topics that are explored in much greater depth in numerous books and full-length studies. Therefore, each chapter concludes with our recommendations for resources that can help you learn more.

This book isn't the final word on the subject it covers, but we hope it is a helpful introduction to some of the people and events that have made American evangelicals who they are today.

—Steve Rabey and Monte Unger

1. A Mighty Wind:
Azusa Street and the Pentecostal
Movement, 1906

Still reeling from Christ's resurrection and ascension, a thoroughly discombobulated group of disciples huddled together in Jerusalem on the Jewish holiday of Pentecost. Then, without warning, all heaven broke loose. "All of them were filled with the Holy Spirit and began to speak in other tongues as the Spirit enabled them," reported the New Testament Book of Acts.

Some skeptics dismissed the antics of history's first holy rollers, saying, "They have had too much wine." But this was no drunken revel or one-time incident. Over the next twenty centuries, aspects of the spiritual energy first experienced at Pentecost would inspire believers like Hildegard of Bingen, Francis of Assisi, Joan of Arc, and Charles Wesley.

In America, the dynamic preaching of the First and Second Great Awakenings was accompanied by spontaneous outpourings of speaking in tongues, jerking, falling, dancing, laughing, and barking. The Pietistic and Holiness movements of the 19th and 20th centuries also emphasized the indwelling and work of the Spirit. By 1906, preacher A. J. Tomlinson had helped give birth to the Church of God of Prophecy, one of the earliest and largest Pentecostal denominations, now known as the Church of God, Cleveland, Tennessee.

Soon, many independent spiritual streams combined to become a raging river that would transform Christianity throughout the world, a renewal that historian Vinson Synan calls "the most important religious movement of the entire 20th century."

Signs and Wonders in Los Angeles

About the only thing William Seymour had going for him was his deep devotion to God. An African-American son of former slaves, he was poorly educated, walked with a limp, suffered from blindness in one eye, and was a poor public speaker.

3

Hungry for a deeper experience of God, Seymour encountered Holiness preacher Charles Parham, who briefly operated a Bible college near Topeka, Kansas, where there was an outbreak of tongues. Parham opened a similar college in Houston in 1905. Although segregationist Jim Crow laws prevented Seymour from registering for classes, he listened from the hallway, gradually accepting Parham's teaching that glossolalia was the external proof of the baptism of the Holy Spirit.

In early 1906, Seymour took these doctrines to a Holiness mission in Los Angeles. Rejected by the pastor there, he began teaching at a private house on Bonnie Brae Drive. After surging crowds caused the home's front porch to give way, Seymour set up shop at a dilapidated building in the city's seedy industrial area, and the Azusa Street revival was officially under way. The *Los Angeles Times* reported on the spiritual outpouring in an April 18 front-page story called "Weird Babel of Tongues":

> Breathing strange utterances and mouthing a creed which it would seem no sane mortal could understand, the newest religious sect has started in Los Angeles. Meetings are held in a tumble-down shack on Azusa Street . . . and devotees of the weird doctrine practice the most fanatical rites, preach the wildest theories, and work themselves into a state of mad excitement in their particular zeal.

Over the next three years, thousands of Christians came to Azusa Street, received the baptism of the Holy Spirit, and returned to their own churches, where they hoped to spread this "latter rain." Some were successful, and by 1914 thousands of Holiness churches had become Pentecostal congregations. Other congregations rejected these new teachings, so devotees formed new Pentecostal denominations, including the Assemblies of God, now the largest Pentecostal group in the U.S.

By 1909 the zeal at Azusa Street had cooled, but Seymour continued teaching there until his death in 1922. The church's dilapidated building was finally torn down in 1929, but the movement's influence continued to be seen far and wide.

Pioneering women preachers like Aimee Semple McPherson and Kathryn Kuhlman helped promote the Pentecostal movement. Today, a diverse group of internationally known Christian leaders like Pat Robertson, Jack Hayford, T. D. Jakes, Bill McCartney, Benny Hinn, and John Ashcroft, the U.S. Attorney General under President George W. Bush, consider themselves spiritual heirs of Azusa Street.

A Worldwide Wave

In 1965 Harvard theologian Harvey Cox boldly predicted the worldwide demise of religion and the ultimate triumph of secularism in his influential book *The Secular City.* "It will do no good to cling to our religious and metaphysical versions of Christianity in the hope that one day religion or metaphysics will once again be back," wrote Cox. By 1995, though, Cox admitted he had been dead wrong. In his introduction to *Fire from Heaven: The Rise of Pentecostal Spirituality and the Reshaping of Religion in the Twenty-first Century,* Cox wrote, "Today, it is secularity, not spirituality, that may be headed for extinction."

> ### A Century of Growth
>
> At the dawn of the 21st century, the worldwide Pentecostal and charismatic movements represent a major force, with:
>
> — over 795 million members (including more people under the age of 18 than adults, and more nonwhites than whites);
> — 15,000 new converts per day;
> — and the majority of the world's megachurches, with more than 50,000 such congregations.
> — Vinson Synan

Throughout the 20th century, Christianity around the globe was reinvigorated by the classical Pentecostal denominations that were founded early in the century, as well as by the neo-Pentecostal or charismatic movement that swept America in the 1960s (see chapter 20).

Today, about 25 percent of the world's Christians are Pentecostal or charismatic, says historian Vinson Synan, dean of the School of Divinity at Pat Robertson's Regent University. Projections developed by researcher David Barrett suggest that by 2005, Pentecostal and charismatic believers will number some 550 million, making them the largest family of Protestant Christians in the world, with a little more than half the numbers of the worldwide Catholic communion.

This growth has been accompanied by controversy, much of it focusing on "oneness" groups. These antitrinitarian, Jesus-only churches, like the United Pentecostal Church International, have been barred from joining the National Association of Evangelicals because of their unorthodox doctrines.

In addition, racism and denominationalism have caused divisions in a movement that once championed a freewheeling egalitarianism. In an effort to heal these rifts, 7,000 leaders and laypeople traveled to Atlanta for Solemn Assembly 2001, a 50-hour prayer vigil designed to rekindle Azusa Street's zeal.

Today that zeal increasingly impacts evangelical churches. Author Peter Wagner and Fuller Theological Seminary professor, coined the term "third wave" to describe the growing movement of evangelical believers who embrace the gifts of the Holy Spirit and practice a deeper, more experiential faith, but do so without changing their denominational affiliation.

Michigan homemaker Julie Frye exemplifies this "third wave." A devoted lay member of a nondenominational evangelical church in Grand Rapids, the Bible belt of Reformed Protestantism, Julie's hunger for "more of the Lord" has taken her to a Vineyard conference in Columbus, Ohio, and revivals at Toronto's Airport Vineyard church and the Brownsville Assembly of God in Pensacola, Florida. "I'm not accepting everything that is out there," she said in 1999, "but I do want everything the Lord has for me."

William Seymour and other Pentecostal pioneers would have uttered a hearty "amen."

> ## Azusa Street's "Fanatical Rites"
>
> Breathing strange utterances and mouthing a creed which it would seem no sane mortal could understand, the newest religious sect has started in Los Angeles. Meetings are held in a tumble-down shack on Azusa Street . . . and devotees of the weird doctrine practice the most fanatical rites, preach the wildest theories, and work themselves into a state of mad excitement in their particular zeal.
>
> — The *Los Angeles Times,* 1906

Resources

Vinson Synan, *The Century of the Holy Spirit: 100 Years of Pentecostal and Charismatic Renewal* (2001).

Synan, *The Holiness-Pentecostal Tradition* (1971, 1997).

Harvey Cox, *Fire from Heaven: The Rise of Pentecostal Spirituality and the Reshaping of Religion in the Twenty-first Century* (1995).

Grant Wacker, *Heaven Below: Early Pentecostals and American Culture* (2001).

Joe Creech, "Visions of Glory: The Place of the Azusa Street Revival in Pentecostal History," *Church History,* September 1996.

Edith L. Blumhofer, *Restoring the Faith: The Assemblies of God* (1993).

2. Fightin' Fundies: Saving Christianity from Modernism, 1910

Fundamentalism is a term that evokes strong and varied reactions from Christian thinkers. Historian George Marsden has called it "militantly anti-modernist Protestant evangelicalism." Joel Carpenter describes it as "a crabbed and parochial mutation of Protestant orthodoxy," and talks about the movement's "cultural alienation, sectarian behavior, and intellectual stagnation." Richard Mouw has written about how fundamentalism's legacy has left the evangelical movement with three common defects: anti-intellectualism, otherworldliness, and a separatistic spirit.

Edward John Carnell, who had been raised a fundamentalist, later received degrees from Harvard University and Boston University and served as president of Fuller Theological Seminary. His critiques of the movement written during the 1950s and 1960s called fundamentalism "orthodoxy gone cultic" and described the movement's creed as, "Believe on the Lord Jesus Christ. Don't smoke, don't go to movies . . . and you will be saved."

In order to understand the origins of fundamentalism and assess its numerous contributions to the later evangelical movement, we need to examine the changes that were transforming America in the late 19th and early 20th centuries.

A Post-Christian America

From its beginning as the first Western nation founded primarily by Protestants, America remained largely a Christian country. Founded "under God" and guided by a Constitution designed to preserve rights given by an almighty Creator, America was considered an evangelical empire until the tumultuous years after the Civil War.

But then a series of destabilizing social transformations (like industrialization) and wrenching cultural conflicts (like the debate over evolution) threatened the nation's formerly unshakable Christian consensus. So severe were the challenges of the modern age that historian Sydney Ahlstrom said they represented "the most fundamental controversy to wrack the churches since the Reformation."

Concerned that modernist ideas were eroding the very foundations of Christian belief, a growing army of conservative believers sounded the alarm. In 1910, these defenders of the faith published the first in a series of books entitled *The Fundamentals,* which would serve as a rallying cry for the emerging fundamentalist movement.

Ultimately, the movement failed to reverse the sweeping changes that raged outside the church, and even its efforts to reform America's major denominations proved largely unsuccessful. Soon, fights broke out between the movement's moderate, evangelical wing and a more militant branch that, in the words of Billy Graham, exhibited an overreliance on "a big stick approach."

At the end of the 20th century, battles still raged over the Bible, evolution, and many other issues that were first raised by the fundamentalists. Even though the movement didn't achieve many of its goals, it correctly perceived that profound changes were afoot in the world, and some of its leaders made a valiant effort to call America and its churches back to their earlier biblical moorings.

From Consensus to Chaos

Charles Darwin's *Origin of Species* was published in 1859 and claimed to present indisputable scientific evidence for evolution, but Darwin's influential book was merely one of many troubling challenges to orthodox Christian assumptions. Higher criticism subjected Scripture to scholarly investigation, leading many to question the reliability of the Bible and its God. Protestant liberalism gained a foothold in many denominations and seminaries. The science of geology wreaked havoc on long-accepted notions about both human and cosmic origins. Psychology and sociology subjected human behavior to unprecedented scientific scrutiny. And new religious movements like Spiritualism, Transcendentalism, Unitarianism, Christian Science, and Mormonism introduced religious diversity on an unprecedented scale.

Meanwhile, immigration and industrialization unleashed drastic social changes. There was an influx of Catholic and Orthodox Christians, as well as Asians and European Jews. Many of these newcomers flocked to America's growing urban centers, where they fueled the industrial revolution and created unique cultural enclaves. Urban despair and poverty helped inspire a mainline Protestant "Social Gospel" movement, which often placed greater emphasis on meeting people's physical needs rather than on securing religious conversions, while fundamentalists responded by organizing evangelistic crusades, promoting temperance, and lobbying for the passage of Sunday "blue laws."

Increasingly, fundamentalists could agree with the words of the revival hymn: "This world is not my home." And the popular Scofield Reference Bible led many to believe that human history was in its final "dispensation" and the end of the world was near.

During these desperate times, pioneering fundamentalist leaders decided something must be done.

A Movement Is Born

The roots of fundamentalism can be found in a loose network of Bible institutes, like the one founded by Dwight L. Moody in 1887, and Bible meetings, like the Niagara Bible Conference. At Niagara, believers wrote their own list of five theological fundamentals: the inerrancy of Scripture, the virgin birth and divinity of Christ, the substitutionary atonement, the bodily resurrection, and the second coming of Christ.

This is the cover of the first of *The Fundamentals* booklets, which expounded on theological "fundamentals" and covered subjects from biblical inerrancy to the efficacy of prayer in 90 articles written by numerous authors.

The Fundamentals booklets expanded on this list. Featuring articles by men like B. B. Warfield and edited by Rueben A. Torrey and others, the 12 booklets, which were published between 1910 and 1915 and are still in print, covered everything from biblical inerrancy to personal testimonials about the efficacy of prayer in 90 loosely organized articles. Thanks to the largesse of oil barons Lyman and Milton Stewart, millions of the booklets were sent to churches, seminaries, and denominational leaders. Though well-reasoned and polite in tone, the booklets did little to sway the opinions of most theological liberals. More needed to be done.

In 1919 some 6,000 conservative Christians gathered for the inaugural meeting of the World Christian Fundamentals Association, which was created to counter the more liberal Federal Council of Churches, founded in 1908. And in 1920 a group of Northern Baptists called "The Fundamentalist Fellowship" became the first to claim the name "fundamentalist" for themselves.

Appreciating the Fundamentalist Heritage

Richard Mouw and Joel Carpenter both criticize fundamentalism for its many flaws, but they also acknowledge its accomplishments.

In *The Smell of Sawdust,* Mouw writes: "Anti-intellectualism is a genuine danger, but so is a highly intellectualized packaging of Christianity. Otherworldliness is a threat to the Christian community, but so is a thoroughgoing this-worldliness. Ecclesiastical separatism is to be avoided, but we must also be on our guard against a vague inclusivism in our understanding of Christian unity."

Carpenter issues the following warning in *Revive Us Again:* "All Christian communities are profoundly shaped by their cultural situation, and revisionists who chide a prior generation for not seeing its own foibles and limitations should know that someday their descendants will say the same of them."

From Theory to Practice

As the fundamentalist movement gathered strength, it sought to translate its ideas into action by taking greater control of Baptist, Methodist, Presbyterian, Congregational, and Episcopalian denominations. But liberal religious leaders like Harry Emerson Fosdick fought back. Fosdick's 1922 sermon, "Shall the Fundamentalists Win?" helped rally moderate and liberal church leaders.

Meanwhile, a rift was growing within the fundamentalist movement. Its more moderate members felt they should continue working within existing denominational structures. More separatist members left to form their own churches, branding those who stayed behind as turncoats and traitors.

Initially, it seemed the separatists would accomplish the most. They engaged in a flurry of institution building, founding many independent Bible colleges, publishing houses, and mission agencies that would later form the foundation of America's sizable evangelical subculture. In the long run, however, the belligerence of leaders like Bob Jones Sr., founder of an influential college, and John R. Rice, editor of a newspaper called *The Sword of the Lord,* led not to greater influence, but instead to increasing isolation.

The divisions within the fundamentalist ranks resulted in the creation of two competing organizations: the more activist (and now largely irrelevant) American Council of Christian Churches, founded in 1941 by Carl McIntire; and the more moderate National Association of Evangelicals, which was founded in 1942 and positioned itself between the contrasting extremes of liberal Protestants and conservative fundamentalists (see chapter 8).

Before their movement splintered, the fundamentalists did their best to resist the tidal wave of modern change, but they were hampered by a siege mentality that led to narrowness, judgmentalism, anti-intellectualism, and self-righteousness. Their emphasis on truth was seldom balanced by an appreciation of grace, and they often chose to engage in confrontation rather than conversation—even with fellow Bible-believing Christians. Their triumphs and failings have left today's evangelicals with a complex and contradictory legacy.

The Quest for an Evangelical Mind

In one of his fiery sermons, fundamentalist preacher Billy Sunday boldly proclaimed: "I don't know any more about theology than a jackrabbit knows about Ping-Pong, but I'm on my way to glory." Unfortunately, such sentiments helped contribute to an anti-intellectualism that continues to haunt present-day evangelicals.

Historian Mark Noll's acclaimed 1994 book *The Scandal of the Evangelical Mind*, detailed the continuing consequences of "the intellectual disaster of fundamentalism." An article published in *The Atlantic Monthly* in 2000 explored the continuing consequences of this disaster: "Of all America's religious traditions, evangelical Protestantism, at least in its twentieth-century conservative forms, ranks dead last in intellectual stature."

Kenneth Kantzer, a former editor of *Christianity Today*, discussed this problem in a 1996 interview for the magazine's 40th anniversary edition. "Most fundamentalists believed that the life of the mind was important," he said, "but they didn't know what to do about it." Some present-day evangelicals understand precisely how they felt.

Resources

The Fundamentals (1910).
J. Gresham Machen, *Christianity & Liberalism* (1923).
Carl F. H. Henry, *The Uneasy Conscience of Modern Fundamentalism* (1947).
Joel Carpenter, *Revive Us Again: the Reawakening of American Fundamentalism* (1997).
Richard Mouw, *The Smell of Sawdust: What Evangelicals Can Learn from Their Fundamentalist Heritage* (2000).
Mark Noll, *The Scandal of the Evangelical Mind* (1994).
Alan Wolfe, "The Opening of the Evangelical Mind," *The Atlantic Monthly*, October 2000.
George M. Marsden, *Fundamentalism and American Culture: The Shaping of Twentieth-Century Evangelicalism, 1870–1925* (1980); and *Reforming Fundamentalism: Fuller Seminary and the New Evangelicalism* (1987, 1995).
Martin Marty and Scott Appleby, *The Glory and the Power: The Fundamentalist Challenge to the Modern World* (companion book to PBS series, 1992).

3. Examining the Foundations: Karl Barth's Commentary on *Romans*, 1918

Rarely—perhaps once or twice a century—does a Christian thinker write a book both timely and timeless enough that it becomes a classic to be savored and discussed generation after generation. St. Augustine's *Confessions* (397–401), the first real spiritual autobiography, continues to move readers today, as does Martin Luther's passionate *Ninety-Five Theses* (1517), which helped ignite the Protestant Reformation.

Karl Barth (1886–1968) wasn't consciously trying to write a classic when he composed his commentary on the apostle Paul's *Epistle to the Romans*, which was published in Europe in 1918 and later revised and translated into English.

The 32-year-old pastor of a Reformed congregation in the small Swiss town of Safenwil, Barth had been engaged in a deeply personal spiritual quest that forced the liberal-trained thinker to reevaluate the very foundations of his faith. *Romans*, which took a fresh and daring look at the Bible and Christian orthodoxy, is the fruit of his struggles. Readers—both liberals and conservatives in the U.S. and Europe—have been wrestling with its implications ever since. As one writer put it, Barth's magnum opus arrived "like a bomb on the playground of the theologians." The tremors can still be felt today.

Barth was one of the founders of an important theological movement called neo-orthodoxy, which sought to restate key Reformation principles in modern terminology. But some conservative critics called his work "no-orthodoxy." Getting behind these confusing and often conflicting labels requires a better understanding of Barth and the turmoil of his time.

The Hype and the Horror

Like Augustine and Luther before him, Barth wrestled with fundamental issues about God and human nature. Trained by some of Europe's most

12

renowned liberal theologians, he inherited a relatively optimistic view of the world: God was immanent and understandable rather than transcendent and aloof; and humanity was innately good, inherently reasonable, morally perfectible, and destined to enjoy near limitless progress.

Such views did little to prepare Barth for the horrors of World War I, some of which he witnessed at close range. Barth was shocked by the savage inhumanity of wartime atrocities as well as the warring powers' use of the latest scientific and technological advances to create ever more malevolent tools of destruction and death. The war forced Barth to examine the near-utopian optimism of liberal Protestantism, and when he did so, he found it wanting.

Many people experience periodic tensions between their core beliefs and the mundane realities of the world around them. Barth's own cognitive dissonance grew so deep and profound that he threw himself upon the two wellsprings of his faith: the Bible and the Calvinist roots of

Karl Barth, one of the founders of neo-orthodoxy, published *The Epistle to the Romans* in 1918. Though trained by liberal theologians, Barth rethought the near-utopian optimism of liberal Protestantism after seeing the atrocities of World War I. He emphasized the importance of the Bible and that the only way to God was through faith in Jesus Christ.

the Reformed faith. From these raw materials he created powerful theological works that borrowed equally from liberal and traditional schools and attempted to restate Christianity for a new and uncertain age.

Restating Traditional Themes

Barth's commentary on *Romans* wasn't even published in English until 1935, but orthodox theologians around the world had long been hearing about Barth's views, and many of them liked what they heard.

For one thing, Barth stressed the importance of the Bible, a book that had played a decreasing role in the work of many liberal theologians.

In addition, Barth affirmed human reason but didn't esteem it as highly as liberals had, arguing that without divine revelation people could know nothing of God. In his descriptions of human nature, he often sounded more like a fiery fundamentalist than a laid-back liberal:

> . . . the trouble in which we find ourselves lies still deeper and extends still further. The true, the real trouble we are in, my dear

friends, consists quite simply in the fact that man is as he is and cannot make himself any different. He is the cause of his own trouble. He suffers from himself. . . . Man is a fallen, perverted being. It is not a matter of the sins which we have committed and are committing, but of the sin from which all sins come, and so of the particular trouble in which all our troubles, the personal and general ones, have their source, just as weeds cannot help growing again and again from a weed root.

As Barth saw it, humanity wasn't good and getting better, but flawed and in desperate need of God's help. Thankfully, God was not only lofty and transcendent but also loving and gracious. Though utterly distinct from humankind, God was clearly revealed to humanity in a most powerful way through Christ, who offered humanity the only way to salvation.

As for the church, its primary obligation was to bear witness to the revelation of God, which required it to be a distinctive and countercultural spiritual institution. Barth's views on the purity of the church, which were spelled out more fully in his magnum opus, *Church Dogmatics,* would be severely tested by the rise of Hitler's Nazi regime. True to his convictions, Barth was a committed member of the Nazi resistance.

Continuing Debates

While many evangelicals found much in Barth they could applaud, others were deeply troubled by certain aspects of his theology. For one thing, Barth expressed a profound ambivalence about whether certain aspects of the Bible were historically true, or whether their historicity even mattered. In addition, Barth's concept of ongoing revelation employed some of the same terminology evangelicals used, but he redefined these terms in uniquely modern ways. For example, he said the Word of God was not necessarily the Bible itself, but rather the Bible becomes the Word of God when its truths are revealed anew to each reader or hearer.

This dynamic, dialectical view of revelation was deeply troubling to many evangelicals who believed it undermined traditional, rational approaches to hermeneutics and biblical interpretation. Later thinkers like Rudolf Bultmann would take Barth's ambivalence about reason to its logical consequences, arguing that Christianity had no relationship to historicity whatsoever, paving the way for the "Death of God" theology of the 1960s.

Barth's views were welcomed by those who rejected both liberalism and fundamentalism, including evangelical theologians like Bernard Ramm and Donald Bloesch, as well as European thinkers like Jacques Ellul and Paul Tournier. But his greatest impact may have been on theologians like Emil Bruner and Reinhold Niebuhr, who turned neo-orthodoxy into one of the most important theological movements of the 1930s, 1940s, and 1950s.

Neither conservatives nor liberals can claim complete ownership of Barth, but members of both camps still appreciate the way he wrestled with the truth. His ability to describe the modern era's crisis of faith helped make him one of the most important Christian thinkers of the 20th century.

> ### Man Is Fallen
>
> The true, the real trouble we are in, my dear friends, consists quite simply in the fact that man is as he is and cannot make himself any different. He is the cause of his own trouble. He suffers from himself. . . . Man is a fallen, perverted being.
>
> — Karl Barth's commentary on Paul's *Epistle to the Romans*

Resources

Karl Barth's *Epistle to the Romans* (1918).
G. Bolich, *Karl Barth and Evangelicalism* (1980).

4. Legislating Morality: The Hollow Victory of Prohibition, 1920

Anyone wanting a crash course on the dangers of using law to promote virtue and curb vice should take a long, hard look at the sad saga of Prohibition. This surprisingly under-studied episode from American history illustrates an important, double-sided lesson. The lesson is that conservative Christians can, with effort and organization, occasionally see some of their moral values enforced through legislation; however, the unintended consequences of trying to outlaw sin can be devastating.

People have been consuming alcohol for eight millennia, and for much of that time there have been sober debates about how to minimize its abuse. America's grand experiment called Prohibition lasted from 1920 to 1933; however, not only did making alcohol illegal fail to decrease drinking, but it also gave birth to organized crime, transforming members of small-time ethnic street gangs into big-time, big-money gangsters. How could such a well-intentioned plan for making things better go so wrong?

From Temperance to Prohibition

Throughout American history, revivals of religion have inspired movements for social and moral reform. The Second Great Awakening, which was actually a decades-long series of spiritual renewals, emphasized both repentance from sin and the possibility of human perfectibility. The belief that people—and perhaps society—could be morally cleansed led to the formation of thousands of voluntary organizations, many of them dedicated to limiting the consumption of alcohol, which had become increasingly cheap, available, and destructive.

The American Temperance Society, which was organized with the support of Protestant churches and clergy, was founded in Boston in 1826, and within a few years, hundreds of similar grassroots groups sprang up around the country. By 1860, nearly a dozen states had passed some form of antiliquor law, but most of these measures were repealed or declared unconstitutional. The battle against booze was resurrected after the Civil War, with many of the new generation of "dry" groups committed to nothing less than national legislation totally banning alcohol.

The Prohibition Party, formed in 1869, was joined in 1874 by the Women's Christian Temperance Union (WCTU), which was founded by Frances Willard, a complex and colorful Methodist educator and feminist leader who combined conservative values with a radical reforming zeal. These two groups would help unleash a tide of female social activism that was unprecedented in American history.

The WCTU's most famous member was Carrie Nation, an energetic and eccentric woman who became an activist after she lost her first husband to drink. Her favored strategy was to stand outside a tavern singing hymns and reading Bible verses before entering the establishment to smash its liquor bottles and destroy its furnishings with her trusty hatchet, crying out, "Smash! Smash! For Jesus' name, smash!"

Behind the headlines, the WCTU's biggest impact came through persuading public schools to teach courses on the evils of alcohol. The Anti-Saloon League, founded in 1895, referred to itself as "the Church in Action Against the Saloon." Like later generations of activists in the Civil Rights and religious rights movements, the league organized sympathetic congregations as its base of operations. "From the Great Lakes to the Gulf a militant majority of American people are crucifying that beastly, bloated bastard of Beelzebub, the liquor traffic," said one Christian prohibitionist.

In March 1917 the U.S. declared war on Germany, and anti-German patriotic sentiment helped turn many Americans against the beer-brewing industry. Andrew J. Volstead, a Republican congressman from Minnesota, introduced the Volstead Act, an amendment to the U.S. Constitution that would prohibit the manufacture or sale of any drink with more than .05 percent alcohol. The act sailed through Congress, where it had enough votes to override a veto by President Woodrow Wilson. Submitted to the states in December 1917, the act received the necessary support of two-thirds of the states in January 1919, when Utah became the 36th state to approve it. After a required one-year waiting period, Prohibition officially took effect on January 16, 1920.

Paradise Postponed

Religious leaders could hardly contain their excitement over the amendment's passage or their hopes for the better future it would certainly bring.

Billy Sunday, who had been a hard-drinking professional baseball player before accepting Christ at the Pacific Garden Mission and deciding to

Evangelist Billy Sunday staged a mock funeral for John Barleycorn, the poster boy for liquor. When the Volstead Act took effect on January 16, 1920, Sunday felt that prohibition would save America and that "Hell will be forever for rent." Instead, liquor became America's largest industry. On December 5, 1933, the 21st Amendment to the Constitution repealed Prohibition.

become an evangelist, even staged a mock funeral service for John Barleycorn, the poster boy for booze, saying, "The slums will soon only be a memory. We will turn our prisons into factories and our jails into storehouses and corncribs. Men will walk upright now, women will smile, and children will laugh. Hell will be forever for rent."

Few people could match Sunday's rhetoric, but many accepted his reasoning. As historian Paul Johnson writes in his *History of the American People:*

> There were many Americans who believed . . . that if only the sale of alcohol could be made unlawful, not only alcoholism and drunkenness could be stamped out but the country could be morally improved in countless other ways.

The arrival of Prohibition's promised paradise would be postponed, however. Far from making America sinless and dry, the effort seemed to make it even wilder and wetter. Some Americans quit drink altogether, but for others, drinking suddenly became fashionable and hip, and millions of formerly law-abiding Americans were downing alcohol at thousands upon thousands of illicit speakeasies. Liquor became America's biggest industry, with billions of dollars going into the pockets of well-organized crime families, some of whom used Prohibition profits to build illegal empires that remain powerful today.

Things certainly hadn't turned out as temperance movement leaders planned, but at least the enactment of Prohibition showed that America's Protestant establishment still had power and influence and shouldn't be counted out. Historian Mark Noll assessed Prohibition's mixed results:

> Prohibition did bring improvements in the nation's health and welfare, but nothing like the utopia its promoters had foreseen. If the results of national Prohibition did not achieve its lofty goals, however, the movement still illustrated the power of the nation's public Protestants—generally evangelical, almost all white, largely

of British background—in translating their moral vision into the law of the land.

After 13 years, most Americans had had enough of Prohibition. On December 5, 1933, the 21st Amendment to the Constitution was ratified, repealing Prohibition and making the manufacture and sale of alcohol legal once again.

Today, the battle continues, even though there are fewer foot soldiers. The national Prohibition Party met in the summer of 1999 to nominate its presidential candidate, just as it had done for 32 previous elections. That's an unprecedented record for an American third party, but only about 30 of the faithful were on hand for the nomination.

Do It for Mom and America

I want every man to say, "God, you can count on me to protect my wife, my home, my mother and my children and the manhood of America."

By the mercy of God . . . I beseech you, make a fight for the women who wait until the saloons spew out their husbands and their sons, and send them home maudlin, brutish, devilish, stinking, bleary-eyed, bloated-faced drunkards.

—Billy Sunday

Resources

N. H. Clark, *Deliver Us from Evil: An Interpretation of American Prohibition* (1976).

Edward Behr, *Prohibition: Thirteen Years that Changed America* (the companion book to a series on the A&E cable network, 1996).

John C. Burnham, *Bad Habits: Drinking, Smoking, Taking Drugs, Gambling, Sexual Misbehavior, and Swearing in American History* (1993).

5. Stations of the Cross: The Rise of Religious Broadcasting, 1921

The emergence of new technologies—from cars to cable television—has typically elicited two distinct responses from evangelicals. A concerned minority raises red flags ("Cars are beds on wheels for immoral kids," or "Ninety-five cable channels equals ninety-five reasons for people not to go to church or read their Bibles"), while pragmatists embrace the latest inventions as tools to further the Christian cause ("It's too bad Jesus didn't have the Internet, but just think what we can do with it").

Radio, which emerged in the 1920s, was no different. Thumbing through their well-worn King James Bibles in search of a definitive passage, skeptics landed on Ephesians 2:2, which called Satan "the prince of the power of the air." Meanwhile, enthusiasts claimed radio would help them accomplish Jesus' command in Matthew 16:15, "Go ye into all the world, and preach the gospel to every creature."

It was these enthusiasts who were among the first Americans to embrace radio, and later, television, seeing the public airwaves as their most efficient means to reach the masses. As historian Dennis Voskuil wrote, "Fundamentalists and Pentecostals, avowed theological antimodernists, eventually became the juggernauts of the electronic media." Today, hundreds of Christian radio programs are distributed by thousands of broadcast outlets to millions of listeners around the world.

Mass-media Messengers

Pittsburgh station KDKA became America's first licensed radio station in late 1920. Its next two challenges were finding listeners and producing programs. An engineer for Westinghouse, KDKA's parent company, sang in the choir at Pittsburgh's Calvary Episcopal Church. He suggested broadcasting one of the church's services, and that's how American religious broadcasting began on the evening of Sunday, January 2, 1921. The popular show was promptly given its own weekly time slot.

Soon, both local stations and nationwide radio networks were giving away free public service time for religious programs, but broadcasters typically favored long-established mainline Protestants over upstart evangelicals, who were forced to pay for their airtime. Still, radio was a relatively cheap way for preachers and teachers to reach the masses, and during the 1920s and 1930s, evangelical broadcasters like Paul Rader in Chicago and Charles Fuller in Los Angeles led the way. Fuller's *The Pilgrim Hour* program aired on a handful of stations in Southern California in the early 1920s, but by the late 1930s he was reaching an estimated 10 million listeners with his *Old Fashioned Revival Hour,* which featured sermons and songs.

The National Religious Broadcasters, founded in 1943, successfully lobbied on behalf of evangelicals, who now dominate religious broadcasting, offering inspiration, information, and entertainment over more than 1,500 stations—which is approximately one of every 10 radio outlets in the U.S. These stations of the cross feature everything from talk and teaching to a wide range of musical formats, including Southern Gospel, praise and worship, and contemporary Christian pop and rock.

Give Me That Prime-Time Religion

Commercial television emerged during the late 1940s, and Christian shows began reaching TV viewers in the early 1950s. One of the earliest and most popular TV teachers was Catholic Bishop Fulton J. Sheen, whose weekly *Life Is Worth Living* and *Mission to the World* programs played to large national audiences from 1952 to 1957.

Standing in a small living room, Sheen stared straight at the camera and talked, his only visual aid being the notes he wrote on a big blackboard. But this low-key approach won Sheen legions of fans, including actor Martin Estevez, who changed his own name to Sheen. The Bishop even bested Jimmy Durante, Lucille Ball, and Arthur Godfrey to win an Emmy Award for TV's Most Outstanding Personality. (Sheen's acceptance speech contained the classic line: "I would like to thank my four writers— Matthew, Mark, Luke, and John.")

Billy Graham also utilized television during the 1950s, but unlike Percy Crawford of Philadelphia and others, he didn't host a regularly scheduled program. Instead, the newly formed Billy Graham Evangelistic Association produced occasional television specials featuring Graham's massive crusades, and paid to air them on the national networks.

In the decades since, religious programming has failed to attract national audiences matching those Sheen and Graham reached, and TV has become increasingly secular and entertainment oriented.

Pentecostal preachers like Oral Roberts and Rex Humbard bought time on numerous local TV stations during the 1950s and 1960s. The medium

> ### A Message for the Masses
>
> I believe that God has raised up this powerful technology of radio and television expressly to reach every man, woman, boy, and girl on earth with the even more powerful message of the gospel.
>
> — Ben Armstrong, executive director of the National Religious Broadcasters, in *The Electric Church*

was a perfect vehicle for their often theatrical preaching and lively music. During the 1970s and 1980s, Pentecostals like Jimmy Swaggart and Jim Bakker dominated the "electronic church" before being brought low by money and sex scandals (see chapter 42).

Unscathed by these failings, Pentecostal Pat Robertson turned his donor-supported Family Channel into an economic powerhouse. A frequent critic of secular entertainment companies like Fox and Disney, Robertson muted these criticisms when these companies began expressing interest in acquiring his television empire.

Broadcasting or Narrowcasting?

The rules of the mainstream broadcasting business are simple and clear-cut: Make profits for owners by developing programming popular enough to attract large audiences so that advertisers will pay big money to reach them.

Things are more complicated for religious broadcasters, who are torn between their desire to reach the lost and the necessity of paying their bills. As a result, most Christian programming is produced for an audience of believers and supported by Christian advertisers who want to reach them.

According to surveys published by George Barna in 1994, Christian broadcasters are succeeding at reaching their core evangelical audience: 70 percent of evangelicals reported listening to a radio program featuring Christian teaching or preaching during the previous week, and 62 percent said they had watched a Christian TV show. As for reaching the unchurched, Christian broadcasts are far less successful.

Still, Christian media remains a force to be reckoned with. According to *Christianity Today,* "The undisputed king of Christian radio is Focus on the Family president James Dobson . . . heard by nearly twice as many listeners as any other in Christian talk radio." Radio has helped put Focus on the map, and its flagship *Focus on the Family* broadcast, which has an estimated 4 million daily listeners, has covered an amazingly broad range of topics while giving increased exposure to deserving ministries, and up-and-coming authors and speakers.

Focus also provides a vital link to a vast network of concerned Christians who spring into action whenever there's trouble brewing in

Washington. All Dobson needs to do is tell his loyal listeners to phone their elected representatives, and the switchboards in D.C. light up—or in some cases shut down—from the large volume of calls (see chapter 28).

Charles Fuller had discovered radio's impact half a century earlier. Concerned about leaving a lasting legacy and frustrated with the direction fundamentalism was taking, the popular radio host founded Fuller Theological Seminary in 1947 and used his show to recruit the first group of 27 students. As historian George Marsden writes in his acclaimed book *Reforming Fundamentalism: Fuller Seminary and the New Evangelicalism,* the school played "a leading role in the original new evangelical attempt to reform fundamentalism." This effort may have been unsuccessful if it weren't for the power of the airwaves.

Critics of Christian broadcasting say it competes with brick-and-mortar churches, reduces the gospel to sound bites, emphasizes style and celebrity over substance, and wraps its listeners in a protective subcultural cocoon that isolates them from the realities of the larger world. But the electronic church's many avid supporters say evangelical broadcasts have introduced untold numbers of people to Christ, given millions of daily doses of encouragement and inspiration, provided information and entertainment free of the mainstream media bias and blasphemy, and served as a vital form of virtual fellowship for those who—for various reasons—can't get out to brick-and-mortar churches.

Resources

Quentin J. Schultze, *Televangelism and American Culture: The Business of Popular Religion* (1991).

Mark Ward Sr., *Air of Salvation* (1994).

Dennis Voskuil, "Power of the Air: Evangelicals and the Rise of Religious Broadcasting," in Schultze, *American Evangelicals and the Mass Media* (1990).

Ben Armstrong, *The Electric Church* (1979).

6. Monkey Business:
Evolution and the Scopes Trial, 1925

Centuries-old tensions between religion and science erupted in a hot and humid Tennessee courtroom in 1925 as fundamentalist firebrand William Jennings Bryan squared off against outspoken agnostic Clarence Darrow in the trial of high school teacher John Scopes, who challenged a state law outlawing evolution.

But the Scopes Trial represents much more than another battle between religion and science. Also at play were long-simmering struggles between fundamentalism and modernism. The case also raised important questions about the role of religion in public life and public education that are still being intensely debated today.

Perhaps more importantly, the trial demonstrated the power of the news and entertainment media to inform—and often inflame—public opinion concerning complex issues. The Scopes trial was the first in American history to be broadcast nationwide via the relatively new technology of radio, and decades later a Broadway play and a Hollywood movie would further color people's perceptions of this historic event.

Science and the Scriptures

If Prohibition represented fundamentalists' effort to control America's drinking behavior through legislation, antievolution laws represented the movement's attempt to dictate what was learned in the nation's classrooms.

In the 1920s, a handful of states enacted laws prohibiting the teaching of evolution. Tennessee's "Butler bill," which took effect in March 1925, declared it illegal to "to teach the theory that denies the story of the divine creation of man as taught in the Bible, and to teach instead that man has descended from a lower order of animals."

Enter the American Civil Liberties Union, which had been founded in 1920 to protect Americans' constitutionally guaranteed rights (even if, as critics have claimed, "its adherence to principle sometimes conflicts with common sense"). ACLU director Roger Baldwin announced that the organization would defend any teacher who challenged the Butler bill.

Clarence Darrow, lead lawyer for the defense of evolution-teaching John Scopes, is seen in the center wearing a white shirt and suspenders and is leaning with his back against the table. The man with the receding hairline and wearing a suit standing behind Darrow is Dudley Malone, the second-most powerful defense lawyer in this trial. Malone made a powerful speech for intellectual freedom, which was called by one writer, "The finest speech of the century." Malone is well known for saying, "I have never in my life learned anything from any man who agreed with me."

John Scopes, a first-year teacher in Dayton, Tennessee, volunteered for the cause, but he never testified during the trial. Instead, Darrow and Bryan took center stage.

Darrow, the most celebrated defense attorney of his day, defended Scopes for free, calling the Scopes trial "the first case of its kind since we stopped trying people for witchcraft."

Bryan assisted the prosecution, which was organized by the World's Christian Fundamentals Association, a group founded in 1919 to combat modernism. A populist politician who had been unsuccessful in three presidential campaigns, Bryan was the era's most prominent fundamentalist and a leading figure in 19th-century efforts to establish a Christian America. For Bryan, the issues raised by the trial went to the foundations of the faith:

> . . . the question, "What shall I do with Jesus?" must be
> answered. A bloody, brutal doctrine—evolution—demands, as the
> rabble did 1900 years ago, that He be crucified.

Testimony about the scientific basis of evolution was largely excluded from the proceedings, which began on July 10, so Darrow and Bryan focused instead on theology. A crucial turning point came when Bryan took the witness stand and Darrow grilled him about alleged inconsistencies in the Bible. Bryan, a powerful orator, who could bring a sympathetic audience to tears, fumbled before his inquisitor, struggling to answer some of Darrow's nagging questions:

Darrow: "What do you think?"

Bryan: "I do not think about things I don't think about."

Darrow: "Do you think about things you do think about?"

Bryan: "Well, sometimes."

Some in the sweltering courthouse laughed at Bryan, according to H. L. Mencken, who was covering the trial for the *Baltimore Evening Sun.* A crusading journalist who cared little for objective reporting, Mencken was an outspoken critic of fundamentalism who once wrote, "Heave an egg out of a Pullman window and you will hit a Fundamentalist almost anywhere in the United States today."

Mencken contributed to the carnival atmosphere surrounding the trial, which one historian said was accompanied by "movie cameras, buzzing aeroplanes, radio installations, clicking telegraph keys (and) chattering typewriters."

Winners and Losers

The trial concluded on July 21 when the jury found Scopes guilty as charged. Bryan and the fundamentalists had won, but their celebration was a muted one. The judge fined Scopes a mere $100. Scopes left Dayton for the University of Chicago, where he was given a scholarship to study geology.

Bryan, meanwhile, planned a national speaking tour to promote biblical creationism. "We must strike while the iron is hot," he said. But five days later he died, and so, too, did many of the hopes of fundamentalists, as Stephen Neill writes:

> Deprived of its major figure, fundamentalism failed in its effort
> to capture the denominations. It survived in the form of minority
> parties in the churches and in splinter bodies, but by the later 1920s
> it was clear that the movement had failed in its principal objectives.

The drama *Inherit the Wind,* which portrayed the Scopes trial as an anti-intellectual witchhunt, opened on Broadway in 1955 during the height of the McCarthy hearings. A movie version starring Spencer Tracy and Gene Kelly followed in 1960, and John Scopes attended its world premiere in Dayton. Bryan was portrayed as a bellicose moron ("I am more interested in the Rock of Ages than I am in the ages of rocks!") and the fundamentalist movement's beliefs were caricatured as "medieval nonsense," all to the accompaniment of a soundtrack featuring the song "Give Me That Old Time Religion."

The Tennessee law under which Scopes was prosecuted was repealed in 1967, but the battle over classroom curricula continued. A newer Louisiana law calling for the "Balanced Treatment of Creation-Science and Evolution-Science in Public School Instruction" was declared unconstitutional by the U.S. Supreme Court in 1987. And in August 1999 the Kansas Board of Education voted to delete Darwinian evolution from the state's testing standards, paving the way for schools to teach Darwin or not, as they saw fit. The decision caused a national uproar, leading to the ouster of three conservative school board members and the overturning of the 1999 decision.

Once upon a time, creationists swore loyalty to a literalist chronology developed by 17th-century Irish Bishop James Ussher, who claimed the Bible taught the world was created in 4004 B.C. But today, there is greater diversity among creationists. While groups like the Institute for Creation Research in El Cajon, California, still promote a "young earth" approach, scientists such as "intelligent design" theorist Michael Behe focus on biochemical cell structures, and Philip Johnson, a law professor at the University of California at Berkeley, critiqued the "false claims of Darwinism" in acclaimed lectures and books.

But 75 years after the Scopes trial, most students in America's public schools today continue to learn a deity-free approach to human origins, even though a public opinion poll released in 2000 found that 79 percent of Americans believe creationism has a place in American schools alongside evolution.

Literary License: How *Inherit the Wind* Got It Wrong

Both the Broadway play and the Hollywood movie changed important facts, which are corrected here:

— Citizens of Dayton, Tennessee, welcomed both William Jennings Bryan and Clarence Darrow to their town, hoping the publicity generated by the trial would provide a financial lift.

— Bryan was not a biblical literalist but rather a "majoritarianist" who believed citizens should be free to decide what their children learned in public school. Nor was he antiscience but in fact was a member of the American Academy for the Advancement of Science.

— John Scopes never actually taught evolution in his classroom and was never put in jail. Citizens didn't burn him in effigy or pelt a jail cell with rocks.

— Bryan certainly had his embarrassing moments on the witness stand, but he was also funny and winsome. He even volunteered to pay Scopes's fine.

—Scopes was not romantically involved with the daughter of a fundamentalist preacher.

Today, parents, concerned Christians, and other creationists who hope to gain a hearing for their views in the court of public opinion still have the ghost of Dayton, Tennessee, hanging like a monkey on their backs.

Resources

Edward J. Larson, *Summer for the Gods: The Scopes Trial and America's Continuing Debate Over Science and Religion* (1997).

Inherit the Wind (1960 theatrical release, not the 1988 TV remake).

Randall Balmer, "In the Beginning: The Creationist Controversy" (1995 PBS program).

Philip Johnson, *Darwin on Trial* (1991) and *Defeating Darwinism by Opening Minds* (1997).

David Livingstone, D. G. Hart, and Mark Noll, *Evangelicals and Science in Historical Perspective* (1999).

7. Costly Grace:
Hitler, the Holocaust, and a Home
for the Jews, 1937

The atrocities of World War I had shocked European thinkers like Karl Barth into questioning the optimism of liberal theology. World War II, complete with the evils of the Holocaust and the systematic extermination of 6 million Jewish men, women, and children, was even more troubling, leading to widespread doubts about the goodness of human nature and even the existence of God.

Most Americans had exhibited a combination of ignorance and indifference about Hitler's Third Reich, which came to power in 1933. The Japanese attack on Pearl Harbor in 1941 put an end to U.S. isolationism and led to America's joining the Allied effort. Back at home, however, most Americans, including many evangelicals, either didn't understand or couldn't face the horrors of the Holocaust, even though there had been numerous warnings, like a 1939 article in *Moody Monthly* entitled "An Appeal for Persecuted Israel." One Holocaust scholar described the prevailing apathy of many believers:

> At the heart of Christianity is the commitment to help the helpless. Yet, for the most part, America's Christian churches looked away while European Jews perished.

Institutional Complicity, Individual Resistance

Germany's Protestant church submitted to Hitler's control, but many individual believers resisted the Nazi juggernaut, often at great personal price.

In 1934 Barth helped write the *Barmen Declaration,* a treatise that challenged German churches to remain faithful to the truths of the gospel and reject the temptations of nationalist religion and totalitarianism. The *Declaration* was adopted by the underground Confessing Church movement and was praised by a young German Lutheran pastor named Dietrich Bonhoeffer.

29

Bonhoeffer, who had occasionally heard Barth speak, became head of a Confessing Church seminary before he turned 30. A series of lectures he delivered at the school was published in 1937 as *The Cost of Discipleship*. Soon, Bonhoeffer demonstrated that "costly grace" was more than an abstract concept.

Lecturing in the U.S. in 1939, he could have remained here, safe and secure from the growing conflagration back home. Instead, he returned to Germany to share the sufferings of his people and serve the resistance movement. Arrested in 1943, Bonhoeffer began writing the documents that would become *Letters and Papers from Prison* (1944). In 1945 he was moved to the Buchenwald concentration camp, and was hanged on April 9, less than one month before Germany surrendered. Bonhoeffer's popularity has continued to grow among American evangelicals, and his sacrificial commitment to Christ has made him a hero among believers around the world, including those who still suffer persecution for their faith (see chapter 49).

Another hero was Corrie ten Boom, who during the 1970s became American evangelicals' strongest link to the horrors of the Holocaust. After the Nazis invaded Holland, Corrie's father, Casper, decided that the family's home and clock shop in Haarlem would be an "open house" for anyone needing help. The family sheltered many Jews and members of the Dutch resistance before being raided by the Gestapo in 1944. Corrie was

Auschwitz II-Birkenau. Roll call of new women prisoners. When the supply of striped clothing ran out, clothes of people who had been gassed upon arrival were painted with a colored stripe or stripes and given to prisoners to wear. This and other horrors of the Holocaust unleashed a wave of pessimistic soul-searching that helped inspire philosophical nihilism and the "Death of God" theology.

sent to the Ravensbruck concentration camp with her sister, who died an agonizing death.

But Corrie survived. Through her book and film, *The Hiding Place*, and an extensive speaking schedule that took her to more than 60 countries before her death at age 100, Corrie stressed two important messages: that God's love is deeper than any human darkness, and that Jesus Christ is the ultimate victor in the battle between good and evil.

In addition to these celebrated individuals, many anonymous Europeans harbored Jews during the worst years of the Nazi regime. Today, more than 11,000 of these "Righteous Gentiles" are honored at Yad Vashem, Israel's national Holocaust memorial.

A Home for the Hebrews

The Holocaust forced many evangelicals to examine anti-Semitic ideas that, according to some scholars, had existed in Christianity ever since Jews were blamed for the crucifixion of Jesus.

> ### A Bonhoeffer Bonanza
>
> Today, Christians around the world still read Bonhoeffer's *The Cost of Discipleship, Letters and Papers from Prison*, and *Life Together*, a work about Christian community.
>
> Recent years have also seen an outpouring of award-winning materials that document the courage and commitment of this unique modern martyr:
>
> — "Bonhoeffer: The Cost of Freedom" (a two-hour program produced for *Focus on the Family*'s Radio Theater, 1997);
> — "Bonhoeffer: Agent of Grace" and "Hanged on a Twisted Cross" are acclaimed video presentations available from Vision Video (1-800/523-0226, www.vision-video.com);
> — and *Christian History* magazine devoted an entire issue to Bonhoeffer (issue 32, vol. X, no. 4).

In the years between the world wars, American believers were among those promoting anti-Semitic conspiracy theories based on *The Protocols of Zion*, a nasty, bogus document that claimed to be the secret minutes of a group of Jews intent on nothing less than total world control. Historian Timothy Weber writes that James M. Gray, a president of Moody Bible Institute, and Kansas prophecy buff Gerald Winrod were among the many evangelicals who fell for the *Protocols* hoax and promoted its lies to other Christians.

The Holocaust was only the latest in a series of tragedies to befall the Jewish people, who rallied worldwide support for the creation of a national homeland in the years after World War II.

The Jewish National Council declared statehood for Israel on May 14, 1948, and almost immediately evangelicals became some of the new nation's biggest boosters. But as Weber points out, it wasn't only sudden regret about anti-Semitism or the Holocaust that caused an outpouring of support for Israel; rather, dispensational understandings of eschatology led evangelicals to "believe that the Holy Land will be ground zero for events surrounding the second coming of Jesus Christ."

Ironically, dispensational theology may have unintentionally contributed to evangelicals' passivity in the face of the Holocaust. After all, didn't biblical prophecy teach that no one could annihilate the Jews, a remnant of whom was needed to establish a Jewish nation and set the stage for the final drama of the end times?

Today, relations between Jews and Christians remain confused and complex. While there has been a move toward more interfaith dialogue and cooperation on common social and political objectives, tensions remain, writes Weber:

> Many American evangelicals pledge their love for the State of Israel, support its claims against those of the Palestinians, and resist anything that might undercut Israel's security. But they also target Jews for evangelism and sometimes blame them for the mess the world is in.

The Holocaust is perhaps the most horrible and most troublesome event in human history. It caused many Jews to abandon faith in the God they believed had abandoned them, and it unleashed a wave of pessimistic soul-searching that helped inspire philosophical nihilism and the "Death of God" theology. No one dare forget the horrors of this period, nor should evangelicals overlook some of its more troubling lessons.

Corrie ten Boom, seen here with Billy Graham, wrote *The Hiding Place*, the story of how her family hid Jews and Dutch resistance members in a narrow "hiding place" in one of the bedrooms in the family home and clock shop in Haarlem, Netherlands.

Resources

Arthur Morse, *While Six Million Died: A Chronicle of American Apathy* (1985).

Timothy P. Weber, "How Evangelicals Became Israel's Best Friend," *Christianity Today* (October 5, 1998).

David P. Gushee, *The Righteous Gentiles of the Holocaust: A Christian Interpretation* (1994).

8. Coming Together: NAE Promotes Evangelical Cooperation, 1942

During the first half of the 20th century, American evangelicals began carving out an identity for themselves. Like a gangly adolescent, however, their initial efforts seemed halting and uncertain. They often defined who they were by describing what they weren't, and defended what they believed by loudly proclaiming what they were against.

There were good reasons for their uncertainty, as early evangelical leaders were cautious about dangers that threatened their embryonic movement from both the "right" and the "left." On the right, fundamentalism was committed to the truth but expressed its zeal in a separatist, self-righteous stance that made it appear harsh and judgmental (see chapter 2). On the left, mainline Protestantism seemed warmer and more welcoming, but its openness to liberal theological ideas made it vulnerable to the corrosive forces of modernism and secularism.

Things began to change for the better in April 1942 when 150 representatives from a variety of churches, ministries, and mission organizations gathered in St. Louis, Missouri, for the National Conference for United Action Among Evangelicals. At a Chicago gathering in 1943, more than 1,000 delegates voted to form the National Association of Evangelicals (NAE), a group that has since helped fix the boundaries of belief and action for its members and a watching world.

Playing Catch-Up

For a variety of reasons, America's evangelicals had initially been slow to seek common bonds. They knew Jesus had prayed that his followers would be unified, warning that "Every kingdom divided against itself will be ruined" (Matt. 12:25); but in conservative Christian circles, it was more common to hear people quoting verses emphasizing doctrinal purity and separation, like Matthew 12:30: "He who is not with me is against me."

In the mid-1800s, a small group of Americans had attended meetings of the Evangelical Alliance (later the World Evangelical Alliance) in London. An American Alliance was formed, but the group was small and underfunded, achieving little in its 40-year history.

Rather, it was mainline Protestants who were the first to organize an effective American association, forming the Federal Council of Churches (FCC) in 1908. The FCC, which would merge with other groups in 1950 to form the National Council of Churches of Christ (NCC) in the U.S.A., was more focused on "the fellowship and catholic unity of the Christian church" than on doctrinal uniformity. Evangelicals criticized the FCC and NCC for giving more attention to advocacy on behalf of social issues like world peace and racial equality than to personal salvation.

Even the fighting fundamentalists organized before the evangelicals did, forming the American Council of Christian Churches (ACCC) in September 1941 and electing Carl McIntire as its first president. The ACCC still exists and publishes the *Christian Beacon,* but it has done little in recent decades to rival its own early achievements, which included helping its members get radio time for their broadcasts and appointments for their military chaplains.

The formation of the ACCC served as a wake-up call for evangelicals, who saw themselves unrepresented as both liberal and more conservative churchmen established national organizations. Ultimately, it wasn't a deep desire for communion that proved sufficient to bring evangelicals together, but rather a desperate need to play catch-up and establish their own distinctive presence on the American scene.

Evangelicalism: New and Old

Even though evangelicals had been slow to unite, the NAE's leaders quickly made up for lost time, helping forge a newfound sense of unity and cooperation that propelled its member churches and organizations into a period of unprecedented growth and effectiveness.

Harold John Ockenga, an emerging young leader, helped herald the dawning of "The New Evangelicalism." In his 1943 presidential speech, he declared that "the United States of America has been assigned a destiny comparable to that of ancient Israel."

As religious historian William Martin says, the emergence of the NAE

> . . . signified a form of conservative Christianity that consciously
> marked itself off from old-line fundamentalism by its tolerance of
> minor theological differences among essentially like-minded believers,
> a conviction that evangelical faith could and should be set forth and
> defended in an intellectually rigorous manner rather than simply
> asserted dogmatically, and with a more positive attitude toward social
> reform than fundamentalists had held during the previous 25 years.

Instead of issuing a long list of narrowly defined theological "fundamentals," the NAE's leaders created a broad-based, seven-point statement of faith covering key theological issues like the Bible, the Trinity, and the nature and work of Christ that members must still affirm today. This statement helped members celebrate the faith's essentials, tolerate disagreements when it came to nonessentials, and avoid the incessant wrangling that had characterized their fundamentalist forefathers.

By the end of the century, though, there were signs that the old battles and struggles for identity weren't completely settled. In 2000, NAE members voted to allow groups to hold dual membership with the NAE and the NCC. "We don't have to define ourselves based on who we're not," said NAE president Kevin Mannoia, who resigned in 2001.

But a year later, the board of the National Religious Broadcasters, a sister organization founded in 1944, voted 80-0 to sever its ties with NAE, saying the two groups "have grown apart." Other NAE members threatened they, too, would leave unless the dual membership rule was reversed. "This does not seem to us to be a clear witness in our post-modern culture where the emphasis is on relativism rather than our standing very clearly for the uniqueness of the Christian faith," said a representative of the Presbyterian Church in America.

Moving Forward

The membership controversy, which contributed to Mannoia losing his job, shouldn't detract from the NAE's major accomplishments during its first six decades. The group opened an Office for Governmental Affairs in the nation's capitol, which helped evangelicals claim their place at the table among liberals and fundamentalists. It launched a number of affiliate organizations, including the Evangelical Press Association and the Evangelical Fellowship of Mission Agencies. And it created commissions focusing on social issues, higher education, stewardship, and the special needs of women, chaplains, and Hispanic believers.

As NAE prepared to enter the 21st century, its members comprised more than 43,000 congregations from 51 member denominations and fellowships along with 250 parachurch organizations and schools.

Making International Connections

In the years after World War II, Christian groups were seeking greater international cooperation, and once again, mainline Protestants and fundamentalists created major world bodies before evangelicals did.

The World Council of Churches (WCC) was formed in 1948 and immediately became the largest and most inclusive Christian body the world had ever seen. The WCC encouraged its largely Protestant member organizations

The NAE's Statement of Faith

1. We believe the Bible to be the inspired, the only infallible, authoritative Word of God.
2. We believe that there is one God, eternally existent in three persons: Father, Son, and Holy Spirit.
3. We believe in the deity of our Lord Jesus Christ, in His virgin birth, in His sinless life, in His miracles, in His vicarious and atoning death through His shed blood, in His bodily resurrection, in His ascension to the right hand of the Father, and in His personal return in power and glory.
4. We believe that for the salvation of lost and sinful people, regeneration by the Holy Spirit is absolutely essential.
5. We believe in the present ministry of the Holy Spirit by whose indwelling the Christian is enabled to live a godly life.
6. We believe in the resurrection of both the saved and the lost; they that are saved unto the resurrection of life and they that are lost unto the resurrection of damnation.
7. We believe in the spiritual unity of believers in our Lord Jesus Christ.

in cooperation, study, fellowship, and worship. Many major evangelical denominations declined to join, as did the Roman Catholic Church, which already saw itself as a unified world Christian body. That same year, Carl McIntire founded the International Council of Christian Churches, an umbrella organization for fundamentalist groups.

Evangelicals responded by founding the World Evangelical Fellowship in 1951. WEF provided Christians with opportunities to support one another in prayer, cooperate in mission programs, and stand together against the worldwide persecution of Christian believers.

So far, NAE and WEF haven't ushered in the kind of unity believers will experience in heaven, but at least the doors to greater communication and cooperation have been opened wide.

Resources

Arthur H. Matthews, *Standing Up, Standing Together: the Emergence of the National Association of Evangelicals* (NAE, 1992).

James Davison Hunter, *American Evangelicalism: Conservative Religion and the Quandary of Modernity* (1983).

Joel Carpenter, *Revive Us Again: The Reawakening of American Fundamentalism* (1997).

William Martin, "Fifty Years with Billy," *Christianity Today* (November 13, 1995).

9. Beyond Kid Stuff:
Youth for Christ and the Youth
Ministry Revolution, 1945

There have always been young people, but "youth" is a much more recent innovation. For millennia, children and teens were treated as junior members of both clan and community, but that drastically changed in the 20th century. Trends like urbanization and industrialization, along with the growth of public education, gave birth to a distinct group with its own unique identities and subcultures. The pace of change has speeded up in recent decades as mass marketers and purveyors of pop culture have targeted America's 32 million teens, who spend $100 billion a year and influence another $50 billion spent by adults.

In the 19th century, Christian leaders began to develop targeted ministries for young people. One of the earliest efforts was England's Young Men's Christian Association (YMCA), which provided urban youth with a positive alternative to the sins of the city. Founded in London in 1844, the YMCA had a Boston branch by 1851. One of the group's biggest supporters was evangelist Dwight L. Moody, who also helped found the Student Volunteer Movement for Foreign Missions in 1886.

British-based InterVarsity Christian Fellowship (IVCF) was founded in 1919 and began working in Canada in 1928 and the U.S. in 1939. Today, IVCF works with more than 30,000 students on more than 600 U.S. campuses. Its Urbana Student Missions Conventions, launched in 1946 and usually held every three years in Urbana, Illinois, attract nearly 20,000 young people and have inspired many to pursue careers in evangelism and missions. The acclaimed InterVarsity Press sells 2 million books a year from its catalog of 700 titles.

A Growing Groundswell

America's first major home-grown youth ministry was Young Life, founded in 1941 by Dallas Theological Seminary student Jim Rayburn, whose success at working with high school students led him to proclaim,

"It is a sin to bore a kid with the gospel." Today, Young Life's weekly meetings in nearly 500 U.S. communities remain lively and energetic (one observer called them "controlled chaos") and reach 80,000 high school students and 17,000 middle schoolers. More than 40,000 young people attend Young Life's summer camp programs.

The most influential of America's youth ministries has been Youth for Christ International (YFC), an organization that emerged from a grassroots movement of evangelistic youth rallies being held in English, Canadian, and American cities during the 1930s and 1940s. In New York, the rallies were called "Word of Life." Kansas City's gatherings were called "Singspirations." The name "Youth for Christ" was allegedly first used in Indianapolis.

Major rallies organized by various independent groups drew huge crowds to venues like Madison Square Garden and Chicago's Soldier's Field. Their success, along with favorable media coverage, led to a growing demand for similar rallies around the country. In 1945, rally organizers met and formed Youth for Christ, which established an office in Chicago to coordinate the rallies and hired its first employee, a then little-known evangelist by the name of Billy Graham.

Through the 1950s, YFC organized Saturday evening city rallies and created Bible clubs, which came to be called Campus Life. Soon, there were 3,600 clubs on high school campuses throughout the country. The organization also expanded geographically and now works with hundreds of thousands of young people in countries around the world.

Though it has had a huge impact on youth ministry, YFC's greatest impact may be its pivotal role in training the leaders that would go on to launch and lead dozens of influential organizations like the Billy Graham Evangelistic Association and World Vision. As *Christianity Today* once put it:

> It is virtually impossible to scratch the surface of any evangelical parachurch ministry today without finding staff personnel whose roots are embedded in the YFC movement.

Man with a Mission

Bill Bright left the business world in 1947 to study at the new Fuller Theological Seminary, but he grew impatient with academia and set out to fulfill the ambitious mission he believed God had given him: to reach every single human being on planet Earth with the gospel message. For the rest of the century, Bright was one of American evangelicalism's most influential personalities.

Bright founded Campus Crusade for Christ (which was modeled after Billy Graham's 1949 Los Angeles Crusade for Christ) in 1951 on the campus of the University of California at Los Angeles. As of October 1999, when CCC was dedicating its new Orlando, Florida, campus, the $368 million international ministry had more than 20,000 full-time staff members and more than 650,000 trained volunteers operating 68 ministries and projects in 181 countries. In the U.S., CCC has full-time staff on more than 150 campuses.

The organization, which calls itself "the world's largest evangelical organization," long ago expanded beyond its original focus on youth and now has targeted ministries for athletes, politicians, business leaders, healthcare professionals, and the entertainment industry. Crusade also fostered projects like the *JESUS* film, which has been translated into 650 languages, and speaker Josh McDowell's ministry of apologetics.

Bill Bright founded Campus Crusade for Christ International in 1951 on the campus of the University of California at Los Angeles.

Along the way, Bright has also been involved in mass evangelism programs like the "I Found It!" campaign and the *Four Spiritual Laws* booklet (see chapter 26), and movements for social renewal through political activism and spiritual revival through prayer and fasting.

By the end of the century, Bright had been slowed by prostate cancer and pulmonary fibrosis of the lung, which required him to turn over Crusade's reins to Stephen Douglass in 2001.

New Challenges, New Movements

Youth culture has continued to evolve, and just as earlier youth ministries were founded by people frustrated with the church's outmoded approaches, a new breed of leaders has created new organizations, including two based in the San Diego area.

The National Network of Youth Ministries organizes events for leaders as well as kids. Its most popular event is the annual "See You at the Pole" high school campus rallies, which began in Texas in 1990 and have spread around the country, involving millions of young people. Youth Specialties, founded by YFC alumni, hosts conferences and publishes products designed to increase the professionalism and effectiveness of youth ministry.

The summer 1994 edition of Youth Specialties' *Youthworker* journal explored the future of youth ministry. George Barna said youth leaders would have to deal with encroaching technology. Tony Campolo discussed issues raised by growing racial and ethnic diversity. And popular speaker Dawson McAllister's comments took on a new relevance as a wave of school shootings broke out at America's high schools: "Because students are hurting so badly and their problems are so deep, youth workers in the 21st century will spend less time entertaining and more time healing the wounds of their students."

Today, Christian groups on secular campuses are under intense pressure to conform to the schools' nondiscrimination policies. In 2000, an InterVarsity group at Tufts University was placed on probation until it redrafted its charter.

No matter how it continues to evolve, youth ministry has already had a profound impact on millions of young people. Even more, its philosophy of targeting ministry to a specific narrowly defined niche has served as a model for specialized ministries to singles, divorcees, members of Twelve-Step groups, and others, providing many more open doors into the redemptive life of the church.

Resources

Mel Larson, *Youth for Christ: Twentieth-Century Wonder* (1947).

James Hefley, *God Goes to High School* (1970).

Joel Carpenter, "Youth for Christ," in *Revive Us Again* (1997).

Carol R. Thiessen, "YFC's Grandest Rally," *Christianity Today* (November 18, 1988).

"Where Are We Headed?" *Youthworker* (summer 1994).

10. Stewards of the Great Commission: The Postwar Missions Movement, 1945

Go and make disciples of all nations," Jesus commanded his followers, "baptizing them in the name of the Father and of the Son and of the Holy Spirit, and teaching them to obey everything I have commanded you." This "Great Commission" not only inspired the early church to boldly proclaim the gospel but has also motivated legions of missionaries to take the Christian message to the uttermost ends of the earth.

Worldwide missionary efforts reached a high point during the 19th century. Church historian Kenneth Scott Latourette has called the years from 1815 to 1914 "the great century" of Christian missions, and during these glory years, new groups like China Inland Mission, Africa Inland Mission, and Sudan Interior Mission penetrated previously unreached areas of the globe. In addition, America's mainline Protestant denominations experienced their own golden age of missions between 1890 and World War I.

But the years between the two world wars witnessed a major shift in U.S. missions activity. Mainline Protestants, influenced by theological liberalism and a changing understanding of the church's role in the world, began to question the importance of evangelizing the world.

Meanwhile, the burgeoning evangelical movement was becoming increasingly organized. The creation of the Interdenominational Foreign Mission Association in 1917 was one example of this trend. And throughout the century, evangelical churches, mission agencies, and parachurch organizations were sending growing numbers of missionaries throughout the world.

"Evangelicals have virtually taken over the field of foreign missions," proclaimed a 1992 article in *Christianity Today.* "Fifty years ago evangelical agencies sponsored 40 percent of all American missionaries; today the figure is over 90 percent." The key to understanding this major shift can be found in the changing attitudes of American evangelicals in the postwar years.

Over There

World War II was a watershed event in world history. Politically, it signified a complete break with earlier U.S. isolationism and paved the way for America to play a greater role in international diplomacy and economics.

Spiritually, World War II ushered in a new age of missionary work. Thousands upon thousands of U.S. servicemen felt compelled to return to the lands where they had once waged war, bringing now a message of peace with God. In addition, a wave of postwar prosperity brought more money to many Christian organizations and causes, in part because many successful capitalists believed one of the best ways to protect the American way of life was to battle Marxism's state-sponsored atheism with Christian evangelism.

This rising tide of missionary interest deeply affected American evangelicals, many of whom increasingly left behind the infighting and division that had been part of their fundamentalist heritage. Casting their eyes to fields that were ripe for spiritual harvest, they began seeking greater cooperation in the urgent challenge of fulfilling Christ's Great Commission.

One of the most powerful examples of this newfound cooperation was the creation of the Evangelical Foreign Missions Association (EFMA) in 1945. An affiliate organization of the National Association of Evangelicals, which had been formed in 1942, the EFMA gathered representatives of 25 sending agencies for its constitutional convention in Chicago in September 1945. Fourteen of the agencies—including denominational missions divisions of the Assemblies of God, the Church of the Nazarene, the Christian and Missionary Alliance, and the Wesleyan Church— became charter members of the EFMA. By the 1990s it represented more than 100 missionary groups, making it the largest association of its kind.

"Onward Christian Soldiers"

The Second World War had an enormous impact on the North American missionary impulse . . . .

Especially for North American evangelicals, the triumph of the Allied forces arrayed around the world excited the missionary imagination, and so did the technological mastery that made these operations possible. Furthermore, the experience of thousands of born-again soldiers and sailors, trained and transported at government expense to serve in faraway lands, led them quite naturally to a greater missions awareness. And thanks to veterans' educational benefits and the abundance of surplus war goods, government spending provided additional support for a postwar missions surge.

—Joel Carpenter

During its first two decades EFMA was guided by Clyde Taylor, who had served as a missionary in Latin America for more than a decade and worked in NAE's Washington, D.C., office. Taylor blazed a course for the new association, giving its members the benefits of research, training, and U.S. government contacts that would have been impossible for most of them to achieve on their own. In time, EFMA would launch the Missionary News Service (later the Evangelical Missions Information Service) and the publication *Evangelical Missions Quarterly*. Resources like these helped member mission agencies know what other groups were up to, and EFMA's regular meetings became an important channel for greater cooperation and effectiveness.

In November 1948 many U.S. evangelicals had their first real contact with committed brothers and sisters from other nations at the First Congress on World Evangelism in Beatenberg, Switzerland. This gathering expanded the vision they had for taking the gospel to all the world.

In a few heady years after World War II, evangelicals in the U.S. launched a host of new missionary organizations and enterprises, including Far Eastern Gospel Crusade (now SEND International), Overseas Crusades, Greater Europe Mission, World Literature Crusade, International Students, TransWorld Radio, and Gospel Films.

In addition, older evangelical groups increased their commitment to world evangelization in the years after the war. For example, InterVarsity Christian Fellowship began hosting its Urbana missions conference, which has inspired thousands of young people to become full-time missionaries. And The Navigators, which had been founded in 1933, spread throughout all branches of the U.S. military during and after the war, helping spawn the ministry's worldwide postwar growth.

A Changing World

At the same time that American evangelicals were increasing their commitment to world evangelization, many mainline Protestant groups were losing their zeal for missions, which had been a cornerstone of the American religious establishment during the late 1800s and the early 1900s.

Part of the decline in mainline missions efforts can be attributed to the growing popularity of liberal theology. American students attending Protestant seminaries were increasingly taught that the Bible was a flawed and largely human work; that the Christian faith lacked historical support for many of its fundamental doctrines, such as the resurrection of Christ; and that U.S. missionaries had no right to practice "religious imperialism" among other faith groups overseas since Christianity had no unique claim to spiritual truth.

The Rockefeller-funded Laymen's Foreign Mission Inquiry investigated the declining mainline interest in missions, publishing its *Rethinking*

Missions report in 1932. The report recommended that Protestant efforts overseas focus on physical and social forms of ministry, much as America's mainline churches had adopted a "Social Gospel" model for their domestic ministries.

At the beginning of the century, virtually all the foreign missionaries sent by U.S. churches were mainline Protestants; however, by the 1990s, nearly all were evangelical. As missions moved into the 21st century, there were no signs of decline in evangelicals' zeal for saving the world.

Resources

Ralph D. Winter, *The Twenty-Five Unbelievable Years, 1945 to 1969* (1970).
Kenneth Scott Latourette, *The 20th Century Outside Europe,* vol. V in *Christianity in a Revolutionary Age* (1962, 1969).
Steve Rabey, *Faith Under Fire: Stories of Courage and Hope from World War II* (2002).

11. From Los Angeles to the World: The Lasting Legacy of Billy Graham, 1949

Billy Graham is one of the world's best-known and most-admired figures and is unquestionably the most influential evangelical of the 20th century. Born—and born again—amidst the contentiousness of fundamentalism, he outgrew what he perceived to be that movement's narrow confines to become an agent of Christian brotherhood throughout the globe. Single-mindedly dedicated to the mission of inviting people to experience a personal relationship with Jesus Christ, he has also become a leader of one of the world's most important parachurch organizations while playing such an important role in the development of evangelicalism that he is often called "a Protestant Pope." An avid critic of Communism during his early years, he transcended politics to become the first Christian to preach in public behind the Iron Curtain after World War II.

Graham's unique accomplishments and the many accolades he has received during half a century of ministry have already been the subject of numerous press profiles and book-length biographies. The most one can hope for from the brief tribute that follows is the sketchiest summary of the milestones that will make up this most unique person's lasting legacy.

Just As He Was

When 16-year-old Billy Graham walked down the aisle at a crusade conducted by fundamentalist Baptist evangelist Mordecai Ham in 1934, nobody knew that the handsome, long-legged boy would preach the gospel more widely than any other figure in church history—personally reaching nearly 200 million people in more than 180 countries, and persuading nearly 3 million souls to accept God's gracious offer of salvation through Christ. It's impossible to estimate how many people have been impacted by Graham's radio, television, and film efforts, but one single event, his 1995 Global Mission Crusade, utilized satellite technology to reach an estimated 1 billion people.

Graham studied at the fundamentalist Bob Jones College and later at the evangelical Wheaton College, where he met wife Ruth Bell, the daughter of missionaries to China. Graham served as a traveling evangelist for Youth for Christ before leading his own crusade in a Los Angeles tent in the fall of 1949. This event, which demonstrated Graham's talent as both a mass evangelist and a mass media figure, would catapult Graham into the national spotlight. "To me it was like a bolt of lightening out of a clear sky," he said. "I was bewildered, challenged and humbled by the sudden avalanche of opportunities that deluged me." One such opportunity, the chance to lead crusades in England in 1954, helped launch Graham's international career.

In 1950 Graham founded the Billy Graham Evangelistic Association, a ministry that would coordinate a host of activities, including the weekly *Hour of Decision* radio program, prime-time television specials, the "My Answer" newspaper column, *Decision* magazine, World Wide Pictures, a book publishing division, international schools of evangelism, and the Billy Graham Training Center at The Cove near Charlotte, North Carolina. Graham also spearheaded the 1974 International Congress on World Evangelization in Lausanne, Switzerland (see chapter 33).

But Graham was more intent on nurturing fellow evangelicals than he was on building up his own empire. In 1956 he played a crucial role in founding *Christianity Today* (see chapter 18), a magazine that helped evangelicalism evolve and mature; and in 1979, his commitment to integrity led to the founding of the Evangelical Council for Financial Accountability, a voluntary organization that has done much to promote fiscal responsibility in Christian ministries (see chapter 39).

For decades, Graham was a towering but kindly father figure around whom far-flung members of the burgeoning evangelical world could flock. He articulated positions on key issues and exhibited Christlike attitudes under the spotlight's intense glare. So great is his impact that one prominent historian concluded that the best definition of an evangelical is "anyone who likes Billy Graham."

A Principled Peacemaker

The fundamentalism from which Graham sprang was contentious and contrarian, but he is revered for his spirit of love and compassion. Still, Graham's role as a peacemaker brought him some of the harshest and most stinging criticism of his career.

A son of the South, Graham was deeply troubled by racial segregation, and he personally removed the ropes separating the seats for whites and "coloreds" at his 1953 Chattanooga Crusade. He also integrated his own organization by hiring African-American evangelist Howard O. Jones to join the preaching team, and even invited Martin Luther King Jr. to lead the prayer at one of his crusades. Such actions were shocking to many Southern whites.

Graham was also willing to extend a hand to Catholics, Anglicans, and mainstream Protestants, inviting them all to participate in the planning for his 1957 New York City Crusade at Madison Square Garden, and directing some of the people who made decisions for Christ during the crusade to their churches. He even endorsed the Revised Standard Version of the Bible, which his fundamentalist brethren had condemned.

For such acts, Graham was dismissed as soft on theological liberalism and called a traitor to the Christian cause. Bob Jones III, a fundamentalist leader and descendant of the founder of Bob Jones University, publicly said the evangelist "has done more harm to the cause of Christ than any other living man." Such criticisms hurt Graham deeply, but characteristically, he didn't strike back or publicly defend himself. Rather, he privately dealt with his own pain while continuing to pursue his calling as a peacemaker.

Billy Graham, the "pastor to presidents," came to national prominence in 1949 at a Los Angeles evangelistic tent meeting. The next year he founded the Billy Graham Evangelistic Association; in 1956 he played a major role in founding *Christianity Today* magazine; in 1974 he spearheaded the International Congress on World Evangelization in Lausanne, Switzerland; and in 1979 his commitment to integrity led to the founding of the Evangelical Council for Financial Accountability.

One of the most controversial aspects of Graham's career has been his unofficial role as "pastor to presidents." Things started off badly when Graham publicly divulged the contents of private conversations he had had with Harry Truman, who called the evangelist a "counterfeit." Graham learned his lesson well, and served as a trusted friend and spiritual adviser to every succeeding U.S. president.

Some politically conservative evangelicals who hadn't been particularly bothered about Graham's cozy relationship with a crook named Nixon raised holy heck about his friendship with a scoundrel named Clinton. Graham was also criticized for remaining aloof from the bare-knuckled political activism of the religious right. "I can identify with them on theology," said Graham, "but in the political emphases they have, I don't, because I don't think Jesus or the apostles took sides in the political arenas of their day." As for the antiabortion group Operation Rescue, which organized massive rallies and protests, Graham said, "I think they have gone much too far, and their cause has been hurt. The tactics ought to be prayer and discussion."

Slowed but Still Standing

During the 1990s, Graham was slowed by advancing age, Parkinson's Disease, and a buildup of fluid on the brain that affected his balance. In November 2000, BGEA's board named son Franklin chief executive officer of the organization. Franklin also filled in for his ailing father by leading a prayer at the inauguration of President George W. Bush.

But no one, not even Franklin himself, believes that anyone will ever be able to fill Billy's unique role as the humble heart and passionate soul of evangelicalism during its formative decades.

At the age of 82, Billy Graham was still preaching at crusades whenever he could, although he had to ride a golf cart to the stage and had to steady himself by gripping the pulpit. But one thing remains the same: the years and miles have neither dimmed his zeal nor altered his message.

"I want to tell you this: as long as God gives me breath, I'm going to continue to preach," he told a crowd of 65,000 people attending a Jacksonville, Florida, crusade in late 2000.

"All you need to understand is that you're a sinner and you need a savior and Jesus is your savior and you're coming to him," he pleaded during the invitation. "We're all looking forward pretty soon to being together up there, and we'll have new bodies."

Resources

Billy Graham, *Just As I Am: The Autobiography of Billy Graham* (1997).
William Martin, *A Prophet with Honor: The Billy Graham Story* (1991).
Marshall Frady, *Billy Graham: A Parable of American Righteousness* (1979).

12. Reds under Our Beds: Confronting the Communist Conspiracy, 1949

Few American evangelicals reacted when the 1917 Bolshevik Revolution brought socialists to power in Russia. Fundamentalist evangelists like Billy Sunday occasionally railed against Marxists, but for most of the first half of the 20th century, the majority of conservative Christians were preoccupied by other matters.

Laypeople seemed more concerned about perceived domestic threats like Catholicism, evolutionary theory, and alcohol abuse than they were about political matters in far-off lands, while Christian leaders were busy fighting theological battles.

By the 1940s, though, evangelicalism was thriving, well organized, and ready to do battle with a growing Communist threat. As the fires of World War II died down and the Cold War began to heat up, two significant events in 1949 helped bring Christian anti-Communism to the boiling point. In August, American scientists discovered fallout from what was believed to be a Russian atomic bomb test; and in October, Communists seized power in the world's most populous nation, establishing the People's Republic of China.

Evangelicals had varied reactions to what was believed by many Americans to be a monolithic Communist colossus intent on world domination. Some studiously analyzed the writings of Karl Marx, who gave the movement its atheistic and materialistic philosophy. Others focused on Communism's aggressive promotion of its values and agenda, or its troubling totalitarian tendencies. Still others succumbed to more paranoid versions of the Red scare. These troubled souls believed that Communism's tentacles had wrapped themselves around nearly every beloved American institution. Their fear-based fantasies led to ceaseless searches for signs of Communist subversion, an approach essayist Richard Hofstadter called "the paranoid style in American politics." Historian George Marsden described this phobia as follows: "All the nation's problems were reduced to communist infiltration of the nation's liberal ecclesiastical, political, and intellectual establishments."

Pulpit Politicos

For much of the first half of the 20th century, most fundamentalists and evangelicals argued that evangelism was the church's top priority and that involvement in politics required worldly compromise; however, many believers were so worried about Communism that they made exceptions. "I would rather win souls to Christ than fight Communism any day," said fundamentalist evangelist Billy James Hargis, "but a man has to do what God calls him to do." Hargis resigned his pulpit in Tulsa, Oklahoma, in 1950 to devote all his energies to combating the Red threat, operating under the motto, "For Christ and Against Communism."

Billy Graham felt Communism was so dangerous that he changed his regular rules of pulpit discourse. During his 1950 Portland crusade, a young Graham told reporters:

> Not once will you hear from this platform an attack, by implica-
> tion or otherwise, against any religious or political group. The only
> one I mention from the platform occasionally is communism, which
> is anti-God, anti-Christ, and anti-American.

Graham made the Red threat a regular feature of his sermons during the 1940s and 1950s, leading one newspaper to call him "Communism's public enemy number one." In 1947, Graham discussed the "domino theory" of country-by-country Communist domination, saying, "Unless the Christian religion rescues these nations from the clutches of the unbelieving, America will stand alone and isolated in the world." The evangelist even hinted he might be willing to leave the pulpit for the presidency, saying, "If the country ever comes close to communism, I will offer myself in any capacity to lead the Christian people of this country in the preservation of their God-given democratic institutions."

Soon, conservative religious leaders launched a host of organizations and efforts. Fundamentalist firebrand Carl McIntire helped found the Christian Anti-Communism Crusade to battle the Red menace. Robert Welch created the John Birch Society, which was named after the Baptist missionary and Army Air Force officer who was killed by the Chinese Communists. The group campaigned to return prayer to the public schools, and even claimed that Presidents Eisenhower, Truman, and Roosevelt were agents of the Communist party. As Peter Lewis wrote in his book *The Fifties*:

> No anti-Communist action or pronouncement could possibly be
> ridiculous. Fear infected Americans with a mass hysteria which had
> not been seen since the Great Crash.

At the height of the anti-Communist hysteria, some conservatives identified America with everything good and godly, equated Communism with everything evil and demonic, and demonized an ever-growing roster of enemies that included Hollywood, labor organizers, the United Nations, the National Council of Churches, the World Council of Churches, peaceniks, public school teachers, promoters of sex education, and the Revised Standard Version of the Bible. One excited crusader even claimed, "The largest single group supporting the Communist apparatus in the United States today is composed of Protestant clergymen."

> ### Stooges in the Pulpit
>
> The largest group supporting the Communist apparatus in the United States today is comprised of Protestant clergymen.
>
> Since the beginning of the First Cold War in April 1948, the Communist Party of this country has placed more and more reliance upon the ranks of the Protestant clergy to provide the party's subversive apparatus with its agents, stooges, dupes, front men, and fellow-travelers. . . .
>
> The international Communist conspiracy aims at the total obliteration of Judeo-Christian civilization.
>
> — "Reds in Our Churches" by J. B. Mathews, published in the *American Mercury,* 1953.

The Lure of Conspiracy Theories

From 1950, when he claimed the U.S. State Department was crawling with Commies, to 1954, when he was condemned by his fellow U.S. senators, Joseph McCarthy fueled the flames of fear and hysteria. His humiliating defeat signaled the end of the worst excesses of the Red scare.

During the early 50s, Donald Grey Barnhouse, editor of *Eternity* magazine, had been one of the few evangelicals to suggest that even though the Red threat must be taken seriously, the fear-mongering of anti-Communists might be an even bigger threat to America's cherished way of life. Most of his evangelical brethren branded him as a liberal or a Communist dupe and ignored his warnings.

During the 1990s, the Union of Soviet Socialist Republics began to unravel at the seams, and Communism appeared to be in a massive retreat. But David Noebel, who assumed leadership of the Christian Anti-Communism Crusade in 1998, warned believers not to be lulled into a false sense of security:

> Indeed, this so-called "quiet" time should be a time for further preparation for the next Marxist threat which is even now raising its ugly head and preparing itself for an assault upon the West.

Senator Joseph McCarthy, United States senator (Republican) from Wisconsin, burst into national prominence when, in a speech in Wheeling, West Virginia, he held up a piece of paper that he claimed was a list of 205 known Communists currently working in the State Department. McCarthy never produced documentation for a single one of his charges, but for the

next four years he exploited an issue that he realized had touched a nerve in the American public. Censured by the Senate in 1954 by a vote of 65 to 22, McCarthy was the most visible political figure of the great Red scare that had dominated the minds of so many evangelicals. McCarthy (left) with lawyer Roy Cohn.

Even though few people take the Communist threat so seriously any longer, its lasting legacy can still be seen in evangelicals' lingering weakness for conspiracy theories that reduce the complexity of modern life to simplistic battles between good and evil.

Long after Communism had ceased to pose a viable threat, evangelicals continued to exhibit their weakness for Manichean dualism and far-fetched conspiracy theories. Throughout the second half of the century, nervous naysayers could be heard proclaiming that the failures in the nation's public schools could be blamed on secular humanists, that the moral decline among young people was due to the lure of rock music played by modern-day pied pipers like Elvis or the Beatles, that the problems plaguing America's families could be laid at the feet of gays and lesbians, or that the long-anticipated end of the world would begin with a computer crisis called Y2K.

Resources

George Marsden, *Understanding Fundamentalism and Evangelicalism* (1987, 1995).

W. Hordern, *Christianity, Communism and History* (1954).

Arnold Forster and Benjamin R. Epstein, *Danger on the Right* (1964).

David A. Noebel, *The Legacy of John Lennon: Charming or Harming a Generation* (1982), and *The Marxist Minstrels: A Handbook on Communist Subversion of Music* (1974).

13. We Buy, Therefore We Are: Prosperity and the Rise of Consumerism, 1950

Wherever true Christianity spreads, it must cause diligence and frugality, which, in the natural course of things, must beget riches! And riches naturally beget pride, love of the world, and every temper that is destructive of Christianity. Now, if there be no way to prevent this, Christianity is inconsistent with itself and, of consequence, cannot stand, cannot continue long among any people; since wherever it generally prevails, it saps its own foundations.

—John Wesley, *Causes of the Inefficacy of Christianity*

In the 1950s an unprecedented wave of prosperity washed over America, and evangelicals—like just about everybody else—dove in, filling their new ranch-style houses in the suburbs with newfangled consumer goods and floating their purchases with credit. Most believers welcomed the nation's newfound wealth, seeing it as both a divine blessing upon a country that had suffered horribly during the Depression and a proof that capitalism—not Communism—would ultimately dominate the world. But most folks didn't give much thought to the causes or consequences of prosperity; they just liked having more stuff.

Ironically, though, a nation that had condemned the Marxists' philosophical materialism fell head over heels for capitalist-style materialism, giving birth to a potent new trinity of Christianity, consumerism, and nationalism that would be America's civil religion for the rest of the century.

Boom Years

Soldiers returning home from Europe's bloody battlefields fueled a postwar boom in births, housing, and higher education; and in 1950, defense spending for the Korean War helped ignite America's economy.

Greed and gluttony, formerly condemned as mortal sins, were now downgraded to lesser offenses. Unbridled consumption was heralded as a patriotic

Larry Burkett is founder and director of Christian Financial Concepts, a nonprofit organization that specializes in teaching Christians biblical principles for managing money. Burkett, heard on more than 1,000 radio outlets worldwide, is author of numerous books, including *The Complete Financial Guide for Young Couples, What Husbands Wish Their Wives Knew about Money, Your Finances in Changing Times,* and *Answers to Your Family's Financial Questions.*

duty that would continue the exponential expansion of America's economy.

But it was advertising, an ancient craft made more effective by experts in the emerging field of psychology, that helped persuade consumers to abandon the older virtues of thrift and self-sacrifice for the new values of self-indulgence and conspicuous consumption. As Vance Packard wrote in his stunning 1957 book *The Hidden Persuaders,* "What the probers are looking for . . . are the *whys* of our behavior, so that they can more effectively manipulate our habits and choices in their favor."

Instead of buying to meet physical needs like food, clothing, and shelter, people began consuming to fulfill more elusive psychological wants and fantasies. According to advertisers, toothpaste wasn't about dental hygiene but about sex appeal. Automobiles didn't merely provide transportation but offered instant status. People didn't buy products; they bought the promise of happiness and self-esteem.

At least for the moment. Planned obsolescence relied on superficial stylistic touches to make people unhappy with last year's purchases—even if they still worked just fine—and make them hanker after the latest models. "We are obligated to work on obsolescence as our contribution to a healthy, growing society," proclaimed an article in *Retailing Daily.*

Author Ron Sider was one of the lone voices crying in the wilderness that unfettered consumerism would corrupt Christianity, heighten class antagonism, deplete finite natural resources, and pollute the environment, but such protests were drowned out by the drone of TV sets and the *ka-ching* of cash registers.

Money, Morals, and Ministry

Tensions between Christianity and capitalism have been a fundamental fact of American life for two centuries. "God gave me my money," claimed oil industry mogul and Baptist layman John D. Rockefeller, who used predatory monopolistic practices to accumulate his wealth during the 19th century and then donated much of it to charitable causes in the 20th century after courts ordered the dissolution of his corporations.

One of the best places to explore Americans' unresolved tensions about God and mammon is around their Christmas trees. In the early 1900s, retailer and Presbyterian layman John Wanamaker made Christmas safe for consumerism by transforming the Grand Court of his Philadelphia store into a "church," complete with a huge pipe organ and a festive nativity scene. Converting his selling floors into shrines, Wanamaker conveyed the message that shopping had now transcended crass commercialism while boosting consumer comfort and sales. In 1950, one happy Wanamaker shopper thanked the store's managers. "I certainly want to congratulate you on your Christmas decorations," she wrote. "It made me feel that Christ my Lord and Savior was in the midst of it all."

In 1952 Norman Vincent Peale's famous book, *The Power of Positive Thinking,* began its three-year stint on national best-seller lists. Peale also wrote an article for *Reader's Digest* in 1953 entitled, "Let the Churches Stand Up for Capitalism."

Stand up they did, for in many ways prosperity was a blessing to the church. As evangelical, fundamentalist, and Pentecostal Christians' fortunes and social standings rose, these believers gave a goodly portion of their earnings to churches and hosts of new Christian parachurch, educational, and missionary organizations. More dollars in the pockets of believers also fueled the growth of the Christian book publishing and retailing industry. Almost overnight, prosperity had given conservative Christians heightened power, popularity, and prestige.

Five Ways Prosperity Changed Evangelicals

1. Old virtues of frugality and self-denial gave way to hunger for financial success.
2. Along with improvements in socioeconomic status came a new "mainstream" prestige along with greater emphasis on this life rather than eternity.
3. Billions of dollars were given to churches and parachurch organizations.
4. These organizations placed greater emphasis on fund-raising and image enhancement.
5. Churches and ministries increasingly stressed their benefits and services rather than asking for sacrificial giving.
   —See "We're in the Money" by Michael S. Hamilton, *Christianity Today,* June 12, 2000, and "Will success spoil evangelicalism?" by Martin Marty, *Christian Century,* July 19–26, 2000.

> ### St. Francis on Possessions
>
> In the 13th century, a simple man by the name of St. Francis of Assisi bucked the prevailing materialism of his day, saying:
>
> "If we had any possessions we should be forced to have arms to protect them, since possessions are a cause of disputes and strife, and in many ways we should be hindered from loving God and our neighbor. Therefore, in this life, we wish to have no temporal possessions."

On the other hand, postwar prosperity and all that came with it raised disturbing questions that American evangelicals would struggle with for the rest of the century. Parachurch organizations trying to meet their ever-expanding budgets debated the ethics of fundraising. Publishers wondered whether they should continue releasing poor-selling books by little-known authors or focus on more lucrative celebrity-driven bestsellers. Thousands of churches adopted seeker-sensitive approaches that emphasized marketing the gospel to increasingly sophisticated religious consumers. And many pastors overlooked troublesome verses like 1 Timothy 6:10 ("the love of money is a root of all kinds of evil"), preferring instead to deliver sermons that equated worldly riches with divine approval.

Never Enough

In 1957 economist John Kenneth Galbraith explored American prosperity in his classic book *The Affluent Society*. Decades later, books and articles talked about the "overspent American," an increasingly common tragic figure whose large paychecks, product-stuffed homes, and gas-guzzling vehicles could keep feelings of insecurity and dissatisfaction at bay.

Trying to find their way out of this economic morass, evangelicals turned to a former electrical engineer named Larry Burkett, who said he had found 700 Bible verses providing "God's perspective on finances." In 1975 Burkett self-published *Your Finances in Changing Times*, the first of more than 70 books. A year later, he left his job at Campus Crusade for Christ to found Christian Financial Concepts. By 2000 the company employed 134 staff members who presented seminars, produced radio shows, and fielded hundreds of thousands of calls from harried believers.

Meanwhile, there were warning signs that America might not be able to sustain good economic times forever. Advertisers were spending more than $300 billion a year to spur greater consumption, but consumers were paying a heavy price, carrying more than $450 billion worth of credit card debt. And in 2001, California suffered an energy crisis. Vice President Dick Cheney, a former oil company executive, rejected as naive the idea that Americans should "do more with less."

Perhaps the most fitting symbol of evangelicals' complex entanglement with the culture of consumerism was the runaway success of *The Prayer of Jabez,* a best-selling book based on 32 previously obscure words from an insignificant Old Testament figure who prayed to God: "Oh, that you would bless me indeed and enlarge my territory."

Author Bruce Wilkinson says he wrote the book with spiritual riches in mind, but many of the consumers who bought more than 8 million copies, along with untold numbers of Jabez coffee mugs, plaques, bookmarks, videos, and companion devotional books, had other things in mind. "Businesspeople say it has increased their profits; single women say it has found them boyfriends; and pastors say it has enlarged their congregations," wrote Laurie Goodstein in the *New York Times.*

Resources

Bruce Barton, *The Man Nobody Knows: A Discovery of the Real Jesus* (1924).
Ron Sider, *Rich Christians in an Age of Hunger* (1977, 1997).
Leigh Eric Schmidt, *Consumer Rites: The Buying and Selling of American Holidays* (1995).
Bruce Barron, *The Health & Wealth Gospel* (1987).

14. Sin or Self-Esteem?: Psychology, Positive Thinking, and the Therapeutic Explosion, 1952

The Power of Positive Thinking, a book about religion and psychology by Reformed Church of America minister Norman Vincent Peale, landed on U.S. best-seller lists in 1952 and stayed there for the next three years. Peale's upbeat approach would help open doors for psychology at many churches, many of which had previously seen Freud, Jung, and everything they stood for as an assault on the true faith.

In 1929 at a Moody Bible Institute conference, minister A. Z. Conrad gave a talk entitled "Modern Psychology, the Foe of Truth." The words he spoke represented the views of most fundamentalists: ". . . of all the modern confederacy of foes which Christianity has to face there is none more subtle, more dangerous than materialistic psychology." A few years later, Moody president Will Houghton decried the worldliness of believers: "Instead of sending for the revivalist, they call in the psychologist."

Soon, though, evangelicals came to see psychology as their friend, not their foe. During the second half of the century, popularizers like James Dobson would convince millions of parents that self-esteem was a necessary ingredient in raising happy, healthy children. Dismissing a "worm" theology that denigrates man, Dobson defended self-esteem as a basic human right: "*Every* child is entitled to hold up his head, not in haughtiness or pride, but in confidence and security," he wrote in *Hide and Seek.*

During the final decades of the century, authors, speakers, and counselors like Larry Crabb, Frank Minrith, Paul Meier, Stephen Arterburn, Dan Allender, Neil Anderson, Robert McGee, and Gary Moon would help make therapeutic terms and techniques an essential component of modern-day ministry.

And thanks to Robert Schuller, who like Peale was a Reformed Church of America minister, pop psychology would become one of the cornerstones of the megachurch movement. Schuller adapted Peale's ideas for his own concept of "possibility thinking" and invited Peale to speak at Garden Grove Community Church, which Schuller opened in an Orange County drive-in theater in 1955.

Evangelical theologians criticized Schuller for rewriting both the Bible (Schuller called the Beatitudes the "Be Happy Attitudes") and ecclesiology (in 1982 Schuller published *Self-Esteem: The New Reformation*), but thousands of evangelical pastors flocked to the $20 million Crystal Cathedral to attend the Robert H. Schuller Institute for Successful Church Leadership, where they received practical instruction in church growth. Among the young pastors Schuller influenced was Bill Hybels, whose Willow Creek Community Church would pioneer the "seeker-sensitive" movement, becoming the most influential congregation of the latter part of the century (see chapter 34).

Don't Worry, Be Happy

Christians had long believed that life's sorrow and suffering were an earthly prelude to heavenly joys, but in the prosperous, postwar 1950s, believers increasingly demanded happiness now. By the end of the century, pastors were preaching fewer sermons on subjects like sin and sanctification, choosing instead to focus on people's "felt needs" and peppering their homilies with references to wholeness, self-actualization, and self-fulfillment.

Even Billy Graham gave salvation a therapeutic update in his 1953 book *Peace with God*; and *God's Psychiatry*, a book by Methodist minister Charles Allen, claimed that happiness could come through "thinking the thoughts" of biblical passages like Psalm 23, which "represents a positive, hopeful, faith approach to life." Christian counselor Clyde Narramore wrote numerous articles on "Your Psychological Needs" between 1954 and 1955, while pioneering psychologists like Paul Tournier and Karl Menninger helped unite the pastor's pulpit with the counselor's couch.

In the 1970s, best-selling authors like Tim LaHaye and James Dobson brought psychological concepts to the evangelical

Dr. Robert Schuller, a Reformed Church of America minister, heads the $20 million Crystal Cathedral, located in Garden Grove, California. The Crystal Cathedral is the home base for the international Crystal Cathedral Ministries, including a congregation of over 10,000 members and the internationally televised *Hour of Power*.

masses, but their work also brought criticism. Dobson said his 1970 book *Dare to Discipline* represented a recovery of traditional biblical principles, but Jay Adams, the leading spokesman for a "Biblical Counseling" movement that rejected the very idea of mental illness, called *Dare* "a godless humanistic book" that merely reworked secular concepts of behavioral modification.

Adams, John MacArthur Jr. Dave Hunt, and other critics argued that the therapeutic movement was inherently anti-Christian and that it exchanged personal responsibility for a mentality of victimization and blame. Meanwhile, Gary Collins, president of the 18,000-member American Association of Christian Counselors, said therapy was a neutral technique, but like everything else, it could be abused.

Fuller Theological Seminary opened its pioneering Graduate School of Psychology in 1964, and soon, students flocked to Christian counseling programs. Three decades later, Denver Seminary began limiting enrollment to its counseling programs, which threatened to overtake other disciplines. "There are a number of people who have graduate school training in psychology, but Sunday-school training in theology," admitted AACC's Gary Collins.

By the mid-1990s, Christian counseling was a growing segment of America's $200 billion mental health industry.

Pastors under Pressure

If self-esteem was supposed to be the new evangelical Reformation, somebody forgot to tell the pastors—70 percent of whom said they felt worse after their years in the pastorate than they did when they began. Many ministers said they were struggling to cope with increasing expectations and decreasing respect.

Parishioners expect their pastors to be superb orators; empathetic counselors; model parents; thoughtful theologians; pioneering church growth gurus; efficient managers of people, programs, and finances; dignified officiators at baptisms, weddings, and funerals; and astute observers of all things spiritual, cultural, and political. Perhaps it should come as no surprise, then, that burnout and discouragement are many pastors' constant companions. A 1991 poll conducted by the Barna Research Group found that less than one percent of pastors surveyed said they were doing "tremendous, highly

> ### The Possibility Thinker's Creed
>
> When faced with a mountain, I will not quit. I will keep on striving until I climb over, pass through, tunnel underneath—or simply stay and turn the mountain into a gold mine, with God's help.
>
> —Robert Schuller

effective work," and an astounding 53 percent said they were having "little positive impact on souls and society." Barna calls pastors "the most occupationally frustrated people in America."

Other recent surveys say 70 percent of pastors don't have close friends they can confide in, and 37 percent say loneliness and isolation have drawn them into inappropriate sexual relationships with members of their churches. Others struggle with the temptations of online pornography.

Like members of their flocks, more pastors have been seeking help through therapy, but a growing number of ministries to ministers say real relief comes only through programs that mix counseling with spiritual formation. "The Bible doesn't show us the workaholism, perfectionism and compulsions we see in the lives of so many pastors," says Bob Sewell, founder of SonScape, a Colorado ministry to hurting pastors. "The Bible shows us how to balance work, worship, play and rest. We're trying to help pastors and their families get off the insidious treadmill that everyone in America is on."

By the end of the century, thousands of churches were offering programs in divorce recovery, sexual abuse, assorted addictions, and other problems. Unlike their fundamentalist predecessors, most evangelicals believed psychology was a beneficial tool that could help them understand and heal people's problems.

Resources

Norman Vincent Peale, *The Power of Positive Thinking* (1952).
Carol V. R. George, *God's Salesman: Norman Vincent Peale and the Power of Positive Thinking* (1993).
Charles L. Allen, *God's Psychiatry* (1953).
Seth Farber, *Unholy Madness: The Church's Surrender to Psychiatry* (1999).

15. Healing Body and Soul: Holistic Ministry through Relief and Development, 1953

Many Christians who returned to America after serving in World War II were inspired to save the souls of people in faraway lands, and their efforts gave birth to a major new phase of missionary activity. Other believers, who were distressed by the poverty and human suffering they had seen during World War II and the Korean War, committed themselves to doing something to relieve people's physical suffering. These caring Christians founded some of America's first evangelical relief and development organizations.

The purpose of such organizations is twofold: providing immediate *relief* for people's suffering, whether caused by war, natural disasters, or governmental incompetence or corruption; and providing the money, expertise, training, and resources for communities to *develop* the institutions and infrastructures they need to get back on their feet and build more hopeful futures.

World Relief, the relief and development arm of the National Association of Evangelicals, was founded in 1944 to provide assistance to victims of World War II, but it would take another decade before most evangelicals embraced the concept of ministering to people's physical needs.

Today, World Relief works hand-in-hand with churches and mission agencies around the world, helping them provide assistance to needy people in the areas where they minister. But this organization was merely the first in a growing number of groups that encouraged evangelicals to begin providing the kind of physical help mainline Protestants had been giving for decades—a point evangelical thinker Carl Henry made in his influential 1947 manifesto *The Uneasy Conscience of Modern Fundamentalism*.

In time, more and more believers were giving heed to Jesus' message—found in Matthew 25—about the importance of meeting people's physical needs. As the passage says, those who feed the hungry, give water to the thirsty, provide clothing for the naked, care for the sick, and visit prisoners are ministering to Christ himself, and are given a reward of eternal life; those who don't do these things are banished to eternal punishment.

Feeling Their Pain

During the first half of the 20th century, most fundamentalists and evangelicals preferred to quote verses like "Man does not live on bread alone," or "The poor you will always have with you."

Not only was citing such verses much easier than actually doing something to address people's physical needs, but also it allowed evangelicals to claim spiritual superiority over liberal Protestants, who were condemned for promoting a "social gospel" that focused more on physical care than on personal salvation.

It took a while for most American evangelicals to realize that caring for the world's physical needs was part of their duty as Christians; however, when they saw the light after World War II, they earnestly began making up for lost time.

One of the people who helped turn the tide was evangelist Bob Pierce. Bob was working on a missions film in China in 1948 when he met a ragged, hungry child named White Jade at a girls' school run by Christian missionaries. The school didn't have money to care for the girl, so Pierce gave them five dollars and promised to send more later. He lost contact with the girl after the Communists seized power in China in 1949, but he never lost the desire to help children like White Jade.

Bob Pierce, first president and founder of World Vision, hugs a boy and girl in Seoul, Korea. He wrote on the flyleaf of his Bible a motto still used today by WV staff around the world: "Let my heart be broken with the things that break the heart of God." Pierce founded World Vision in 1953. World Vision is working today in nearly 100 countries, giving aid and relief to the poor and needy.

By early 1950, Pierce was preaching in Korea, which had been divided after World War II, and saw war erupt in 1950 when the South was invaded by soldiers from the North. When he went home to America, Pierce regularly told American audiences about the hardships endured by Korean Christians, begging his listeners to do what they could to help.

When Billy Graham heard of their plight, he publicly proclaimed that he was canceling an order to buy a shiny new Chevrolet and giving the money instead to help the Koreans. As more money came in, Pierce founded World Vision in September 1953, writing these words in the flyleaf of his Bible: "Let my heart be broken with the things that break the heart of God."

After a Korean cease-fire was declared in 1953, World Vision began helping war orphans by recruiting Americans to "sponsor" them at the cost of a few dollars a month. Today World Vision's U.S. operations have an annual budget of nearly $350 million, and its international partners, who work in nearly 100 countries, have a budget of more than $650 million and a staff of 10,000 people.

Bob Pierce wasn't the only American evangelist in Korea in the early 1950s. Everett Swanson went there to preach to American servicemen and wound up falling in love with the needy children he saw. When he talked about Korea during his American revival meetings, people gave him money, which he used to found Compassion International in 1953. By 2000 the ministry had an annual budget of $92.5 million and was helping a quarter-million children in 22 countries.

Seeing the Connection

For much of the first half of the 20th century, American evangelicals labored under a Gnostic misconception that God cared greatly about people's souls but cared little about their bodies. Such confusion never infected William Booth, the evangelist who founded the Salvation Army in a London slum in 1865. Today, the Army is the world's largest charity, taking in more than $600 million in private support and millions more in government grants, which it uses to care for bodies and minister to souls. "We have a burning desire to meet their needs, both material and spiritual," said an Army leader. "One is not complete without the other."

During the 1970s, Franklin Graham would come to the same conclusion. The son of world-renowned evangelist Billy Graham, Franklin became the president of the relief and development organization called Samaritan's Purse

Franklin Graham, son of evangelist Billy Graham, became president of the relief and development organization called Samaritan's Purse in 1976 after the death of its founder, World Vision's Bob Pierce.

in 1976 after the death of its founder, World Vision's Bob Pierce. "My father has never suggested that my ministry should mirror his, though our common priority is evangelism," Franklin told the *Saturday Evening Post* in 1985. "While my father pursues this objective through city-wide crusades, I do it individually."

The following year the two Grahams gave a powerful demonstration of how the two forms of ministry could work together. Billy's ministry hosted 8,000 preachers at his International Conference for Itinerant Evangelists in Amsterdam, and Franklin Graham's ministry gave each of the 7,500 men in attendance two shirts, a tie, a pair of socks, and tennis shoes. "I've been praying for some shoes," one delighted man told *TIME* magazine.

> ## Ministering to Bodies and Souls
>
> In response to the Great Commission, Compassion International exists as an advocate for children, to release them from their spiritual, economic, social, and physical poverty and enable them to become responsible, fulfilled Christian adults.
>
> — Compassion International 1995 mission statement

Still, groups like Samaritan's Purse continued to receive criticism for their work. In 2000, the AD2000 & Beyond movement released a report arguing that many relief and development ministries weren't religious enough. As a result, the report said the people they help "will experience the greatest disaster in the universe; going to hell." On the other hand, in 2001 Samaritan's Purse came under fire from the U.S. Agency for International Development, which claimed the group's work was too religious. The agency threatened to withdraw government relief funds from the ministry's work with El Salvador earthquake victims unless Samaritan's Purse did more to avoid the appearance that tax dollars were being used to fund prayer proselytizing.

But for growing numbers of evangelicals, meeting people's physical needs in the name of Christ continued to be a powerful means of proclaiming the gospel by demonstrating its transforming truths.

Resources

Franklin Graham with Jeanette Lockerbie, *Bob Pierce: This One Thing I Do* (1983).

John Stott, *Involvement: Being a Responsible Christian in a Non-Christian Society* (1985).

16. From Procreation to Recreation: Seeds of the Sexual Revolution, 1953

Sex was a subject Americans once found too confusing and embarrassing to discuss in polite company, but the 1960s sexual revolution brought the subject to center stage, and the silent majority no longer had the luxury of remaining silent. Suddenly, controversial issues like abortion, pornography, and homosexuality were front-page news, inspiring millions of evangelicals to unprecedented levels of social and political activism. By the 1980s and 1990s, many folks concluded that sex was the main thing evangelicals thought about.

Pinpointing the birthplace of the sexual revolution isn't easy, but a good place to start may be the laboratory of biologist Alfred Kinsey. Not content studying the reproduction techniques of birds and bees, Kinsey focused instead on the sex lives of men and women. He founded the pioneering Institute for Sex Research at Indiana University in 1942, and his two groundbreaking reports, *Sexual Behavior of the Human Male* (1948) and *Sexual Behavior of the Human Female* (1953), indicated that things were wilder behind bedroom doors than people typically let on.

While Kinsey gave Americans clinical data, Hugh Hefner gave them breasts. A cheesecake photo of Marilyn Monroe was the highlight of the fall 1953 debut issue of *Playboy*, a magazine that aimed to take female nudity out of the realm of porn shops and stag films and make it an essential element of a more mainstream "good life." *Playboy* packaged smiling, wholesome-looking, nearly-nude women alongside articles by respected writers like Norman Mailer and Isaac Asimov. It conducted interviews with national leaders like Martin Luther King Jr. and Jimmy Carter in a glossy, glitzy magazine that editor Hefner said was designed to "thumb its nose at all the phony puritan values of the world in which I had grown up." By 1969 *Penthouse* was making *Playboy* look prudish by bringing genital nudity to newsstands nationwide. And by the 1990s, the Internet was delivering graphic sexual material—including depictions of pedophilia and bestiality—to home computers.

While some Americans were content looking at sexy photos, others wanted action, fueling a boom in extramarital sex that was aided by the birth control pill, which had been developed in the 1950s and first went on sale in 1961. Greater sexual openness, combined with the pill's chemical "insurance policy," changed the way Americans dated and mated. As George Marsden said, "When the sexual revolution of the 1960s had run its course, both private and public sexual mores had changed dramatically."

Out of the Closet

Some evangelicals were still waking up to the heterosexual revolution when they were forced to confront another major challenge to traditional teachings on marriage and family.

New York City police officers executing a raid at Greenwich Village's Stonewall Inn on June 28, 1969, were in for a surprise when the bar's mostly gay patrons fought back. Today, the "Stonewall Riots" are seen as the opening salvo in the campaign for gay rights, and the inn is listed on the National Register of Historic Places.

Hugh Hefner, surrounded by "playmates of the month," started *Playboy* magazine in 1953 that showed nude photographs amidst literary articles by the likes of Norman Mailer and fiction by Isaac Asimov. Playboy featured lengthy interviews with national celebrities, such as Rev. Martin Luther King Jr. and former President Jimmy Carter. As part of the sexual revolution of the 1950s, Hefner said his magazine was designed to "thumb his nose at all the phony puritan values of the world in which I had grown up."

One year before Stonewall, Pentecostal preacher Troy Perry saw that one of the biggest battlegrounds for gays was churches where Old and New Testament passages opposing homosexuality held sway, so he founded the gay-friendly Universal Fellowship of Metropolitan Community Churches, which now has hundreds of congregations and thousands of members worldwide.

Throughout the 1970s, 1980s, and 1990s, Christian denominations had heated debates about the origins of same-sex orientation, the morality of homosexual behavior, and civil rights and ordination for gays. "This is not just another moral issue, this is the issue on which we defend or abandon the authority of the Bible," said David Seamands, who led the effort to maintain the United Methodist Church's historic bans on gay sex and ordination.

Others, like evangelical singer Anita Bryant, weren't debating but were taking action. Bryant led a controversial Florida campaign against the gay movement while Exodus International, an umbrella movement of ministries to gays and ex-gays, promoted the message that gays could go "straight." "I have no doubt, based on my own life and the experiences of hundreds of people I know personally, that homosexuals can change," said Exodus International executive Bob Davies. But Mel White, who worked as an evangelical author and filmmaker before coming out of the closet, vehemently disagreed with the claims of such groups. White had spent decades in prayer and counseling in an unsuccessful effort to change his orientation. "I was a victim of their false hope," he said, "and I almost ended up killing myself because I believed them."

Conservative Christians' attitudes toward gays contributed to their failure to respond compassionately when the AIDS epidemic struck in the 1980s. Pat Buchanan, a Catholic, was among the most outspoken: "The poor homosexuals. They have declared war on nature and now nature is exacting an awful retribution." It was also widely reported that Jerry Falwell called AIDS "the wrath of God upon homosexuals," although he denied it. Regardless, in late 1999, Falwell met with Mel White and other homosexuals, and he urged evangelicals to tone down their hateful, homophobic rhetoric.

From the Bedroom to the Public Square

The 1960's sexual revolution forced evangelicals to rethink their theology of sexuality. Many denominations approved a variety of mechanical and chemical approaches to birth control, parting ways with the Roman Catholic Church, which maintains that such efforts are unnatural and counter to God's purposes for marriage.

Evangelicals also acknowledged that Hugh Hefner had been partially right about at least one thing: pleasure was an important part of sex. During the 1970s and 1980s, Christian publishers created sanctified sex manuals like Tim and Beverly LaHaye's *The Act of Marriage: The Beauty of Sexual Love,* and Ed and Gaye Wheat's *Intended for Pleasure.* As writer Carol Flake said, "Christians hoped to wrest the joys of sex, like the powers of TV, from the exclusive possession of secular humanists."

Meanwhile, some believers waged war on the sexual revolution. Donald Wildmon's American Family Association led the campaign against porn, targeting 7-11 stores in one successful nationwide effort. Others tried to promote purity through legislation and met with mixed results. James

Dobson, who participated in Attorney General Meese's pornography commission, once declared the battle against porn "a winnable war," but home video, cable TV, and the Internet made sexually explicit material almost universally available to anyone who wanted it.

Opposition to abortion, long a central plank in the conservative Christian political agenda, yielded few tangible results, leading many evangelicals to throw their support behind efforts like Crisis Pregnancy Centers, which ministered to pregnant women nationwide.

As for the fight against the "gay agenda," evangelicals thought they had a major victory in 1992 when 53 percent of Colorado voters approved Amendment 2, a measure that limited gay rights in the state. But the U.S. Supreme Court ruled the measure unconstitutional in 1996, saying, "Amendment 2 classified homosexuals not to further a proper legislative end but to make them unequal to everyone else."

Frustration with such setbacks caused some desperate radicals to take matters into their own hands, launching violent attacks on gays, abortion clinics, and their personnel. Meanwhile, young people were proving even more desperate for love and intimacy than their parents' generation had been during the 1960s. By the 1990s, news reports described how school districts around the country were confronting previously unimaginable levels of teen and preteen sexual behavior, along with the outbreaks of sexually transmitted disease that often accompany such experimentation. Once unleashed, the sexual revolution showed no signs of stopping.

Resources

Final Report of the Attorney General's Commission on Pornography (1986).
Ed and Gaye Wheat, *Intended for Pleasure* (1977).
Mel White, *Stranger at the Gate: To Be Gay and Christian in America* (1994).
James R. Petersen, *Playboy's History of the Sexual Revolution: 1900–1999* (illustrated, 1999).

17. The Missionary Martyrs: Love and Death in Ecuador's Rain Forest, 1956

The five men and their families were enjoying the best years of their lives, but their happiness wasn't due to America's newfound prosperity, complete with its cornucopia of consumer goods. Instead, like thousands of fellow evangelicals, these men and women in their 20s and 30s were serving Christ on foreign soil during an unprecedented postwar boom in American missionary activity.

In their case, the foreign soil was the lush, tropical rain forests of Ecuador. From a primitive base named Shell Mera—a former oil exploration camp located on the Pacific side of the rugged Andes Mountains—the missionaries worked among the Quechua, the Jivaro, and other tribes, preaching the gospel and providing medical services, sanitation training, and language instruction.

But the work of cross-cultural evangelism was demanding and difficult, and the five missionaries were restless. Out of a combination of youthful exuberance and evangelistic zeal, they set their sites on reaching out to the Huaorani people, an isolated and violent tribe better known among many people as the Acuas, a term that meant "savages." "Wherever you are, be all there," said Jim Elliot, who had been sent to Ecuador by the U.S. organization, Christian Missions in Many Lands. "Live to the hilt every situation you believe to be the will of God."

The Huaorani's reputation for bloodshed was a cause for concern, but hadn't Jesus instructed his followers to go into *all* the world and preach the gospel? "He is no fool who gives what he cannot keep to gain what he cannot lose," said Elliot.

Nate Saint, who toiled alongside Elliot and the others, was an airplane pilot with the U.S.-based Mission Aviation Fellowship. During his years in the jungle, Saint had experienced more than his share of close calls, but his zest was unquenchable. Following one near-fatal accident, he returned to his cockpit wearing a cast that extended from his neck to his thighs. "Every time I take off, I am ready to deliver up the life I owe to God," Saint had said.

Who knew how eerily prophetic those words were? And who could imagine the worldwide impact those five dedicated missionaries would have?

Reaching the Unreachable

After months of seeking God's guidance about how to reach the Huaorani, the five men settled on an elaborate strategy that included weekly flights over the remote village in Saint's small propeller plane to drop gifts for the villagers. After three months of fly-overs, all seemed to be going well. So in January 1956 the men landed on a beach near the village and set up camp. Faith and fear intermingled as the men prepared to approach the Huaorani and tell them about God's love face-to-face.

On Friday, January 6, things went well. There was a brief and friendly meet-

Elisabeth Elliot, wife of Jim Elliot, wrote *Through Gates of Splendor,* a book that tells the story of the ministry and martyrdom of five missionaries killed in Ecuador in 1956.

ing with a few of the villagers. Then on Sunday, everything went horribly wrong. A group of Huaorani, with their long, handmade spears, attacked and instantly killed all five men.

It took days for a ground party combing the dense jungle to find the men's bodies and the vandalized remains of their plane. But shortly after news of their deaths was transmitted to the waiting widows, the killing of the missionaries became an international media event. In time, the episode inspired books, TV shows, a film, and even a musical drama.

Many Americans had heard of Billy Graham, but few knew about the work of missionaries around the globe. That all changed as people read reports of the missionaries' deaths in newspapers and magazines. Even those people who didn't subscribe to the dead men's theology expressed admiration for their courage and idealism and applauded their commitment to help civilize primitive people in faraway lands.

Within evangelical circles, the men were hailed as modern martyrs, and their deaths inspired even more young people to leave the comforts of home for Christian service in remote and dangerous places. Nearly two dozen young men reportedly volunteered to take Nate Saint's place as a pilot in Ecuador.

Elisabeth Elliot, the wife of Jim Elliot, wrote about the whole episode in her 1957 book, *Through Gates of Splendor,* saying the men's death "motivated many to join the evangelistic enterprise." Elliot, who would go on to become a popular writer and lecturer, added an update in a 25th anniversary edition of the book:

> At least hundreds were jolted by the sacrifice of five young men to whom obedience to their Lord was quite literally a matter of life and death. In a civilization where, in order to be sure of their manhood (or, alas, even their 'personhood'), men must box, lift weights, play football, jog, rappel or hang-glide, it was startling to realize that there was such a thing as spiritual commitment as robust, as total, and perhaps more demanding than the most fanatical commitment to physical fitness. It was a shock to learn that anybody cared that much about anything, especially if it was invisible.

The dead missionaries' bodies were buried in a spot near where they died. In 1959, Elisabeth Elliot and Rachel Saint, Nate's sister, returned to the jungle with their families to continue the unfinished work of reaching the Huaorani. As Elliot pointed out in her book *The Savage My Kinsman*, the Indians had been moved by the sacrifice of the five men, who could have—but didn't—shoot the Indians with their rifles. In time, they even developed an interest in the message the men had tried to bring, as did much of the watching world.

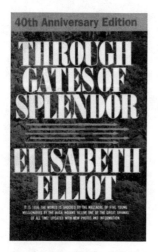

In *Through Gates of Splendor,* five young men dared to make contact with a stone-age tribe deep in the jungles of Ecuador. The goal was to establish communication with a people whose only previous response to the outside world had been to attack all strangers. The men's mission combined modern technology with innate ingenuity, sparked by a passionate determination to get the gospel to a people without Christ.

As Stephen Saint, the pilot's son, put it, the event "became a primary narrative for the young evangelical movement, reinforcing and illustrating to the world our core ideals."

As growing numbers of committed young Christians went throughout the world to spread the gospel, many of them carried in their hearts the words of Jim Elliot, who had said, "When it comes time to die, make sure all you have to do is die."

Resources

Elisabeth Elliot, *Through Gates of Splendor* (1956) and *The Savage My Kinsman* (1961).
Stephen E. Saint, "The Unfinished Mission to the 'Aucas,'" *Christianity Today* (March 2, 1998).

18. Finding a Voice:
Christianity Today Builds an Evangelical Consensus, 1956

Quick: Who was Henry Knox Sherrill, Franklin Clark Fry, Eugene Clarkson Blake, or Henry Pitney Van Dusen? We're not sure ourselves, but these four pillars of the mainline Protestant establishment graced the cover of *TIME* magazine during the 1950s. Meanwhile, the movers and shakers of the emerging evangelical movement remained largely unknown, and many conservative Christians felt isolated even from like-minded believers.

Billy Graham determined to help change all that. "Repeatedly in those days I came across men and women in virtually every denomination who were committed to the historic biblical faith," said Graham. "And yet they had no standard around which to rally, and no place they could look for spiritual encouragement and intellectual challenge. *Christianity Today* came into being to help fill that vacuum."

With Graham leading the way, *Christianity Today* sought to articulate a broad-based evangelical consensus on both the foundations of the faith and their application to contemporary life. The magazine would not only help evangelicals understand the breadth and depth of their growing movement but also it would provide curious observers with reliable information about who evangelicals were and what they were up to. As the editors stated in "Why *Christianity Today*," their slightly defensive editorial in the October 15, 1956, debut issue:

> *Christianity Today* has its origin in a deepfelt desire to express historical Christianity to the present generation. Neglected, slighted, misrepresented—evangelical Christianity needs a clear voice, to speak with conviction and love, and to state its relevance to the world crisis.

To fulfill these lofty goals, *CT*'s editors assembled a team of international correspondents ("Swift airmail service speeds their reports to the

73

news desk") and enlisted the help of a group that few people knew existed: "evangelical scholars." Using these resources, along with generous funding from John Howard Pew, a theologically and politically conservative oil mogul and industrialist, the editors set out to help pastors "return to truly biblical preaching" and promote "true ecumenicity" among "believers in Jesus Christ," all the while avoiding "controversial denominational differences." Even trickier, *CT* aimed to "apply the biblical revelation to the contemporary social crisis." As its editors added, "This, Fundamentalism has often failed to do."

Within a decade, *CT* had replaced the *Christian Century,* its older mainline Protestant competitor, as the most widely read religious magazine in the nation. Even more, *CT,* which was headquartered in Washington, D.C., gave evangelicals hope that their movement might one day be considered part of America's religious mainstream. "The editors daily look down Pennsylvania Avenue and glimpse the White House," read the debut editorial. "Thus *Christianity Today* is a symbol of the place of the evangelical witness in the life of the public."

An Ideological Barometer

Throughout its history, *CT* has explored both the fundamentalist heartland and the progressive hinterlands of American evangelicalism. It has featured articles by authors as varied as FBI director J. Edgar Hoover and Ron Sider of Evangelicals for Social Action, and it has alternately praised and criticized evangelicalism's leading lights.

CT's first executive editor was L. Nelson Bell, who had served 25 years in China as a medical missionary and was Graham's father-in-law, but it was initial editor-in-chief Carl Henry who made most of the decisions about what ran in the magazine. Although Graham had worried that Henry might be too conservative, he proved to be too liberal for Pew, who used his influence to have Henry replaced by Harold Lindsell in 1968. According to one scholar, Lindsell righted the ship and "readily provided Christianized versions of the rhetoric of Spiro Agnew during the Nixon era."

Lindsell, who had become a leader of the biblical inerrancy movement, was replaced by Kenneth Kantzer in 1978, but by then *CT*'s conservative tone had already inspired the emergence of competing evangelical publications. As George Marsden said:

> In 1971, dissident students at Trinity Evangelical Divinity School (a leading center for 'establishment evangelicalism') organized The People's Christian Coalition and founded an underground newspaper, *The Post-American,* later becoming *Sojourners,* published by the radical evangelical Sojourner's Community in Washington, D.C.

Senator Mark Hatfield became the best-known supporter of this movement.

By 1999 *CT* was a thick, glossy magazine published 18 times a year and enjoying a paid circulation of nearly 200,000. Its parent company, CTi, published magazines for pastors (*Leadership* journal), women (*Today's Christian Woman*), youth (*Campus Life*), church administrators (*Your Church*), couples (*Marriage Partnership*), and other specialized titles like *Christian History, Computing Today, Christian Parenting Today,* and the thoughtful journal *Books & Culture.* CTi also supports a popular and award-winning Web site (www.christianity today.com).

> ## "Why *Christianity Today*"
>
> *Christianity Today* has its origin in a deepfelt desire to express historical Christianity to the present generation. Neglected, slighted, misrepresented—evangelical Christianity needs a clear voice, to speak with conviction and love, and to state its relevance to the world crisis.
>
> — from an editorial in the magazine's debut issue

Meet the Press

As evangelicalism grew and prospered, so did Christian publishing. In April 1998, members of the Evangelical Press Association (EPA) gathered in Chicago to celebrate the 50th anniversary of their group, whose 300-plus member publications represent denominations, parachurch organizations, missionary groups, and private publishing houses and have a combined circulation of over 20 million.

Big anniversaries give people a chance to debate the past and predict the future, and EPA50 was no exception. "In the early days, most editors were retired pastors, and many magazines published sermon excerpts," says Doug Trouten, an EPA board member, editor, and journalism instructor. "Today the organization is dominated by journalists who have little theological background."

Among the many interesting tidbits Trouten uncovered when he researched EPA was that in the early years it passed resolutions opposing formal diplomatic ties with the Vatican, interstate liquor advertising, and federalization of school funding. Unlike the National Religious Broadcasters, EPA soon stopped debating such resolutions at its annual meetings.

Instead, EPA editors and writers routinely discuss issues like how to serve two masters: their own sense of Christian truth and their employer's particular version of it. "There is always some tension there," said John Walker, a former editor for LifeWay Christian Resources, an agency of the Southern Baptist Convention.

Christian editors also wrestle with how to cover complex and controversial issues. A conference-opening workshop entitled "News Priorities: Advocacy, Balance, or the Party Line?" illustrated EPA's diversity by bringing together editors from the right-wing *World,* the left-leaning *Sojourners,* and *CT,* which tries to stake out a more moderate position.

Following that heated discussion, *CT* associate editor Douglas LeBlanc hosted a session entitled "Speaking the Truth in Love":

> There are two great temptations. We can say cultural questions are irrelevant and hide our heads in the sand. Or we can engage these questions in a belligerent way. There is also a middle way, which tackles these subjects, but does so in the spirit of Christ.

Intentionally or otherwise, LeBlanc was echoing the words of publishing pioneer Billy Graham, who said, "The one badge of Christians is not orthodoxy, but love."

Resources

Douglas Sweeney, "Christianity Today," in Mark Fackler and Charles H. Lippy, eds., *Popular Religious Magazines of the United States* (1995).

Quentin J. Schultze, editor, *American Evangelicals and the Mass Media* (1990).

19. Catholicism Goes Mainstream: John F. Kennedy and Vatican II, 1960

Catholics came to North America before British Protestant colonists sailed for the New World. And by the mid-1990s, there were 60 million Catholics in the U.S., their numbers dwarfing the membership figures for any one of the dozens of major Protestant denominations.

Still, Protestants have long outnumbered Catholics, who remained outside the mainstream of American society until the 1960s.

Some conservative Protestants had long equated the Catholic Church with the prophesied Prostitute of Babylon, called the pope the Anti-Christ, and referred to lay Catholics as "Papists." Scholar David Harrington Watt describes this animosity: "Fundamentalists regarded Catholicism as a perverted form of Christianity and they were seldom inclined to minimize the enormity of those perversions." Even in some secular circles, people questioned whether Catholics were true-blue Americans.

Many of these long-standing prejudices disintegrated after a man with Irish Catholic roots ascended to the nation's highest office and the church's hierarchy radically changed what it meant to be a Catholic.

Keeping Church and State Separate

For much of the 20th century, conservative Christians watched nervously as Catholics struggled for respectability and political power. Some of the tensions were class-based. Middle-class Protestants felt lower-class Catholics from Ireland and Germany were dirtier, less literate, and more inclined to drunkenness than good Christians ought to be. Clyde Taylor, an early leader in the National Association of Evangelicals, spoke for many people when he claimed that Catholics and Communists were essentially the same.

In the 1970s evangelicals would become increasingly active in politics, but in the preceding decades they opposed Catholic activism, saying their main concern was to preserve a constitutionally mandated separation of church and state.

President-elect John F. Kennedy shakes hands with Father Richard J. Casey, the pastor of Holy Trinity Church, after attending mass there prior to the 1961 inauguration ceremonies. Kennedy, America's first Catholic president, didn't become a puppet of the pope, as many Christians believed he would be.

In the 1940s and 1950s, evangelicals vigorously opposed President Harry Truman's efforts to appoint a personal envoy to the Vatican. And in 1960, NAE unsuccessfully opposed candidate John F. Kennedy. "We were absolutely unable to convince the press that the Protestant concern was the continued separation of church and state and that we were not entering politics nor attacking a person," said NAE's Clyde Taylor.

Evangelicals weren't alone in opposing Kennedy. Norman Vincent Peale and other prominent mainline Protestants worried that the pope was pulling Kennedy's strings like some papal puppet master—a view that was conveyed with frightening urgency on a mass-produced booklet entitled "If America Elects a Catholic President."

Kennedy addressed these concerns in a historic speech before the Houston Ministerial Alliance, reassuring his hearers that his faith was a personal matter, not a political one. In a later presidential proclamation supporting the National Day of Prayer, Kennedy said:

> This country was founded by men and women who were dedicated or came to be dedicated to two propositions: first, a strong religious conviction; and second, a recognition that this conviction could flourish only under a system of freedom.

Evangelicals were not reassured. Some believed that Catholicism was part of a vast, international conspiracy bent on destroying America, and that a Kennedy victory would usher in the end times. Protestants voted overwhelmingly for Republican candidate Richard Nixon, but Kennedy won anyway, becoming America's first Catholic president.

Fresh Air for the Church

Shortly after John XXIII was named pope in 1958, he announced that he would organize the Second Vatican Council, a series of meetings held over the course of four years and attended by more than 2,500 church leaders and invited guests. John died in 1963, but by the time the council concluded in 1965, it had forever changed the church.

The pope claimed the goal of the council was *aggiornamento,* an Italian word meaning "bringing up to date." As he said, "We need to open the windows and let some fresh air blow into the church." Certainly there were millions of Americans who considered the church stuffy and irrelevant.

Vatican II ushered in a series of sweeping changes and altered the ways Catholics expressed their faith. There was a relaxing of once-rigid rules about eating fish on Fridays and fasting before Mass and during Lent. And while the content of the Mass wasn't altered, its form certainly was. In the past, priests officiating at the Eucharist prayed quietly to God with their backs toward the parishioners. Now, priests faced their flocks. Even more surprising, Mass could now be said in the vernacular languages of the people, not the largely unintelligible Latin that had been used for centuries. Laypeople, including women, were given a larger role in the rituals of the church, and members were encouraged to read the Bible, which the council affirmed was the ultimate source of Christian truth and doctrine.

The church also formally acknowledged the existence of "separated brethren" in the Orthodox and Protestant traditions. Before Vatican II, these non-Catholic believers were viewed as being beyond the pale, but now they were seen as fellow disciples, and church officials initiated dialogue with other Christian leaders (see chapter 45).

Within the span of a few short years, the Catholic Church had not only transformed the ritual practices of its American members, but also built important bridges to those outside its fold, including evangelicals.

A Changing Church

Within the course of a few short years, the once-static Catholic Church had opened itself to the winds of change and diversity, and depending on one's perspective, the change was either frightening or liberating. Traditionalists were devastated by the sudden changes in their church, which had long served as an unchanging bulwark against the vicissitudes of time and circumstance. Others greeted the changes with open arms.

The campaign of modernization was costly. Between 1965 and 1975, U.S. attendance at Mass fell 35 percent. There was also an exodus of priests and nuns, with thousands leaving public ministry. Even more worrisome to some was the growing number of so-called "cafeteria Catholics," who cheered the demise of the old, authoritarian church and exercised their free will, picking and choosing which aspects of church doctrine they would obey. When Pope Paul VI released his 1968 encyclical forbidding most forms of birth control, many of these independent members simply ignored it.

It had taken centuries, but by the 1960s Catholicism had finally become part of the American mainstream, a process that involved wrenching transformations. Still, it would take a few more decades before many evangelicals felt a closer kinship to their Catholic neighbors.

Resources

Jay Dolan, *The American Catholic Experience: A History from Colonial Times to the Present* (1992).
Charles R. Morris, *American Catholic* (1997).
Andrew Greeley, *The American Catholic: A Social Portrait* (1977).

20. Where the Wind Blows:
The Charismatic Movement, 1960

Evangelicals who enjoy closing their eyes and raising their hands during worship services, or who experience moments of intense spiritual vitality praying alone to God, or who sing contemporary praise choruses ought to thank Dennis Bennett. This Episcopalian priest was a pioneer in the charismatic movement that swept over evangelical, mainline Protestant, Catholic, and nondenominational churches during the 1960s, bringing millions of believers into a deeper encounter with the reality of a living, loving God.

Bennett was the rector of the thriving St. Mark's Episcopal Church in tony Van Nuys, California, in 1959 when members began telling him about something called "the baptism of the Holy Spirit." Studying the New Testament, he saw that Jesus promised his disciples they would receive this baptism, and even the Anglican *Book of Common Prayer* contained numerous references to the Spirit's role in the life of churches and believers. Bennett sought and experienced the baptism himself, describing the experience in his 1970 book, *Nine O'Clock in the Morning:*

> . . . a very strange thing happened. My tongue tripped, just as it
> might when you are trying to say a tongue twister, and I began to
> speak in a new language!

Soon, a hundred members of St. Mark's were speaking in tongues, but not everyone at the church was rejoicing. Bennett was forced to resign and the congregation split, a schism that was covered in both *TIME* and *Newsweek*. Charismatics from St. Mark's started their own congregation and launched the Blessed Trinity Society, *Trinity* magazine, and the "Christian Advance" seminars to promote their movement, which soon began to take on a life of its own.

By the end of the century, the charismatic movement would influence every major denomination and play a major role in a trend Harvard's Harvey Cox called "the Pentecostalization, or partial Pentecostalization, of American Protestantism." Together, old-line Pentecostals and charismatic—

or neo-Pentecostal—believers would constitute a global fellowship nearly half a billion strong.

Movers and Shakers

The charismatic movement offered all believers the blessings of Pentecost without the historical and cultural baggage of old-line Pentecostalism. Still, the movement probably wouldn't have taken off without the work of bridge-builders like Demos Shakarian, David du Plessis, and David Wilkerson.

Shakarian was an Armenian Pentecostal who worked with Oral Roberts in the early 1950s before founding the Full Gospel Business Men's Fellowship International in 1952. The organization, now operating in nearly 100 countries, introduced thousands of non-Pentecostals to concepts like divine healing and Spirit baptism.

South African native du Plessis came to America in 1949 and was such a tireless promoter of charismatic spirituality that he was nicknamed "Mr. Pentecost." Convinced the Holy Spirit could break down walls dividing denominations, he enthusiastically promoted ecumenical cooperation, which led to both problems (the Assemblies of God denomination, fearing he was compromising the faith, revoked—and later reinstated—his ministerial credentials) and praise (Pope John Paul II acknowledged du Plessis's "service to all Christianity" with the "Good Merit" medal, making "Mr. Pentecost" the first non-Catholic to receive the honor).

David Wilkerson, Assemblies of God pastor and author of the 1963 best-seller *The Cross and the Switchblade,* showed that spiritual gifts could help turn drug addicts to Christ.

Wilkerson, an Assemblies of God pastor, came to fame with the publication of his 1963 best-seller *The Cross and the Switchblade,* which demonstrated that spiritual gifts weren't merely for the enjoyment of believers but could also help gang-hardened drug addicts turn to Christ and stay off the stuff.

Another 1963 best-seller, *They Speak with Other Tongues,* was written by *Guideposts'* editor John Sherrill, an Episcopalian who originally set out to discredit the charismatic movement before becoming persuaded of its authenticity.

Books like Wilkerson's and Sherrill's, along with Roman Catholic support of charismatic gifts as one aspect of "the charisms of the faithful," helped inspire the Catholic Charismatic Renewal movement, which began with a 1967 meeting at the University of Duquesne in Pittsburgh and spread rapidly to Catholic communities elsewhere. The Catholic Fraternity of Charismatic Covenant Communities and Fellowships, which represents more than a dozen groups, was formally recognized by the church in 1990.

Beyond Movements

The Azusa Street revival of 1906 helped spawn most of today's major Pentecostal denominations, but the revival's leaders had originally hoped to promote renewal within existing churches, not create new ones.

The leaders of the 1960s' charismatic movement learned from their Pentecostal predecessors. While the Calvary Chapel and Vineyard denomination did spring from the movement, charismatics were also successful at infusing many existing evangelical and Protestant groups with newfound spiritual zeal. "We urged people who visited us not to leave their own churches," said Dennis Bennett, "but to go back and share with them what was happening."

Bennett's own Episcopal denomination originally reacted negatively to the charismatic movement but later embraced it. Today, one fifth of American Episcopalians are involved in programs sponsored by Episcopal Renewal Ministries.

Author Larry Christensen was instrumental in promoting the charismatic movement within the American Lutheran Church, which issued guidelines for neo-Pentecostal members in 1963. And the General Assembly of the Presbyterian Church (U.S.A.) embraced the movement with its 1970 report, "The Work of the Holy Spirit." But not all denominations were so welcoming. Charismatic believers in the Lutheran Church-Missouri Synod and the Southern Baptist Convention say they have routinely faced opposition.

Outside denominational channels, spiritual renewal was being promoted through praise and worship music, publications like *Charisma* magazine, and ministries like Alpha, a popular evangelism program that was developed by a charismatic Anglican congregation and which includes lessons on the Holy Spirit.

By the 1980s, C. Peter Wagner and others were describing a "third wave," which incorporated the best elements of Pentecostal and charismatic spirituality but rejected the necessity of Spirit baptism or tongues. For many evangelicals, this growing openness to the moving of the Spirit was a welcome antidote to the dead orthodoxy that some felt had been all too common at too many churches for much too long.

Resources

John Sherrill, *They Speak with Other Tongues* (1963).
Dennis Bennett, *Nine O'Clock in the Morning* (1970).
Richard Quebedeaux, *The New Charismatics* (1976, 1983).
Vinson Synan, *The Holiness-Pentecostal Tradition* (1971, 1997).

21. Readin', Writin', and Religion: The Battle Over God in the Public Schools, 1962

A wise man named Solomon once said, "Train a child in the way he should go, and when he is old he will not turn from it." That's exactly what believers have attempted to do for most of the past 2,000 years—training their young themselves or entrusting their education to church-run schools. These Christian schools were the predecessors of America's system of public schools, which was introduced in the 19th century and came to dominate education in the 20th.

In the 1960s, though, a series of controversial Supreme Court decisions on issues like school prayer and Bible reading left many evangelicals feeling betrayed by the schools they had trusted to train their children. In the decades since, parent groups and major Christian organizations have advanced a variety of strategies to "bring God back into the classroom"; while others, believing such efforts are doomed to failure, have fueled a rapid growth in the Christian schools and home schooling.

A Century of Conflict

Christians have been involved in struggles over religion and education since the early 1900s. In the Scopes trial of 1925 (see chapter 6), the century's most celebrated education case, the fundamentalists won the battle but lost the war. Tennessee affirmed that teaching Darwinian evolution was illegal, but the ban was ineffective, and fundamentalists wound up suffering a humiliating public defeat.

Things only got worse during the 1960s, when three important Supreme Court decisions made many evangelicals feel as if their nation's schools had declared their deepest beliefs and values off-limits.

In *Engel v. Vitale* (1962), the court disallowed a classroom prayer that had been approved in the 1950s by the New York State Regents. Ten parents sued a school district over the invocation, which said, "Almighty God, we acknowledge our dependence upon Thee, and we beg Thy blessings upon us, our parents, our teachers and our country." The case reached the High Court, where the justices ruled that the prayer violated the constitutional wall of separation between church and state. The following year, the court ruled in *Abington School District v. Schempp* that daily classroom devotionals incorporating Bible readings were unconstitutional. And, in its 1964 ruling in *Chamberlin v. Public Instruction Board,* the court disallowed classroom readings from the Bible and the recitation of the Lord's Prayer.

Perhaps anticipating a major reaction, the court explained that its decisions shouldn't be interpreted as hostile toward religion, and that students could still pray alone or in groups, discuss their faith in the classroom, and share it with others in appropriate ways. Such explanations failed to sway most evangelicals, who were soon fighting education battles on many fronts.

Many schools adopted sex education courses that focused more on the mechanics of birth control than they did on sexual morality, making many people feel that the state had intruded on the sacred duties of parents. New battles erupted over curricula that sought to change children's beliefs, including programs involving values education, multiculturalism, self-esteem, life skills, and guided imagery techniques.

In the South, where there was deep concern about desegregation and busing, it was issues of race that led to the founding of some of the country's earliest private Christian academies.

One study described how evangelicals felt increasingly alienated from many of the major institutions of their own country:

> What appears most objectionable to fundamentalist critics is their perception that Christianity not only has been de-emphasized in American culture but has been supplanted by a rival religion.

Pat Robertson even detected the outlines of a vast cultural conspiracy:

> This plundering of traditional morality and Christian values was never accidental. It has been a deliberate and methodical assault on the tenets of society . . . and has proliferated from the classrooms to the courtrooms, and from the newsrooms to the living rooms of America . . . .
>
> The end has not just been to supplant Christian values with humanism, but to weaken American sovereignty and supplant it with a one world socialist government.

During the final decades of the century, classrooms and school board meetings would become battlegrounds where seemingly simple debates over curricula, textbooks, and procedures exploded into all-out "culture wars" between conservative Christians and their liberal opponents, both of whom could resort to overheated rhetoric.

Liberal combatants included the National Education Association, the American Library Association, the American Civil Liberties Union, and People for the American Way, whose 1993 report on "The Religious Right and School Boards" said that "in towns and cities in every region of the nation, right-wing activists are using school boards as their point of access to curricular decisions and to reintroduce sectarian views and influence into America's classrooms."

Evangelical combatants included Robertson's Christian Coalition, James Dobson's Focus on the Family, Phyllis Schlafly's Eagle Forum, and Citizens for Excellence in Education, whose president Robert Simonds once thanked a group of donors for helping "our Christian parents save their beautiful innocent children from atheistic indoctrination, immorality and the occult new age."

Phyllis Schlafly (at microphone) became one of the most vocal and influential members of the Christian Right by founding the Eagle Forum. The forum produces *Education Reporter,* a publication that supports parents' rights in education, as well as reports on what's happening in education across the nation.

Religious Education Reborn

While these battles raged, many believers put their energies into private schools or home schooling, both of which experienced an unprecedented boom. By century's end, there were more than a million students in an estimated 10,000 evangelical schools, and nearly that many are being home schooled.

In addition, graduates from these programs fueled the expansion of Christian colleges, which grew five times as quickly as private and public institutions.

That's not how things worked out for America's Catholic parochial schools, which had as many as 5.5 million students during their mid-1960s boom years. By the end of the century, Catholic schools had less than half that many students.

Continuing Battles

Evangelicals didn't give up on redeeming the public schools, and a number of legal battles continued to rage.

A string of decisions issued during the 1980s and 1990s didn't bring much encouragement. The Supreme Court overturned a law requiring the posting of the Ten Commandments in school rooms (1980), a statute authorizing student "volunteers" to lead classroom prayers (1982), a state-mandated moment of silence (1985), and Louisiana's act for "Balanced Treatment for Creation-Science and Evolution-Science in Public School Instruction" (1992).

But there were significant victories too. A 1993 decision in *Lamb's Chapel v. Center Moriches Union Free School District* declared that adults should not have been barred from using a school building for an after-hours showing of a Focus on the Family film series. And in 2001, the High Court extended the same privileges to Child Evangelism Fellowship, whose Good News Club had been banned from a Milford, New York, school.

Meanwhile, there was little progress on one of Christian activists' top educational priorities: giving Christian parents government-funded vouchers to cover the expenses of private schooling.

Some evangelicals were encouraged in 1995 when President Bill Clinton declared, "the First Amendment does not convert our schools into religion-free zones," spelling out ways students could exercise their faith at school.

On April 20, 1999, Cassie Bernall and Rachel Scott were among the 12 students and one teacher gunned down at Colorado's Columbine High School. Both were the subject of popular Christian books (*She Said Yes* and *Rachel's Tears,* respectively), and in time, these two Christian students would be honored as modern-day martyrs by millions of Christian young people. Meanwhile, many adults saw Columbine and other school killings as a sobering symbol of the sorry state of American public education.

Resources

Stephen Bates, *Battleground: One Mother's Crusade, the Religious Right, and the Struggle for Our Schools* (1993).

Barbara B. Gaddy, T. William Hall, and Robert J. Marzano, *School Wars: Resolving Our Conflicts Over Religion and Values* (1996).

22. A Dream Deferred:
Martin Luther King Jr. Fights for
Civil Rights, 1963

Martin Luther King Jr. whose resounding voice and righteous zeal made him one of the most influential figures of the 1950s and 1960s, once said that the most segregated hour in America was from 11:00 to 12:00 on Sunday morning. Nearly four decades after his death, many evangelical churches have failed to live out the radical implications of this simple song:

Red and yellow, black and white,
They are precious in his sight;
Jesus loves the little children of the world.

America, at least outwardly, is a much different place than it was when King was born in 1929. Blacks don't have to ride at the back of the bus anymore, and they can vote. Still, race remains a deep and divisive issue. Blacks are more likely than whites to drop out of school, wind up in jail or on welfare, or die from disease, gunfire, or suicide. Meanwhile, race-based entitlement programs, first created in the 1960s to address centuries of racism and segregation, are coming under increasing fire.

In 1963, King held much of a nation spellbound when he said, "I have a dream that my four children will one day live in a nation where they will not be judged by the color of their skin but by the content of their character." In reality, though, America largely remains two nations: one black and one white. King's dream remains unrealized.

The Gospel of Freedom

King's deep faith in God and radical commitment to freedom combined to forge a vision so strong that it survived incredible odds and inspired a nation.

Licensed to preach by the time he was 18, King was a divinity student when he heard a lecture about Mahatma Gandhi and the faith-based, non-violent passive resistance that transformed India from a British colony to

89

an independent nation. King adopted Gandhi's nonviolent methods, and for the next decade and a half he was at the forefront in the battle for civil rights.

In 1954 the U.S. Supreme Court declared segregation in public schools unconstitutional. That same year, King was called to pastor the Dexter Avenue Baptist Church in Montgomery, Alabama. And the following year, Rosa Parks ignited the Montgomery bus boycott, generally regarded as the first major campaign of the modern Civil Rights movement. King became the boycott's leader and was later named the first president of the Southern Christian Leadership Conference, which cosponsored 1961's Freedom Rides.

The August 1963 March on Washington brought more than 250,000 people to the nation's capitol. There, participants heard King's rousing "I Have a Dream" speech, which seamlessly blended biblical and American allusions:

> I say to you today, my friends, that in spite of the difficulties and frustrations of the moment, I still have a dream. It is a dream deeply rooted in the American dream.
>
> I have a dream that one day this nation will rise up and live out the true meaning of its creed: "We hold these truths to be self-evident: that all men are created equal."
>
> I have a dream that one day on the red hills of Georgia the sons of former slaves and the sons of former slaveowners will be able to sit down together at a table of brotherhood.
>
> I have a dream that one day even the state of Mississippi, a desert state, sweltering with the heat of injustice and oppression, will be transformed into an oasis of freedom and justice.

King was named *TIME* magazine's man of the year in 1964 and awarded the Nobel Peace Prize in 1965. He continued to fight for civil rights until he was assassinated April 4, 1968, one day after telling a Memphis audience: "I've seen the promised land. I may not get there with you, but I want you to know tonight that we as a people will get to the promised land." Outrage over King's killing ignited riots in more than 100 U.S. cities.

Enemies and Roadblocks

Although praised by many, King had many enemies, both white and black. FBI Director J. Edgar Hoover considered him a Communist, and most members of the "silent majority" believed the "Negro problem" would simply disappear if "uppity" agitators like King only quieted down. Meanwhile, many in the black community felt King was too passive and patient. Black Muslim leader Malcolm X exploited these anxieties before his own violent death in 1965.

King knew controversy and criticism came with his calling, but he was most deeply troubled by the failure of white Christians to embrace his crusade. Four months before the March on Washington, King wrote his "Letter from Birmingham Jail" from a cell where he was held in solitary confinement. Addressed to "My Fellow Clergymen," and quoting the Old and New Testaments, Augustine, Martin Luther, Abraham Lincoln, Martin Buber, and Paul Tillich, the letter expresses King's mounting frustration:

Rev. Martin Luther King was named *Time* magazine's man of the year in 1964 and awarded the Nobel Peace Prize in 1965. When he was assassinated in 1968, there were riots in more than 100 U.S. cities. The third Monday of January is now a national holiday in honor of Rev. King. His tombstone is inscribed with the words: "Free at last! free at last! thank God Almighty, we are free at last!"

> I have almost reached the regrettable conclusion that the Negro's great stumbling block in his stride toward freedom is not the White Citizen's Counciler or the Ku Klux Klanner, but the white moderate, who is more devoted to "order" than to justice.

Billy Graham was more outspoken on issues of race than many of his evangelical brethren, but even Graham complained that King was "going too far too fast." King disagreed, saying, "There comes a time when the cup of endurance runs over." He wrote:

> For years now I have heard the word "Wait!" It rings in the ear of every Negro with piercing familiarity. This "Wait" has almost always meant "Never." We must come to see, with one of our distinguished jurists, that "justice too long delayed is justice denied."

During the 1960s, evangelicalism remained a white man's world. Harlem evangelist Tom Skinner broke through the color barrier at InterVarsity Fellowships Urbana '70, but he alienated whites when he called them to convert their religious platitudes into social action.

The 1990s saw many white evangelicals repenting for their failures. The Southern Baptist Convention confessed its sins of racism and announced it would intentionally recruit more black members. National Association of

Evangelicals president Don Argue said, "White evangelicals were, for the most part, absent from the civil-rights struggle." Pastor/activist Eugene Rivers agreed, saying, "White evangelicals blew an opportunity."

Today, Argue, Rivers, and groups like Promise Keepers are working to promote racial reconciliation, but the work is painfully slow, and the sorrow and suspicion that took centuries to create won't disappear overnight. "Real reconciliation requires more than a few hugs at a big gathering," said Carl Ellis, a black evangelical.

By 2001, U.S. Census figures showed that nearly half of the country's 100 largest cities were home to more blacks, Hispanics, Asians, and other minorities than whites. But evangelical churches remained largely segregated.

King's ideal of a color-blind society wasn't achieved in his lifetime, and it remains to be seen whether reconciliation can be achieved in ours, or only in the next life. Perhaps that was the message of King's tombstone, which is inscribed with the words of the old Negro spiritual: "Free at last! free at last! thank God Almighty, we are free at last!"

Resources

Charles Marsh, *God's Long Summer: Stories of Faith and Civil Rights* (1997).

Mervyn A. Warren, *King Came Preaching* (2001).

Edward Gilbreath, "Catching Up with a Dream: Evangelicals and Race 30 Years after the Death of Martin Luther King, Jr.," *Christianity Today* (March 2, 1998).

Tom Skinner, *How Black Is the Gospel?* (1970).

Eyes on the Prize (PBS series and companion book, 1987).

Craig S. Keener and Glenn Usry, *Black Man's Religion: Can Christianity Be Afrocentric?* (1997).

Michael O. Emerson and Christian Smith, *Divided by Faith: Evangelical Religion and the Problem of Race in America* (2000).

23. Wit and Wisdom from Oxford: Evangelicals Embrace C. S. Lewis, 1963

One must keep pointing out that Christianity is a statement which, if false, is of no importance, and if true, of infinite importance. The one thing it cannot be is moderately important.

This pointed prose, with its uncanny combination of wisdom, wit, and winsome conviction, is vintage C. S. Lewis, as the writer's legions of fans can attest. Lionized by American evangelicals but less celebrated in his native England, Irish-born Lewis was a scholar, teacher, literary historian, critic, apologist, novelist, children's writer, science fiction author, poet, and radio celebrity whose books have sold more than 100 million copies.

The author of dozens of books and more than a hundred essays, Lewis first became popular in America during the 1940s and 1950s following the publication of *Miracles, Mere Christianity,* and the *Chronicles of Narnia* children's novels. A 1947 *TIME* magazine cover story marveled at his "heresy," which was to affirm supernatural Christianity in academia's hallowed—and secular—halls.

According to a 1993 article in *Christianity Today,* "Lewis . . . was not an evangelical. He was not even familiar with the word." Instead, he preferred the term "Classic Christianity." In addition, his "worldly" habits (he smoked a pipe and hung out in pubs with literary types) would have made him unwelcome in many of the conservative churches where people excitedly devoured his books. Yet American evangelicals overlooked Lewis's many idiosyncrasies, embracing him at a time when they were desperately looking for cultural legitimacy and rapidly distancing themselves from the anti-intellectualism of fundamentalism.

Lewis's fame only grew after his death on November 22, 1963, even though news of his passing was drowned out by eulogies for two other men who died the same day: U.S. President John F. Kennedy and English writer

Aldous Huxley. Lewis's literary estate has issued more than three dozen posthumous books, and the writer has been the subject of both an acclaimed drama and a major theatrical film. A 1998 story in *Christianity Today* declared Lewis "our patron saint."

Reason and Religion

Born near Belfast and raised in a religious home, Lewis was a precocious child who loved literature. After his mother died when he was nine, he became an atheist. Years later, in *Mere Christianity,* he would declare atheism untenable:

> My argument against God was that the universe seemed so cruel
> and unjust. But how had I got this idea of *just* and *unjust?* A man
> does not call a line crooked unless he has some idea of a straight line.

Fittingly, it was books that helped Lewis come to faith: first in God, and then in Jesus. He devoured the work of children's writer George MacDonald (whom Lewis claimed "baptized" his imagination) and Catholic apologist G. K. Chesterton (from whom Lewis learned to use humor as an intellectual rapier).

In England, Lewis's reputation was based on his literary scholarship. *The Allegory of Love,* his 1935 study of medieval literature, was hailed by the *Times Literary Supplement* as "scholarly, fascinating, and original." His academic peers couldn't comprehend how a man of letters could write popular Christian tracts and children's books, and biographer Lyle Dorsett says these works "caused so much disapproval that he was more than once passed over for a professorship at Oxford." A Fellow at Oxford's Magdalen College for 29 years, Lewis finally received a full professorship at Cambridge University, where he taught medieval and Renaissance literature until his death.

Lewis's *Screwtape Letters* still stirs considerable controversy. He wrote from the perspective of a devil giving advice to another devil on how to tempt a Christian. In doing so, he reveals to us how we let evil into our own lives. Lewis's work has influenced three generations of Christian thinkers and will continue to be a seminal Christian work.

Lewis called himself a "literary evangelist," and his books have played an important role in bringing many to faith, or confirming them in it. "*Mere*

Christianity was instrumental in my own conversion," says Charles Colson. J. I. Packer says, "I owe him much," adding, "*The Screwtape Letters* and the three small books that became *Mere Christianity* brought me, not indeed to faith in the full sense, but to mainstream Christian beliefs about God, man, and Jesus Christ." When *Discipleship Journal* magazine asked Elisabeth Elliot how evangelicals could learn to think more deeply about their faith, she replied, "Study the Bible. And study C. S. Lewis. He covered the whole field of theology in popular, understandable language." Syndicated columnist George Will said Lewis "ranks among the century's most influential writers."

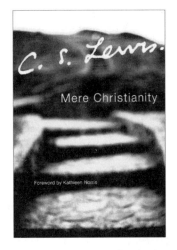

Mere Christianity is a book about basic Christianity. It has been read by Christians and non-Christians internationally. An apologetic, it provides people of all denominations with a basic understanding of essential Christian theology. The book was instrumental in the conversion of Charles Colson, the special counsel to the White House during Richard Nixon's presidency.

He certainly had a profound influence on Joy Davidman Gresham, an American Jew and former Communist who had come to faith in Christ while reading Lewis. She corresponded with him for years before meeting and, in 1956, marrying him. A year later she was diagnosed with cancer, and by 1960 she was dead. Lewis says his carefully crafted theology collapsed "like a house of cards," a crisis of faith powerfully portrayed by Anthony Hopkins in the acclaimed 1993 film *Shadowlands*. After Joy's death, Lewis turned to words for solace, writing *A Grief Observed* under the pen name N. W. Clerk as a "safety valve against total collapse."

An Unlikely Hero

American evangelicals, like their fundamentalist predecessors, have long exhibited a profound ambivalence about "secular" literature and other intellectual pursuits. But Lewis wasn't hindered by such problems, as Charles Colson observed:

> What was it that made him such a keen observer of cultural and intellectual trends? Why was Lewis so uncannily prophetic? The answer may be somewhat discomfiting to modern evangelicals: One

reason is precisely that Lewis was not an evangelical. He was a professor in the academy, with a specialty in medieval literature, which gave him a mental framework shaped by the whole scope of intellectual history and Christian thought. As a result, he was liberated from the narrow confines of the worldview of his own age—which meant he was able to analyze and critique it.

Lewis even challenged his students to read two old books for every new book they read. He wasn't an older-is-better absolutist, but he believed earlier writers could help readers understand and critique the errors of their own day.

Throughout much of his life, Lewis met weekly at an Oxford pub called The Eagle and Child with J.R.R. Tolkien, Charles Williams, and members of a group calling themselves the Inklings. Tolkien, a committed Catholic, was a scholar of Anglo-Saxon literature who enjoyed international popularity in the 1960s and 1970s with the fantasy novel *The Hobbit* and his *The Lord of the Rings* trilogy which was turned into a popular film series beginning in 2001. Williams was a writer of mystery and suspense novels overflowing with sensational depictions of invisible spiritual realities. In addition to reading—and sometimes harshly criticizing—drafts of one another's work, the Inklings engaged in lively debates and, in the words of a biographer, "let their imaginations run wild."

The work of these imaginative Christians inspired believers and intrigued seekers throughout the second half of the century. As writer Kathleen Norris put it, "Lewis betrays a deep faith in the power of the human imagination to reveal the truth about our condition and bring us to hope."

Lewis's work remains as refreshing and relevant today as it was decades ago, even though his literary legacy has been an embattled one. Scholar Kathryn Lindskoog has charged his literary custodians with fraud and forgery. And publisher HarperCollins caused a stir in 2001 when it announced plans to publish new Narnia novels by unidentified authors and to downplay Lewis's religion in new marketing plans.

C. S. Lewis said, "People don't write the books I want, so I have to do it for myself." There are seven books in the *Chronicles of Narnia,* the magical world behind the wardrobe where four children meet a Lion, the White Witch, and other characters. The series is allegorical, with obvious Christian meanings.

Some evangelicals cried foul, but Douglas Gresham, one of Joy Davidman's two sons, wasn't alarmed. "What is wrong with trying to get people outside of Christianity to read the Narnian chronicles?" he asked. "The Christian audience is less in need of Narnia than the secular audience."

Resources

C. S. Lewis, *Mere Christianity* (1952).
Christian History magazine (vol. IV, no. 3 is an all-Lewis issue).
Humphrey Carpenter, *The Inklings* (1978).
Shadowlands (1993 movie).
The C. S. Lewis Foundation (www.cslewis.org).

24. The Guru of True Truth: Francis Schaeffer Visits Wheaton, 1965

As the conventional 1950s gave way to the controversial 1960s, nobody in America seemed quite sure what to do about a growing youth movement and its social rebellion, drug experimentation, and sexual exploration.

Meanwhile, high in the mountains of Switzerland, a man *Newsweek* magazine called the "Guru of Fundamentalism" was opening his doors to thousands of spiritually restless young people, listening to their stories, showing compassion on their confused lives, and telling them how Christ offered hope, healing, and a "true truth" that was both comprehensible and transcendent.

From 1965 until his death from cancer in 1984, Francis Schaeffer exerted a profound influence on millions of Christians, including movers and shakers like Prison Fellowship founder Charles Colson, musician Larry Norman, Moral Majority founder Jerry Falwell, and author Os Guinness. "Perhaps no intellectual save C. S. Lewis affected the thinking of evangelicals more profoundly; perhaps no leader of the period save Billy Graham left a deeper stamp on the movement as a whole," wrote historian Michael S. Hamilton, who claims Schaeffer "reshaped American evangelicalism."

A Fundamentalist Philosopher

Born in Philadelphia, Schaeffer sampled agnosticism during his youth before coming to a firm faith in Christ at a time when battles between fundamentalists and modernists were tearing apart Presbyterian churches. Schaeffer sided with the fundamentalists, becoming the first ordained minister in the separatist Bible Presbyterian Church, serving U.S. pastorates for a decade before moving to Switzerland in 1948 with his wife Edith to serve as a missionary.

Soon, talking with young people about their beliefs became an increasingly important part of the Schaeffers' ministry. In 1955 the Schaeffers founded L'Abri (French for "shelter"), an innovative outreach to spiritual seekers housed in a chalet nestled in the Swiss mountain town of Huemoz.

At first L'Abri welcomed only a trickle of visitors, but after an article in *TIME* magazine in the early 1960s, a flood of mostly young seekers (along with a few older pilgrims, like psychedelic guru Timothy Leary) flocked to the Schaeffers' mountain outreach, where they experienced loving hospitality, Christian community, creative worship, stimulating lectures on subjects like racism and the environment, and a welcoming atmosphere that encouraged them to open their hearts and minds. As the influx of pilgrims grew, L'Abri expanded its facilities and formalized its programs.

In 1965 Schaeffer visited America for a series of groundbreaking lectures, including talks at Wheaton College that became *The God Who Is There* (1968), the first of his more than two dozen books that sold more than 3 million copies. Even before he said a word, Schaeffer made quite an impression with his knickers, knee-length socks, long hair, and beard.

His words were even more riveting. Quoting Bob Dylan while critiquing European intellectuals, Schaeffer demonstrated the importance of exegeting both the Bible and secular culture. If C. S. Lewis had given evangelicals

Francis Schaeffer founded L'Abri (French for "shelter") in Switzerland in 1955 as an outreach to spiritual seekers. In 1965 he visited Wheaton College, giving lectures that eventually became *The God Who Is There,* a book published in 1968. He wrote over two dozen books, which have sold more than 3 million copies. Historian Michael S. Hamilton said that Schaeffer "reshaped American evangelicalism."

Frank, the son of Francis and Edith Schaeffer, is a painter, filmmaker, and writer. In addition to helping his father create a popular Christian film series, he wrote *Addicted to Mediocrity: 20th Century Christians and the Arts* in 1981 and a critically acclaimed novel, *Portofino,* in 1992. He has now converted to Eastern Orthodoxy.

permission to love literature, Schaeffer challenged them to examine mainstream culture. As he would write in his 1973 booklet *Art and the Bible:*

> As evangelical Christians we have tended to relegate art to the very fringe of life. . . . Despite our constant talk about the Lordship of Christ, we have narrowed its scope to a very small area of reality.

Although academic specialists have harshly criticized Schaeffer's penchant for superficiality and sweeping generalizations, a generation of evangelicals was transformed by his talks and books. "At Wheaton College, students were fighting to show films like *Bambi,* while Francis was talking about the films of Bergman and Fellini," writes historian Michael S. Hamilton.

In 1977 Schaeffer crisscrossed America to lecture about his book *How Should We Then Live?* and show a companion film series produced by his son, Frank. These popular projects, which explored the decline of Western civilization and the urgency of a Christian response, increased Schaeffer's visibility and popularity.

From Cultural Critic to Culture Warrior

Schaeffer's next major opus, a collaboration with future U.S. Surgeon General C. Everett Koop, was 1979's book and film *Whatever Happened to the Human Race?* which focused on the issues of abortion and euthanasia. During the last five years of his life, Schaeffer, who had been diagnosed with cancer, spent less time with spiritually hungry young people and more time working with leaders of the nascent religious right, including Pat Robertson, D. James Kennedy, and Jerry Falwell (who said he was inspired to start the Moral Majority after hearing Schaeffer).

Some thought the man who once hung out with hippies was suddenly changing his stripes, but his opposition to abortion was consistent with his long-held views about the inability of "secular humanism" to provide an adequate basis for life, morals, or government. Just as Schaeffer had earlier introduced many evangelicals to art and philosophy, he now challenged them to roll up their sleeves and slow the West's rapid slide into moral relativism.

Later books like *A Christian Manifesto* (1981) and *The Great Evangelical Disaster* (1984) upped the ante. Schaeffer railed against evangelical complacency, challenging believers to political activism and even civil disobedience. This clarion call inspired a new breed of radical activists, including Operation Rescue founder Randall Terry.

All in the Family

Meanwhile, wife Edith developed an extensive speaking ministry and wrote nearly a dozen books, including the autobiographical *L'Abri* (1969) and *The Tapestry* (1981), as well as works on art, family, and hospitality.

Son Frank, who had helped his dad create popular Christian film series, tried his hand at mainstream movie making with 1986s' embarrassing *Wired to Kill* and authored increasingly shrill diatribes criticizing evangelicalism before converting to Eastern Orthodoxy and becoming an acclaimed novelist. His 1992 work, *Portofino,* was a humorous but biting look at his parents' religious idiosyncrasies and marital hang-ups.

Unlike Frank, all three of Francis Schaeffer's daughters and their husbands remained involved in the ongoing work of L'Abri communities around the world.

In the end, Schaeffer's uncanny ability to see into the heart of both people and contemporary culture would continue to inspire Christian thinkers for many years to come.

Resources

Michael S. Hamilton, "The Dissatisfaction of Francis Schaeffer," *Christianity Today* (March 3, 1997).

Francis A. Schaeffer, *The Complete Works of Francis A. Schaeffer: A Christian Worldview* (five volumes, 1982).

Edith Schaeffer, *L'Abri* (1969).

Lane T. Dennis, *Francis Schaeffer: Portraits of the Man and His Work* (1986).

Ronald W. Ruegsegger, ed., *Reflections on Francis Schaeffer* (1986).

25. Let's Make a Deal: Evangelism Campaigns and the Commodification of the Gospel, 1967

D. James Kennedy was fresh out of seminary when he set out for tiny Coral Ridge Church in Fort Lauderdale, Florida. After nearly a year in the pulpit, the congregation had shrunk from 45 to 17 souls. Clearly, this was not the kind of church growth his seminary professors had in mind.

When a congregation in Georgia invited Kennedy to lead a series of evangelistic services, he happily accepted the offer. After he got to Georgia, though, he learned that in addition to preaching nightly meetings, he would accompany church members during the day as they shared the gospel with people individually in their homes.

"I was petrified," said Kennedy, "for I knew I had no ability whatsoever to do this." But the experience transformed him, and much of the American evangelical church, as well. "I went back to Fort Lauderdale a new man, and I began to do just what I had seen done."

Kennedy began personally recruiting and training members of his congregation to do one-on-one evangelism. The church experienced rapid growth, and soon people from other churches wanted to hear Kennedy's vision of "mobilizing and equipping the vast lay army of the church to do the work of ministry." In 1967, three dozen pastors attended Evangelism Explosion's first leadership training clinic, and 1970 saw the publication of the *Evangelism Explosion* textbook, which *Christianity Today* called "probably the most widely used single guide" for lay evangelism. By 1973 the program had gone international, and by 1995, Evangelism Explosion International (EE) proudly proclaimed it had fulfilled the ministry's goal and was now operating in all 211 of the world's nations.

EE has helped thousands of Christians around the world overcome their fears and present the gospel to millions. At the same time, the program exhibits problems that have bedeviled many of the mass evangelism campaigns that became increasingly popular during the 1960s and 1970s:

it converted Christianity into a commodity and marketed it like any other consumer product, emphasizing its immediate benefits and downplaying its long-term costs.

"There are five great laws of selling or persuading: attention, interest, desire, conviction, and close," wrote Kennedy in *Evangelism Explosion*. "It does not matter whether you are selling a refrigerator or persuading men to accept a new idea or philosophy, the same basic laws of persuasion hold true."

1-800-SALVATION

America's early Puritan colonists didn't have much faith in sudden conversions. They believed receiving God's gift of salvation was the result of a long and difficult period of internal struggle. America's Great Awakenings and the techniques of revivalist preachers like Charles Finney changed all that, and by the 20th century, most conservative Protestants emphasized the individual's free will to accept immediate regeneration.

James Kennedy, pastor of Florida's Coral Ridge Church and founder of Evangelism Explosion, said, "There are five great laws of selling or persuading: attention, interest, desire, conviction, and close." Using these laws, *Evangelism Explosion* became the most widely used single guide for lay evangelism.

Bill Bright, who had been so anxious to win the world to Christ that he cut short his studies at Fuller Theological Seminary, founded Campus Crusade for Christ in 1951. Bright boiled down the salvation message to "Four Spiritual Laws," which emphasized the benefits of individual salvation ("God has a wonderful plan for your life"). Originally used as a training device for crusade staffers, the *"Four Spiritual Laws"* were first published in tract form in 1965. Since then, more than 2 billion of the tracts have been printed in more than 200 languages and distributed throughout the world, making this little booklet the most widely distributed document in evangelical history.

Bright was a businessman who had achieved success selling gourmet food products before his conversion to Christianity through the outreach ministry of Hollywood Presbyterian Church. "Marketing has had a special fascination for me," he said in a 2001 interview.

In the mid-1970s, Bright took the selling of salvation to unprecedented heights with his "Here's Life, America!" campaign, which aimed at nothing less than the evangelization of America by 1977 and the world by 1980. A 1977 article in *TIME* magazine summarized the campaign:

> "Here's Life" markets Jesus the way others might introduce a new brand of soda pop to a city. I FOUND IT! tease the TV and newspaper ads, billboards, buttons, bumper stickers. Found what? The ads offer a telephone number that will provide the answer: Jesus.

By 1978 the campaign had reached more than 100 countries and recorded more than 3.5 million decisions for Christ, but its tactics generated criticism. Billy Graham, whose evangelistic crusades were characterized by widespread participation among local churches, asked Bright to remove his name from the "Here's Life, America!" campaign's list of supporters, saying the parachurch powerhouse seemed to be "in competition with the churches." An article in *The Christian Century* criticized the campaign's gimmickry and exploitation of people's emotions as well as its incomplete theology of both witness and salvation:

> Christ's claim of Lordship over the whole of human history and the costly call to discipleship become lost in the presentation of "new life" as a possession to be added to the other possessions of television viewers and telephone callers. . . . The glorious gospel becomes a commodity sold and delivered to the doorstep like a brush or a bar of soap.

Green Weenies and Gospel Blimps

Evangelicals have tried nearly everything in their efforts to proclaim the Christian message. The novel *Portofino*, Frank Schaeffer's

---

Domesticating Belief

While the doctrinal creed of conservative Protestantism has remained largely unchanged by the encounter with modernity, the cognitive style has changed, and changed in significant ways.

An important consequence of Evangelicalism's accommodation to modernity has been its increased marketability in a highly competitive religious marketplace. The packaging of Evangelical spirituality has made it easy to adopt. . . . Yet the most notable consequence of the accommodation to modernity has been the domestication of conservative Protestant belief.

The rationalization of the conversion experience and all other dimensions of Evangelical spirituality has had the effect of harnessing the ecstatic, taming the predictable, and pacifying the "unruly" qualities of Evangelical faith.

— James Davison Hunter in *American Evangelicalism: Conservative Religion and the Quandary of Modernity* semi-autobiographical account of growing up the son of Francis and Edith Schaeffer, features vivid portrayals of Edith's trusted gospel walnut—a hollowed-out shell containing a printed paper tape bearing the message of salvation. More recently, a line of Christian clothing called "Witness Wear" has exposed people everywhere to messages like this:

> In case of RAPTURE
> this T-shirt will be empty.

Some of the more laughable evangelism efforts have been lambasted in the satirical magazine *The Wittenburg Door*, which awarded the worst offenders with its "Green Weenie" award.

The Four Spiritual Laws

1. God loves you and offers a wonderful plan for your life.
2. Man is sinful and separated from God; thus he cannot know and experience God's love and plan for his life.
3. Jesus Christ is God's only provision for man's sin. Through Him you can know and experience God's love and plan for your life.
4. We must individually receive Jesus Christ as Savior and Lord; then we can know and experience God's love and plan for our lives.

— Bill Bright of Campus Crusade for Christ

The most damning critique of evangelism campaigns was a 1960 book called *The Gospel Blimp* written by Joseph Bayly. Bayly's impeccable evangelical credentials (on the staff of InterVarsity Christian Fellowship, editor for David C. Cook Publishing Co. and both *Eternity* and *His* magazines) lent credibility to his uncomfortably accurate spoof of a group of earnest believers trying to replace one-on-one outreach with mass media bombast. The book's protagonists ignore their flesh-and-blood next-door neighbors to spend obscene amounts of time, energy, and money creating elaborate programs to evangelize "the world."

For those who didn't get the message, Bayly explained everything in the book's concluding chapter. "The wonderful Gospel Blimp is every impersonal, external means by which we try to fulfill our responsibility to witness to our neighbors," he wrote. "Jesus Christ didn't commit the gospel to an advertising agency; He commissioned disciples. And He didn't command them to put up signs and pass out tracts; He said that they would be His witnesses."

Going into All the World

Criticism of evangelism programs will likely continue as long as believers devise new ways to reach the unchurched. In 2001, the Christian Research Institute's *Christian Research Journal* critiqued the theology of the Alpha program, which was developed in the Anglican church in London and has been used in 20,000 churches in 20 countries.

Still, the programs developed since the 1960s have three things in their favor. They have talked about God's loving grace, while many earlier approaches concentrated on damnation and judgment. They have helped many laypeople see that they have an important role to play in carrying out Jesus's Great Commission to "go into all the world." And they have given millions of people around the world a chance to hear and respond to the gospel message—or at least a truncated version of it.

David McGaw, a former Campus Crusade staffer who worked on a 1999 revision of the *Four Spiritual Laws* booklet, has ambivalent feelings about its Cliff Notes-style summary of Christian theology. In the final analysis, though, he believes it has served as a helpful tool to bring millions to Christ. "Call the booklet dorky, choose not to use it if you want," he says, "but I'm still glad those souls came to know God."

Resources

D. James Kennedy, *Evangelism Explosion* (1970, 1973).

Michael Richardson, *Amazing Faith: The Authorized Biography of Bill Bright* (2000).

Richard Quebedeaux, *I Found It! The Story of Bill Bright and Campus Crusade for Christ* (1979).

Joseph Bayly, *The Gospel Blimp* (1960).

George Barna, *Evangelism That Works* (1995).

26. In Gods We Trust:
Pop Culture and the
"Spiritualization" of America, 1968

The four British mop-haired young men named John, Paul, George, and Ringo certainly didn't invent the cafeteria approach to spirituality that became increasingly popular in the 1960s. But they probably did more than anyone else to promote it to the youth counterculture through the lingua franca of popular music.

During their meteoric decade-long career, the Beatles helped revolutionize rock both musically and lyrically. Once a Top 40 radio-oriented genre that had confined itself to exploring puppy love or launching a succession of short-lived dance crazes, rock began turning its attention to weightier subjects like politics, social justice, war, sexuality, and even religion and philosophy.

In groundbreaking albums like 1966's *Revolver* and 1967's *Sgt. Pepper's Lonely Hearts Club Band,* the Beatles gave voice to the Eastern spirituality and psychedelic mysticism that they and so many other young people had been exploring. In the process, they created influential pop culture commodities that doubled as sacred artifacts.

In February 1968, nearly a year after John Lennon had said, "We're more popular than Jesus Christ right now," the Beatles—along with actress Mia Farrow and musicians Donovan and Beach Boy Mike Love—made a pilgrimage to Rishekesh, India, headquarters for Maharishi Mahesh Yogi, the bearded, long-haired guru who gave the West a watered-down form of Hinduism called Transcendental Meditation. "News of the group's retreat was greeted with a fascinated anticipation not seen since Moses' trek up the mountain," wrote Davin Seay and Mary Neely. "The Beatles were ascending to the abode of the gods to bring Truth to a waiting world."

The retreat ended abruptly after the Maharishi revealed himself unduly interested in grasping the Beatles' wealth and grabbing their female companions. (Their song "Sexy Sadie" chronicles the guru's fall from grace.) They hurriedly left India behind, but not their hunger for meaning and transcendence, a hunger that motivated millions of young people to shop for faith in the 20th century's burgeoning pop culture metaphysical bazaar.

Never before had such a cornucopia of non-Christian religions seemed so alluring to so many spiritual seekers, bringing about a transformation in American religious life that historian Martin Marty called a "seismic shift." We are still feeling its aftershocks today.

From Religion to Spirituality

America was a religious melting pot long before the "Asian invasion" of the 1960s. Transcendentalist writers like Thoreau and Emerson inspired many people to look to the East during the 19th century. In 1893 the World Parliament of Religions brought representatives of many Eastern faiths to Chicago. And in the 20th century, increasing numbers of Hindu and Buddhist "missionaries" set their sights on the Christian West.

This process of religious diversification accelerated rapidly during the 1960s. A combination of imported religions, new concoctions like Scientology, and the spiritual narcissism of the human potential movement beckoned to people who were dissatisfied with establishment-style Christianity and were hungry to explore something new, or old, or merely different. Some used the term "New Age movement" to describe the emerging religious scene, which often mixed the novel with the ancient, adapted the pantheism and some of the disciplines of Eastern faiths, and viewed Jesus as merely one of many incarnations of God.

There was also a profound change in the way people embraced religion. Sociologist Wade Clark Roof says the baby boomers who fueled the 1960s spiritual explosion made a distinction between "religion" (which was often associated with legalism, institutionalism, hypocrisy, and death) and "spirituality" (which conveys life, growth, balance, and personal development).

Many boomers turned their back on the faith of their fathers to sample Krishna Consciousness, Rev. Moon's Unification Church, Neopaganism, Zen Buddhism, feminist spirituality, earth-based Native American traditions, new-fangled Creation Spirituality, Twelve-Step support groups, Wicca, and a host of systems mixing metaphysics, New Thought, and divination.

In 1998, the authors of *Shopping for Faith* wrote, "Many Americans say they want to become 'more spiritual' but have little interest in 'organized religion.'" Alister McGrath, an evangelical theologian, believes that the absence of a viable and vibrant form of Christian spirituality was a major reason for the 1960s spiritual shift:

> As we look back, the remarkable growth of the New Age movement in areas previously dominated by mainline Christianity can, at least in part, be put down to the headlong rush of radical writers

and preachers to totally eliminate the supernatural and transcendent from Christianity. Lots of Americans got bored with the result, and, yearning for precisely those supernatural and transcendent elements, they turned to the mystical religions of the East, to paganism and to astrology.

Another major factor in the transformation of America's religious landscape was the changing face of the nation's population. Immigrants from Asia and the Middle East brought their temples and mosques to main-street America, and by the late 1990s, there were more Muslims in America than Episcopalians.

Confronting the Cornucopia

American evangelicals, who had financed missionary efforts throughout the world, were shocked to see their own country embrace alien faiths. Many responded by treating their own country as a mission field. Walter Martin pioneered evangelical research into other belief systems, writing 1965's best-selling *Kingdom of the Cults* and founding the Christian Research Institute. (After Martin's death in 1989, successor Hank Hanegraaff has increasingly focused on exposing alleged theological errors within the church.) Meanwhile, Campus Crusade for Christ staffer Josh McDowell wrote *Evidence that Demands a Verdict* and took his popular apologetics to college campuses throughout the country.

Many churches responded to America's new "quest culture" by adopting a "seeker sensitive" ecclesiology that attempted to make Christianity a more appealing consumer choice, but baby boomers aren't the joiners their parents

Hank Hanegraaff became president of the Christian Research Institute (CRI) after founder, Walter Martin, author of the 1965 best-selling *Kingdom of the Cults,* died in 1989. CRI focuses on exposing alleged theological errors within the church.

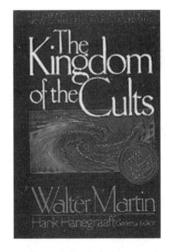

Kingdom of the Cults' comprehensive analysis of major cult systems has helped it become a recognized classic in its field.

were. Boomer believers are highly individualistic, and 80 percent say one can be a good Christian without regularly attending church.

Increasingly, spiritual seekers cobbled together their own personal creeds without relying on traditional religious institutions or authority figures to guide them.

By the 1990s, church membership figures were flat, but there was a major boom in spiritual books (*Conversations with God* and *The Celestine Prophecy*), films (*The Sixth Sense* and *Seven Years in Tibet*), and chart-topping musical recordings (Creed's God-haunted hard rock and Santana's *Supernatural* album). Shopping for faith had never been so easy, and the search didn't even require traveling to India.

Resources

Davin Seay and Mary Neely, *Stairway to Heaven: The Spiritual Roots of Rock 'n' Roll* (1986).

Andrew Greeley, *God in Popular Culture* (1988).

Robert S. Ellwood, *The Sixties' Spiritual Awakening: American Religion Moving from Modern to Postmodern* (1994).

Wade Clark Roof, *A Generation of Seekers* (1993).

Richard Cimino and Don Lattin, *Shopping for Faith* (1998).

William Romanowski, *Pop Culture Wars: Religion & the Role of Entertainment in American Life* (1996).

27. Pass It On: Reinventing Church for the Woodstock Nation, 1969

July 1969 was an important month for two distinct branches of the youth counterculture. In upstate New York, half a million people gathered for Woodstock, a three-day festival of music, mud, and merrymaking. And in Berkeley, California, printing presses were churning out some of the first copies of *Right On,* an underground newspaper published by the Christian World Liberation Front, one of the most intriguing of the hundreds of independent Jesus movement groups that were popping up across the country.

After seeing that free love could be costly, self-appointed gurus could turn out to be con men, and drug trips could escort one to the heart of spiritual darkness, millions of young people decided to accept the challenge offered by Larry Norman, a long-haired musician and Jesus movement troubadour who sang: "Why don't you look into Jesus, he's got the answer."

As early as 1965, countercultural youth had begun attending First Baptist Church of Mill Valley, California, right across the bay from San Francisco. Under the guidance of Ted Wise, these believers founded a Christian coffeehouse in the heart of the Haight-Ashbury district during August 1967's fabled "Summer of Love." A June 1971 cover story in *TIME* magazine on "The Jesus Revolution" signified that the movement had come of age.

At first, many mainstream evangelicals had problems distinguishing long-haired Jesus people from their secular counterculture counterparts. But Ron Enroth, one of the earliest chroniclers of the movement, was on to something when he wrote, "Theologically, the Jesus People are fundamentalists; sociologically, they are not."

Decades later, it's clear that the Jesus movement permanently altered the church's music, worship, and antiestablishment ecclesiology.

Finding a Spiritual High in California

The Christian World Liberation Front (CWLF), whose name was inspired by a Bay Area socialist group, was one of the most impressive pioneering ministries in what would become a varied, geographically dispersed, decentralized, and spontaneous movement that spawned coffee houses, communes, and congregations all across America.

Campus Crusade for Christ worker Jack Sparks, who was concerned about the inability of evangelicals to reach countercultural youth, helped start CWLF in 1968. Soon the group was offering a wide range of programs, including drug counseling, Bible studies, free food distribution, a literature ministry, campus outreach to U. C. Berkeley, crash pads and youth hostels for street kids who had no place to stay, long-stay houses where young Christians could be discipled, and the Rising Son Ranch located in the hills north of San Francisco. The group would also give birth to *Radix,* an acclaimed magazine relating faith to art and culture, and the Spiritual Counterfeits Project, which provided a Christian perspective on the burgeoning number of Eastern, cultic, occultic, and human potential groups that were attractive to so many young people.

Though evangelical in theology, CWLF and other groups expressed the ancient faith in new and culturally relevant ways. One can get a taste of their efforts by reading an excerpt from *The 2nd Letter to the Street Christians,* which is part of a Jesus-movement-style paraphrase of the New Testament:

> Dig it! God has really laid a heavy love on us! He calls us his children and we are! The world system doesn't recognize that we're His children because it doesn't know Him. Right on, brothers and sisters, we are God's children, even though we're a long way from being what He's going to make us. Don't get hooked on the ego-tripping world system. Anybody who loves that system doesn't really love God.

Billy Graham was able to look beyond the Jesus movement's unorthodox sociological trappings and see the orthodox theology at its core. In his 1971 book *The Jesus Generation,* Graham praised the young people's focus on Christ, commitment to the Bible, anticipation of the second coming of Christ, and emphases on evangelism and discipleship. Graham also praised the young people's interest in the Holy Spirit and their hunger for experiencing God, even though these very characteristics could sometimes lead to faddishness, excessive emotionalism, and cultic tendencies.

One pastor who opened his arms and his church to the Jesus people was Chuck Smith of Calvary Chapel in Costa Mesa, California, the congregation that would become the mother church of the Calvary Chapel denomination. Officially founded in 1969, the congregation had more than a thousand people attending services by 1971. While older members sat in pews, the Jesus people sat on the floor and filled the aisles. Love Song, one of the many new bands that got its start at Calvary Chapel, described the congregation in their song, "Little Country Church":

Long hair, short hair, some coats and ties
People finally comin' around
Lookin' past the hair and straight into the eyes
People finally comin' around.

Music of a Movement

Love Song and other Calvary bands made their recording debut on 1971's *The Everlastin' Living JESUS Music Concert,* an album that launched Maranatha! Music, which would soon become the most influential contemporary Christian music label.

Love Song would also join Andrae Crouch, Randy Matthews, Johnny Cash, the Speer Family, and Larry Norman at EXPLO '72, a week-long event sponsored by Campus Crusade for Christ that ended with a Jesus music festival attended by nearly 200,000 young people.

Norman, who combined Charles Wesley's gift for popular hymnody and Bob Dylan's incisive wit, is generally considered the father of Jesus music. His groundbreaking 1969 recording, *Upon This Rock,* was released by Capitol Records. Over the next decade Norman's own Solid Rock Records label would introduce important new artists like Randy Stonehill, Mark Heard, and the band Daniel Amos. Still, Norman is best known as the author of many classic Jesus-music anthems, including "Why Should the Devil (Have All the Good Music)," "I Wish We'd All Been Ready," "One Way," and "The Outlaw," which encapsulated the Jesus movement's countercultural Christology:

Larry Norman, one of the Jesus movement's early leading singers, gave this advice to millions of young seekers: "Why don't you look into Jesus, he's got the answer." The movement caught the nation's attention when a June 1971 *TIME* magazine cover story entitled "The Jesus Revolution" hit the stands. Billy Graham praised the work of the youth and wrote *The Jesus Generation* in 1971. The impact of the Jesus movement can still be heard in church music today.

Some say He was an outlaw
That He roamed across the land
With a band of unschooled ruffians
And a few old fishermen.

In time, such retellings of the timeless Christian story would help inspire popular Broadway musicals and movies like *Jesus Christ Superstar* and *Godspell*.

While aspects of the faith of the Jesus people were institutionalized in the Calvary Chapel and Vineyard denominations, even older denominations and a host of new, nondenominational congregations were influenced by the movement's music and methods.

In Chicago, one can still see one of the few surviving communities: Jesus People USA, whose members inhabit a north-side hotel where they host worship services, feed the homeless, publish *Cornerstone* magazine and books, and coordinate the annual Cornerstone Christian music festival.

Still, one needn't go to Chicago to see the lasting influence of the Jesus movement. During the 1990s, massive Promise Keepers rallies and evangelist Greg Laurie's Harvest Crusades featured the Maranatha! Praise Band. And at thousands of evangelical churches throughout the land, contemporary praise and worship choruses were sung every Sunday morning.

Resources

Ron Enroth, et. al., *The Jesus People: Old-Time Religion in the Age of Aquarius* (1972).

Edward Plowman, *The Jesus Movement in America* (1971).

Paul Baker, *Contemporary Christian Music* (1985).

Larry Eskridge, "One Way: Billy Graham, the Jesus Generation, and the Idea of an Evangelical Youth Culture," *Church History* (April 1998).

28. Family Man:
James Dobson's Moral
Crusade, 1970

In the late 1960s, James Dobson looked at America and didn't like what he saw. Members of the youth counterculture were igniting and fueling "a very serious worldwide revolution" set on destroying "authority in all its forms." As he wrote in *Dare to Discipline* (1970), the first and most popular of his nearly two dozen books that have sold some 20 million copies:

> They have no program of reform; their platform includes nothing but universal destruction . . . .
>
> These young militants are angry because America has the audacity to be imperfect, and they wish to annihilate its leaders and institutions.

Unlike other members of the "silent majority," Dobson spoke out, and he tried to do something about America's perceived ills. In the decades since, his approach has focused on two overlapping activities: reintroducing people to the timeless principles of the Bible and battling the moral relativism he feels endangers the family and society.

Today, Focus on the Family is one of the largest parachurch organizations in the world, with an annual budget of nearly $130 million. Dobson has helped millions of people practice principled parenting, becoming one of the most loved and trusted evangelical leaders of the century. Still, his ventures into partisan politics and his dogged advocacy of his conservative "family values" agenda have caused controversy, both inside and outside the evangelical community.

A Mass Media Ministry

When three-year-old James Dobson walked forward and committed his life to Jesus at a Nazarene church one Sunday morning, it was his father, James Sr. who was preaching the sermon. Shortly before his death in 1977,

Dobson's father said God spoke to him, promising that his only son would reach millions of people.

Focus on the Family has helped Dobson do just that. After earning a doctorate in child development from the University of Southern California, Dobson—who has no specialized theological training—left a secure post with USC's medical school to found Focus in Arcadia, California.

The first Focus on the Family radio program aired March 15, 1977, on approximately three dozen stations. Today the show, which highlight's Dobson's "warm and folksy manner," airs on thousands of stations in the U.S. and around the world, reaching millions of listeners. In 1994, *Christianity Today* called Dobson "the undisputed king of Christian radio."

In addition, Focus publishes nearly a dozen carefully targeted periodicals, including award-winning magazines for children (*Clubhouse* and *Clubhouse, Jr.*), teens (*Brio* and *Breakaway*), parents (*Plugged In* and *Single-Parent Family*), teachers (*Teachers in Focus*), and doctors (*Physician*). The ministry has also produced high-quality video series for young people ("McGee and Me!" "Adventures in Odyssey," and "Last-Chance Detectives") and film and video series for adults ("Turn Your Hearts Toward Home" and "That the World May Know").

While many evangelical ministries use high technology primarily to improve their ability to solicit donations, Focus is a high-tech, high-touch ministry that employs hundreds of people to personally answer the hundreds of thousands of phone calls and letters that flood Focus's offices every year. These workers provide Dobson's insights on everything from ambiguous genitalia to zits. *The Chronicle of Philanthropy* and other publications have praised Focus's uncommon responsiveness to its constituents, and the ministry's client communications operations have been studied by both Fortune 500 companies and the White House.

Culture-War Crusader

Dobson has always been concerned about the social and political implications of biblical faith. According to his authorized biography, this concern grew more intense during the 1980s when Dobson served on U.S. Attorney General Edwin Meese's pornography commission: "James Dobson became involved in public policy because the family needed to be defended from those who disrespected its heritage and the value system on which it rests," says a 1989 biography. Or as Dobson himself put it in the 15th anniversary edition of his ministry's flagship magazine, "This is where the battle for righteousness is being fought. I don't think I had any choice."

In *Children at Risk*, the 1990 book he wrote with former Reagan administration official Gary Bauer, Dobson proclaimed:

Nothing short of a great Civil War of values rages today throughout North America. Two sides with vastly differing and incompatible world-views are locked in a bitter conflict that permeates every level of society.

Dobson devised a series of weapons to help his side win the war. The ministry's Public Policy division publishes *Citizen* magazine, produces a radio show, issues regular special reports, conducts research, and coordinates the activities of dozens of state-based Family Policy Councils, which promote Dobson's positions on local legislation.

In 1980 he was among a small group of concerned Christian conservatives who founded the Family Research Council (FRC). Originally formed as a division of Focus, the FRC became independent in 1992 so its political lobbying activities would not jeopardize Focus's nonprofit tax status. Based in Washington, D.C., FRC works with legislators and the media to promote its positions.

During the 1990s, director Gary Bauer was the FRC's most visible spokesman, but he and Dobson parted ways during Bauer's unsuccessful 2000 presidential campaign and eventual endorsement of

James C. Dobson is founder and president of Focus on the Family, a nonprofit organization that produces his internationally syndicated radio programs heard daily on more than 3,000 radio facilities in 12 languages in more than 95 other countries. Dr. Dobson served 14 years as associate clinical professor of pediatrics at the USC School of Medicine and a concurrent 17 years on the attending staff of Los Angeles Children's Hospital in the divisions of Child Development and Medical Genetics.

John McCain. (Dobson never endorsed Bauer's candidacy, and Charles Jarvis, a Focus executive who had served as Bauer's campaign manager, left to work for candidate Steve Forbes.)

Although he is a fiscal and cultural conservative, Dobson has had a love-hate relationship with the Republican party. After supporting Ronald Reagan and other Republican candidates, Dobson grew increasingly impatient with their failure to support his specific policy agenda. He threatened to leave the GOP, taking as many people with him as he could.

Focus helped found the Alliance Defense Fund, a conservative Christian legal group; and Dobson's wife, Shirley, served as the chairman of the

National Day of Prayer, an annual event designed to encourage Americans to pray for their government.

Kudos and Criticism

Although Dobson's tireless efforts on behalf of family values and better parenting techniques have drawn praise from millions of devoted supporters, he has also been a lightning rod, drawing criticism from many quarters. Even some Christian thinkers have suggested that the family values movement promotes the idolatry of the family by placing greater emphasis on familial bonds than the spiritual ties that link believers to one another and to the worldwide church.

Even more controversial, his forays into politics have drawn fire, both nationally and in Colorado Springs, where Focus relocated in 1991. Some evangelicals fear that Dobson and other leaders of the "religious right" have unduly politicized the church. Other critics claim he has attempted to transform a constituency that turned to him for help with family problems into a political phalanx. Gil Alexander-Moegerle, who once cohosted Focus's radio show with Dobson before becoming one of the ministry's harshest foes, claims Dobson has occasionally used his considerable clout to bully fellow believers and Christian organizations with whom he disagrees.

It's still too early to tell if Dobson's crusade for America and its families has been successful, but early results are not promising. In 1993, fellow culture warrior William Bennett's *Index of Leading Cultural Indicators* concluded that America was in the grips of a "palpable cultural decline." And in an August 2001 issue of *Focus on the Family* magazine, Dobson said recently released U.S. Census figures showed that "the institution of the family is unraveling at a faster pace than ever."

Still, Dobson has probably done more than any other evangelical leader to try to knit families back together and put "family values" front-and-center on the national agenda.

Resources

James Dobson, *Dare to Discipline* (1970).
Rolf Zettersten, *Dr. Dobson: Turning Hearts Toward Home* (1989).
James Dobson and Gary L. Bauer, *Children at Risk* (1990).
Gil Alexander-Moegerle, *James Dobson's War on America* (1997).

29. Pop Apocalypse: Fear, Hype, and the Longing for Armageddon, 1970

After the wrenching social upheavals of the 1960s had left millions of Americans wondering what the world was coming to, a series of pundits and prophets offered to explain the recent past and predict the distant future.

Future Shock, Alvin Toffler's 1970 best-selling look at the accelerating pace of change, foretold a brave new world where permanence would be replaced by transience; settled living patterns would give way to a new nomadism; and both individuals and families would be inundated by a sea of information, leading to a paralyzing condition called "overchoice":

> The flood of novelty about to crash down upon us will spread
> from universities and research centers to factories and offices, from
> the marketplace and mass media into our social relationships, from
> the community into the home. Penetrating deep into our private lives,
> it will place absolutely unprecedented strains on the family itself.

The best-selling book of the 1970s, however, wasn't Toffler's grim futuristic tome, but Hal Lindsey's 1970 ominous end-times scenario, *The Late Great Planet Earth,* which has sold nearly 30 million copies in more than 100 printings. Both chilling and fantastic, frightening and oddly comforting, *Late Great Planet Earth* confirmed evangelicals' worst fears about the world going to hell in a hand basket, but at the same time it assured readers that God was still in control.

For Lindsey, a former bartender who accepted Christ and worked as an evangelist for Campus Crusade for Christ, the doomsday clock began ticking in 1948 with the creation of the state of Israel. Blending prophetic passages from the Old Testament's book of Daniel and the New Testament's book of Revelation with a mishmash of current events, Lindsey boldly predicted that the second coming of Christ would occur within a generation of 1948, and probably no later than 1988.

OVER 15 MILLION COPIES SOLD

HAL LINDSEY

WITH C. C. CARLSON

Hal Lindsey's *The Late Great Planet Earth* was the best-selling book of the 1970s, which has since sold over 30 million copies in more than 100 printings. The *New York Times* called it the "no. 1 non-fiction best-seller of the decade."

Updating outmoded dispensationalist end-times scenarios promoted during the 19th century by John Nelson Darby and found in the pages of Scofield's reference Bible, Lindsey concocted a new-and-improved eschatological drama, casting the Soviet bloc as the biblical northern confederacy, Communist China as the kings of the East, and the European Common Market as the Antichrist's revived Roman Empire. As for the Bible's "fire and brimstone," Lindsey said this referred to an imminent nuclear holocaust that would wipe out the world.

Changing events forced Lindsey to repeatedly revise his predictions. But like the promotional slogan for the 1970 movie *Love Story* ("Love means never having to say you're sorry"), he never acknowledged or apologized for his errors; rather, he merely released a dozen more apocalyptic books, including *1980s: Countdown to Armageddon*. By the 1990s, Lindsey was leading trips to the Holy Land, hosting shows on Christian TV and radio, and continuing to predict that "this generation is going to see the climax of history as predicted by the prophets."

Some would dismiss Lindsey's predictions as religious fiction, but the boom in apocalyptic novels wouldn't hit America until the 1990s.

Pre-trib, Pre-mil Potboilers

As his crowded 747 cruises high over the Atlantic, pilot Rayford Steele's thoughts turn to seducing perky senior flight attendant Hattie Durham. But when Hattie approaches him, she is clearly distraught.

"People are missing," she tells Rayford. "Their shoes, their socks, their clothes, everything was left behind."

Before long, Rayford, Hattie, and globe-trotting journalist Buck Williams realize that millions of people from all walks of life and all corners of the globe have vanished without a trace.

Experts attribute the mystery of the missing masses to UFOs or a terrorist attack. But as the central characters in this fictional drama wind their way through burning neighborhoods and wreck-strewn, corpse-lined highways, they begin to see the truth: "The Rapture had taken place. Jesus Christ had returned for his people." Among the lost and unraptured are liberal preachers, pew-sitting churchgoers, newspaper editors, and other skeptics.

So begins *Left Behind*, a fast-paced, 468-page end-times novel coauthored by Tim LaHaye and Jerry Jenkins that inspired a resurgence of end-times enthusiasm in the years before the Millennium. Over the next few years *Left Behind* spawned a mini-industry of best-selling sequels, children's novels, board games, clothing (T-shirts proclaim: "Don't Be Left Behind," while baseball caps use the shorthand "DBLB"), a video, a companion musical anthology, a syndicated radio series, a popular www.leftbehind.com Web site, and a nonfiction booklet intended to be used in evangelistic crusades or by churches studying Bible prophecy. In May 2001, trade magazine *Publishers Weekly* reported: "Almost 39 million copies in books and related products later, the Left Behind series shows no signs of slowing."

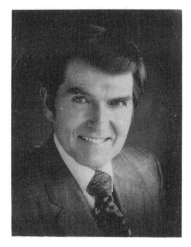

Dr. Tim LaHaye has written over 40 books and is a noted author, minister, and nationally recognized speaker on Bible prophecy. He is the founder of both Tim LaHaye Ministries and the Pre-Trib Research Center.

Adored by readers, the series is widely believed to have scared thousands of people into accepting Christ in the 1990s, much as Lindsey's books and

Jerry B. Jenkins describes himself as the "most famous writer no one's ever heard of." He is former vice president for publishing and writer-at-large for the Moody Bible Institute of Chicago, and is the author of more than 100 books, including the best-selling *Left Behind* series. Also the former editor of *Moody Monthly* magazine, his writing has appeared in *Reader's Digest, Parade,* and dozens of Christian periodicals.

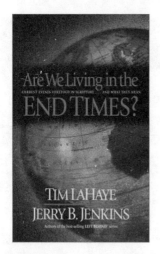

In *Are We Living in the End Times?* best-selling author and prophecy scholar Tim LaHaye and coauthor Jerry B. Jenkins examine the signs of the end times and present 20 reasons why they believe the current generation could see the rapture. LaHaye and Jenkins lead the reader through the basics of prophecy, then present their 20 reasons in detail.

inexpensively produced end-times films like *A Thief in the Night, The Prodigal Planet,* and *A Distant Thunder* did during the 1970s and 1980s.

A film adaptation called *Left Behind: The Movie* debuted on video in 2001 before opening in theaters in 2001 to a critical drubbing. One reviewer called *Left Behind: The Movie* "Cheesy. Silly. Moronic. Dull. Plodding. Torturous." More excitement was generated by a lawsuit LaHaye filed against the filmmakers, who reportedly failed to deliver on a promised blockbuster.

Ready for the Rapture

The *Left Behind* books drew additional criticism from theologians, like D. James Kennedy of Coral Ridge Presbyterian Church, who said, "I believe that it is better to get one's theology from the Bible than from novels."

Kennedy and others say the Bible is at odds with the novels' pretribulational, premillennial theology, which teaches that faithful believers will be "raptured" from the earth *before* a seven-year period of trouble and tribulation, which occurs *before* Christ's millennial reign.

Still, there's no arguing that pre-trib, pre-mil eschatology offers greater dramatic opportunities for car crashes and bloodshed than other end-times views.

Christians have long anticipated the culmination of human history. In the first century, St. Paul warned against predicting "time and dates," but the warning hasn't been heeded. Over the years, detailed predictions have been made by the Shakers, Alexander Campbell and the Disciples of Christ, William Miller and the Adventists, Chuck Smith of Calvary Chapel, television evangelist Jack Van Impe, and engineer Edgar C. Whisenant, author of *88 Reasons the Rapture Will Be in 88.*

Some thinkers believe that end-times books only serve to distract believers from more pressing matters, but they have certainly been a financial blessing to the Christian publishing industry. Zondervan sold a million copies of *Armageddon, Oil, and the Middle East* while tensions about the

1991 Persian Gulf War ran high, and according to a 1999 article in *USA Today,* publishers planned to release "as many as 100" end-times books and novels before the year 2000.

Evangelicals' longing for Armageddon during the last decades of the millennium made these good times for books about bad times.

Resources

Hal Lindsey, *The Late Great Planet Earth* (1970).

Tim LaHaye and Jerry Jenkins, *Left Behind* (1995).

Timothy P. Weber, *Living in the Shadow of the Second Coming* (1979, 1987).

Paul Boyer, *When Time Shall Be No More: Prophecy Belief in Modern America* (1992).

30. The Lesser among Equals: Evangelicals Confront the Women's Movement, 1972

The civil rights struggle of the 1950s and 1960s was still simmering when the battle over women's rights heated up in the 1970s. The Civil Rights Act of 1964 had prohibited discrimination on the basis of sex, but millions of women felt the act's promises hadn't become reality in the male-dominated worlds of work and worship.

The mainstream women's movement forced many Americans to reevaluate traditional ideas about women's roles, responsibilities, and rights; while its evangelical counterpart revealed deeply entrenched sexism in churches and parachurch organizations. Evangelicals struggled to interpret hundreds of complex and seemingly contradictory biblical passages. Some suggested that women had ministered as equals to men in the early church. Others demanded that women remain silent and submissive. And at least one passage—Galatians 3:28—taught that the gospel transcends all social distinctions: "There is neither Jew nor Greek, slave nor free, male nor female, for you are all one in Christ Jesus."

The Congregationalists were the first to ordain women to the ministry in 1853, and during the 20th century, most mainstream Protestant denominations followed suit. Few evangelical denominations ordained women, even though organizations as diverse as the Salvation Army and Moody Bible Institute had earlier done so.

Debates over gender issues, while not as highly publicized as battles over abortion and gay rights, would divide evangelicals throughout the final decades of the century. "No issue has caused evangelicals more consternation in the second half of the twentieth century than feminism," wrote Randall Balmer.

Called to Lead or Follow?

Women were at the forefront of the major Christian reform movements arising out of the Second Great Awakening, but after leading the battles for abolition and prohibition, many women decided it was about time they were given the right to vote, too. The struggle for suffrage, which began in the 19th century, was condemned by Catholic leaders but embraced by most Protestants, in part because they believed women, long regarded as the conscience of the home, would only elevate the morality of politics if given half a chance. The 19th Amendment to the Constitution gave women the right to vote in 1920, and during the coming decades, women would fight for an even greater role in society.

Women achieved a measure of equality in many American churches. Groups like the Puritans, Quakers, Wesleyans, and the Holiness and Pentecostal movements gave women great freedoms to teach and preach; and between 1861 and 1910, the Women's Missionary Movement sent thousands of single women to the mission field. Fundamentalist churches, though, enforced strict gender distinctions, allowing women to teach children but not adult men. Fundamentalists like John R. Rice, author of *Bobbed Hair, Bossy Wives and Women Preachers* (1941), condemned "uppity" women.

In 1972 the Equal Rights Amendment, which had languished in Congress for half a century, was approved and sent to the states for ratification. Evangelical women typically found themselves in one of two opposing camps. On the "right," traditionalist "counterfeminists" lobbied against the ERA, opposed the growing feminist movement, and argued that women should spend less time worrying about their rights and more time being good wives and mothers. On the "left," an emerging group of "evangelical feminists" founded the Evangelical Women's Caucus and began publishing the groundbreaking journal *Daughters of Sarah*.

Throughout the 1970s, conservative and feminist groups battled one another and sought influence among evangelicalism's male leaders. In 1973 Marabel Morgan's *The Total Woman* argued that evangelical women were

The Total Woman by Marabel Morgan sold over 3 million copies in the 1970s. Published in 1973, the book argued that evangelical women could compete against men in the workplace but should remain submissive to their man at home. In 1974 it was the nation's top best-seller (369,315 sold), beating out James Michener's *Centennial* (330,289 sold). Mrs. Morgan tells the reader she believes it is possible for almost any wife to have her husband absolutely adore her in just a few weeks' time.

Beverly LaHaye, wife of Dr. Tim LaHaye of the current best-selling "Left Behind" series, founded Concerned Women for America. She called the organization a "positive alternative to the militant feminism that threatens American society." The group promised to "expose movements seeking to weaken the family," among other issues.

quite capable of competing against men in the workplace, but at home they should concentrate on being submissive and seductive. The book sold 3 million copies and enraged both feminists (who called it reactionary) and fundamentalists (who called it worldly). *All We're Meant to Be,* a book *Eternity* magazine hailed as the most important work of 1974, was an insightful and influential defense of evangelical feminism by Letha Scanzoni and Nancy Hardesty.

In 1979 Beverly LaHaye, wife of Moral Majority board member Tim, founded Concerned Women for America as "a positive alternative to the militant feminism that threatens American society." The group promised to "expose movements seeking to weaken the family," "educate women in the principles for living according to the Word of God," and "provide representation on family and moral concerns in Washington, D.C."

Meanwhile, evangelical feminism was fracturing from within. In 1986 the Evangelical Women's Caucus recognized the presence of a "lesbian minority" in its ranks and adopted a stand in favor of civil rights protection for homosexuals. This move led Catherine Clark Kroeger and others to abandon EWC to form Christians for Biblical Equality in 1987. The same year saw the founding of an opposing traditionalist group, the Council on Biblical Manhood and Womanhood.

People on both sides were reading the Bible for clues to God's views on gender and debating questions like this one: Was Adam's headship of Eve part of God's original plan, or a result of the fall?

Battle of the Books

Throughout the centuries, the Bible has played an important role in the debates about the role of women. In the 1890s, suffragist leader Elizabeth Cady Stanton created controversy with *The Woman's Bible,* which dismissed portions of Scripture that had been used to hold women in their "divinely ordained sphere." A century later, a dispute over a much different Bible illustrated evangelicals' ongoing divisions over gender.

In 1997 controversy erupted when the International Bible Society (IBS) announced its plan to publish a "gender-accurate" version of its popular New International Version. The text would maintain male references to God but use gender-neutral language when referring to groups that included both men and women.

The feisty *World* magazine charged IBS with creating a "stealth" Bible and aiding the "feminists' seduction" of evangelicalism. The controversy was a public relations nightmare for IBS, and some offended believers even defaced their old copies of NIV and mailed them to the ministry. (*World* was later rebuked by the Evangelical Press Association for slanted and inflammatory journalism.)

James Dobson, who had criticized IBS, invited 11 male scholars to Focus on the Family's headquarters in Colorado Springs where they drafted guidelines for translating the Bible. But later, Dobson announced that Focus was withdrawing its own *Adventures in Odyssey Bible* for children, which contained "some unnecessary gender changes." (In 2002, IBS released its new "gender-accurate" *Today's New International Version* to similar controversy.)

A Continuing Conflict

While battles over nouns and nuances raged, larger issues concerning the role of women in the church remained largely unanswered.

Even more frustrating for many evangelical women was the sexism that seemed to reign supreme at most evangelical parachurch organizations. These ministries were organized as businesses—not churches—so theoretically, women should have been free to rise up in the ranks. In practice, though, men held the vast majority of parachurch executive and board positions. In 1992, for example, only two of Campus Crusade for Christ's 164 campus directors were female, and these were at all-women colleges.

Whatever it was that Paul meant when he wrote that there should be neither male nor female in the kingdom of God, by the end of the century, most women understood that restrictive gender distinctions were a deeply entrenched tradition within the evangelical subculture.

Resources

Letha Scanzoni and Nancy Hardesty, *All We're Meant to Be* (1974).
Patricia Gundry, *Woman, Be Free!* (1977).
Bonnidell Clouse and Robert G. Clouse, eds., *Women in Ministry: Four Views* (1989).

31. Matters of Life and Birth: *Roe v. Wade* and the Dawn of Evangelical Activism, 1973

On January 22, 1973, the U.S. Supreme Court delivered a startling wake-up call to millions of Americans with *Roe v. Wade,* a controversial decision that said a woman could legally terminate her pregnancy as part of a constitutionally protected "right of privacy." The ruling changed not only the law but led to a transformation of U.S. politics.

The *Roe* decision, written by Justice Harry Blackmun, a Republican appointed to the court by Richard Nixon, did three major things: it overturned state laws prohibiting abortion during the first six months of a pregnancy; it declared that a fetus was not a "person"; and it said the government must have a compelling reason to prevent an abortion.

For many evangelicals, *Roe* was a watershed event. As they saw it, their government had now sanctioned the killing of unborn babies. The shock broke many believers out of their traditional isolation and—more than any other single event in the century—gave birth to the evangelical political activism that would play an important role in the life of both church and state in the last quarter of the century.

Joining the Battle

"Jane Roe" was a pseudonym for Norma McCorvey, who in 1969 was a poor, single, and pregnant 21-year-old. In 1970 women's groups had helped McCorvey challenge an 1854 Texas antiabortion law. By 1995, though, she had given the antiabortion side one of its rare public relations victories by accepting Christ and joining the staff of Operation Rescue. "I'm pro-life," announced McCorvey, who would later convert to Catholicism. "I think I always have been pro-life. I just didn't know it."

Catholics had been at the forefront of the fledgling antiabortion movement long before most evangelicals were even aware such a movement existed. The National Conference of Catholic Bishops founded the National Right to Life

Committee in 1968. Evangelicals were spurred into action by Francis Schaeffer, who coauthored the 1979 book *Whatever Happened to the Human Race?* with pediatric surgeon C. Everett Koop, who would later become U.S. surgeon general. Schaeffer and Koop toured the country, lecturing on the book and a companion film series. "The reason we are writing this book is that we strongly feel that we stand today on the edge of a great abyss," they wrote. They were not alone. Historian Mark Noll explains:

> Many religious conservatives viewed the *Roe v. Wade* decision legalizing abortion on demand as an explicit affront to Judeo-Christian reverence for life and an implicit sanction of the morally reprehensible sexual revolution.

Francis Schaeffer and C. Everett Koop coauthored the 1979 book *Whatever Happened to the Human Race?*, helping spur evangelicals into action against abortion.

As a result of *Roe,* conservative Christians—most of whom had been politically passive—were transformed into some of the country's most passionate activists.

Teaching and Tactics

The Bible makes no specific mention of abortion, even though it was practiced during Old Testament and New Testament times. Through the ages, most Christian thinkers have opposed abortion. During the 1970s and 1980s, mainline Protestants debated about what to do in cases of rape, incest, or potential injury or death to the mother. But for most of America's evangelicals, there was no point in debating such questions. For some, opposition to abortion in all its forms was a litmus test used to evaluate fellow believers' faithfulness to God.

As judges, politicians, and medical ethicists debated complex issues like when human life begins, evangelicals turned to passages like Psalm 139 (". . . you knit me together in my mother's womb. I praise you because I am fearfully and wonderfully made . . . ."). Pro-life theology emphasized the inherent value of each life and challenged women to view their procreative powers as a divine gift rather than a legal entitlement.

As evangelicals began rolling up their sleeves and joining the battle that raged on many fronts, they focused on politics. At first, the emphasis was on putting the right man in the White House (it was thought his appointees to the Supreme Court might reverse *Roe*), or the right people in Congress (they could pass parental consent laws or "partial-birth" bans). As the evangelical voting bloc grew in size and influence, Republican politicians promised them the moon but were either unable or unwilling to deliver on their promises.

Some evangelicals looked beyond political solutions, seeking instead to decrease the number of abortions by supporting Crisis Pregnancy Centers, promoting adoption instead of abortion, or engaging in dialogue with pro-choice supporters about ways the two groups could work together.

For others, failure to halt abortions led to frustration as many conservative evangelicals lost faith in the American system. As an editorial in *Christianity Today* put it, *Roe* proved that "the American state no longer supports, in any meaningful sense, the laws of God."

Ratcheting Up the Rhetoric

This frustration led to a ratcheting-up of rhetoric, as abortion providers became "baby killers," abortion clinics were called "abortuaries," and abortion-related deaths were likened to the Holocaust, a comparison that angered many Jews, even evangelical-friendly conservatives like Michael Medved.

Growing numbers of otherwise law-abiding believers embraced civil disobedience, taking to the streets in a series of increasingly contentious clinic confrontations. "God never gave the government a blank check to do what it wants to do," said Randall Terry, a controversial and colorful character who founded Operation Rescue in 1986 and rapidly became one of the pro-life movement's most visible leaders.

The organization staged clinic protest rallies in cities across the nation, claiming victories when clinics were closed in New York City, Philadelphia, and Cherry Hill,

---

Colson Questions Prolife Tactics

I have fervently supported the efforts of the thousands of Christians who protest abortion clinics. We should all be fighting this battle for unborn lives.

But I have grown increasingly uneasy about the conduct of some involved in this movement and how Christians have accordingly been portrayed in the mass media. Rather than piercing anyone's conscience, I wonder if we are not stabbing both our neighbors and our cause instead. News footage of Christians screaming and waving their Bibles, faces twisted with hate and anger, hardly helps our cause.

We must work on a more fundamental level than legislation alone, painting a fresh moral vision on our dingy national canvas, a vision of hope and human dignity. We must woo people's hearts toward righteousness. But we cannot woo unless we love.

— adapted from "How Prolife Protest Has Backfired," *Christianity Today,* Dec. 15, 1989.

New Jersey. In Wichita, Kansas, Terry led a long-running showdown that nearly shut down the entire city and resulted in more than 2,700 arrests.

Quick-tongued and short-tempered, Terry was renowned for his intemperate comments. "What it is coming down to is who runs the country," he said in a 1992 speech. "It's us against them. It's the good guys versus the bad guys." In a 1993 speech to antiabortion activists, Terry was reportedly even more provocative: "I want you to just let a wave of intolerance wash over. I want you to let a wave of hatred wash over you."

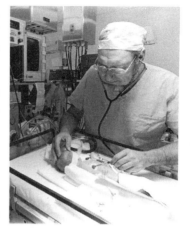

Dr. C. Everett Koop, a pediatric surgeon, later became the U.S. surgeon general. He and coauthor Francis Schaeffer wrote about abortion and other issues.

Some critics argue that Terry's inflammatory rhetoric may have helped inspire clinic violence and the killing of abortion providers. While such violence led to the closing of many clinics, it also turned many Americans against the pro-life cause and inspired Congress to pass the 1994 Freedom of Access to Clinic Entrances Act, or "bubble law," which protected abortion providers and their clients from the kinds of demonstrations Terry once organized.

Terry would go on to wage an unsuccessful campaign to win a seat in the New York house, divorce his wife of 19 years, marry an assistant 16 years his junior, and be ostracized by both his church and Operation Rescue (which changed its name to Operation Save America and began battling pornography and homosexuality). In some ways, his setbacks were symbolic of the larger problems besetting the pro-life movement at the end of the century.

Life More Abundantly

Nearly three decades after *Roe v. Wade,* abortion remained legal and available while the movement that rose up to oppose it appeared dejected and divided.

Theological thinkers argued that part of the problem was that evangelical activists had been too narrow in their focus. Catholic leaders like Cardinal Joseph Bernardin, for example, had articulated a more expansive "seamless garment" approach to "a consistent ethic of life":

Nuclear war threatens life on a previously unimaginable scale; abortion takes life daily on a horrendous scale; public executions are fast becoming weekly events in the most advanced technological society in history . . . .

Ironically, many American evangelicals opposed gun control, supported capital punishment, and advocated increased military spending. Pope John Paul II and other world religious leaders believed that such positions contributed to the West's "culture of death."

The evangelical pro-life movement also struggled to keep pace with medical and scientific developments including the RU-486 abortion pill and human cloning. And by 2001, President George W. Bush's support for government funding of stem cell research had further divided pragmatists from purists. As the *New York Times* reported, "The president's decision to use government funds for stem cell research appears to have divided the large, long-reliable coalition against abortion."

Resources

Francis Schaeffer and C. Everett Koop, M.D., *Whatever Happened to the Human Race?* (1979).
Ron Sider, *Completely Pro-Life* (1987).
Harold O. J. Brown, *Death Before Birth* (1977).
Laurie Goodstein, "Abortion Foes Split Over Plan on Stem Cells," *New York Times*, August 12, 2001.

32. God's Word in Our Words: The New International Version and the Babel of Bibles, 1973

Translating Bibles used to be hazardous work. John Wycliffe was found guilty of heresy and forced to leave public life. His death from a stroke in 1384 may have saved him from the fate that befell a later biblical translator, William Tyndale, who was imprisoned, convicted of heresy, and killed by strangulation in 1536 before his lifeless body was thrown onto the flames.

Today, Christians in some countries are persecuted for owning or reading Scripture. Still, the work of translation continues as missions-minded linguists create the first Bibles in hundreds of lesser-known languages. As a result of their work, the Bible is the world's most widely translated, published, and disseminated text, with portions of it available in more than 2,000 languages. A seminary student even created a Bible in Klingon, the language of TV's *Star Trek*. In addition, computers and the Internet make scholarly resources available to more people than ever before.

In the U.S., Bibles are big business. Every year, Christian publishers release dozens of new versions and editions, like the million-selling *Precious Moments Bible,* which includes 24 pastel illustrations of the big-eyed Precious Moments kids; *Serenity: A Companion for 12-Step Recovery,* which integrates New Testament verses with the lessons of Alcoholics Anonymous; and Robert Schuller's upbeat *The Possibility Thinker's Bible.* There are more than 7,000 editions of the Bible in English, including target-marketed niche versions for fathers, feminists, and fundamentalists.

Ironically, this Babel of Bibles has done little to reverse a staggering decline in biblical literacy, among both the churched and the unchurched. Three recent examples demonstrate this point:

—*Christianity Today* reports that incoming freshmen students at Wheaton College have problems placing biblical characters like Abraham, Moses, Jesus, and Paul in their proper chronological order.

—Pollsters asking Americans to identify Joan of Arc were shocked when one in ten respondents said she was wife of the biblical Noah.

—And when David Koresh, the ayatollah of the Branch Davidian compound near Waco, Texas, said God's plan for the world had something to do with "seven seals," FBI agents thought he was referring to fin-footed mammals, not apocalyptic prophecies from the book of Revelation.

Bibles for Every Tongue and Taste

The 20th century has seen an unprecedented level of Bible translation activity. In 1934, Cameron Townsend founded the Summer Institute of Linguistics, which trained foreign missionaries to translate the Bible into the languages of "unreached" people groups. In 1942 this group became Wycliffe Bible Translators, which has since created Bibles in hundreds of languages.

Tyndale House Publishers, Inc., was founded in 1962 by editor and author Dr. Kenneth N. Taylor. Concerned that his 10 children weren't understanding the family's devotional reading of the 17th-century English in the King James Version of the Bible, Taylor wrote what has become the Living Bible so they could hear and understand the Scriptures in everyday English. Half a million copies were given away through the Billy Graham crusades.

Back in America, one of the most important new English versions was the Revised Standard Version. Sponsored by dozens of Protestant groups and published between 1946 and 1952, the RSV was condemned by some conservative Christians who called it a "Communist Bible." Still, the RSV has sold more than 50 million copies.

Many fundamentalists believe the King James Version (KJV) is the only reliable version, but evangelicals looking for an alternative to the RSV and KJV formed the Committee on Bible Translations in 1965 to create the New International Version (NIV). The NIV New Testament was published in 1973, followed by the Old Testament in 1978. Within a decade, the NIV would become the best-selling U.S. Bible.

The 1970s also saw the publication of various colloquial paraphrases of the Bible. Kenneth Taylor founded Tyndale House Publishers to market his Living Bible version, which emphasized ease of readability. Taylor began work on the project in 1954, creating it with his own

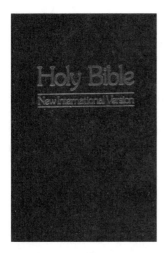

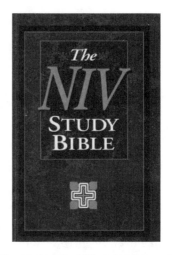

The New International Version of the Bible was born out of a group of evangelicals who formed the Committee on Bible Translations in 1965 to create a more internationally understood version. The New Testament was published in 1973, followed by the Old Testament in 1978. During the remainder of the 20th century, the NIV became the best-selling Bible in the U.S.

The NIV Study Bible is a Bible and a reference library in one, including a complete verse-by-verse commentary. It has over 20,000 in-text study notes, complete with maps, charts, diagrams, and illustrations. It has become a top Bible aid for in-depth study.

children in mind. Completed in 1971, the Living Bible was an immediate success, and soon there were special editions for children, Catholics, and Spanish-speaking believers. Also popular was the reader-friendly Good News Bible (Today's English Version, 1966-1976), which was designed to help both young readers and new believers better understand Scripture.

New idiosyncratic versions were created for specific audiences. *Letters to Street Christians* (1971) was a Jesus movement-style paraphrase of St. Paul's epistles attributed to "two brothers from Berkeley":

> *Now dig this! When we were helplessly wasted, Jesus the Messiah came by God's plan to die for every rotten one of us. Now that's really far out . . . .*

The Black Bible Chronicles (1994), which aimed to make the Bible relevant to contemporary, urban African Americans, referred to God as "one mean dude," and restated the Decalogue's injunction against taking the name of the Lord in vain like this:

> *You shouldn't diss the Almighty's name, using it in cuss words or rapping with another. It ain't cool, and payback's a monster.*

Some of the most profitable new Bible products were some of the many niche-market study Bibles, which combined biblical texts with notes, study aids, and often endorsements or contributions from Christian celebrity authors. Unfortunately, a study presented at the 1997 Christian Booksellers Association convention revealed that many Bible consumers spent more time studying the extra-biblical aids than they did reading the biblical texts.

The Battle over Inerrancy

While Bibles were flying off of publishers' presses, evangelicals began arguing over whether or not the Bible was inerrant, or free from any error. For much of the century, fundamentalists and many evangelicals had been committed to inerrancy, even though it is not a concept explicitly taught in Scripture.

Harold Lindsell, the editor of *Christianity Today,* believed that some evangelicals were drifting away from inerrancy toward theological liberalism, a problem he tried to correct in his 1976 bombshell of a book, *The Battle for the Bible.*

Lindsell was particularly concerned about two perceived problems at Fuller Theological Seminary. In 1967 Fuller had removed the word *inerrancy* from its statement of faith, replacing it with the word *infallible,* which allowed for some textual inconsistencies. And Fuller professor Paul Jewett wrote a 1975 book called *Man as Male and Female,* which claimed that the apostle Paul was mistaken when he taught that women should be subordinate to men.

Lindsell was concerned not only about Jewett's approach to the

---

Good Book Spawns "Bad" Books

When *The Christian Century* magazine asked some of its contributors to identify some of the worst religious books of recent years, two Bible projects made the list.

The collective works of the Jesus Seminar, a liberal group that questions the historicity of much of the Bible, didn't represent "the cutting edge of biblical scholarship," as the publicity-savvy seminar had claimed. Still, the group's efforts had sown enough doubts that many believers "hold their faith with a kind of bad conscious."

Also making the list was The Living Bible, which was dismissed as "a sanitized Bible, one rendered safe from all ambiguity and provocation."

— *The Christian Century,*
May 2001 spring books
issue

Bible, which was common among liberals but relatively unheard of in more conservative circles, but he also feared that evangelicals wouldn't be able to withstand challenges like the women's movement unless they resisted moral relativism and stood firm on the revealed and infallible Word of God.

Many evangelicals shared Lindsell's concerns, but they didn't like the combative approach he employed against his theological opponents. Evangelical leader Carl Henry accused Lindsell of "relying on theological atom bombing" to attack his foes, and the result, Henry said, was that "as many evangelical friends as foes end up as casualties."

Evangelicals continued to debate inerrancy throughout the 1980s, and the issue was also a source of division within both the Southern Baptist Convention and the Lutheran Church-Missouri Synod.

By the end of the century, though, tempers had cooled, as had many people's interest in reading God's revealed Word.

Resources

Harold Lindsell, *The Battle for the Bible* (1976).
Nathan Hatch and Mark Noll, eds., *The Bible in America* (1982).

33. Lausanne and Beyond: Helping the World Reach the World, 1974

For much of the 19th and 20th centuries, missionary work was largely the "white man's burden," as residents of the emerging Western superpowers of Britain and the United States went out to save the world. By the 1970s, though, that was beginning to change.

In 1974, 2,700 Christian leaders representing denominations, mission agencies, and parachurch organizations from more than 150 countries gathered in Lausanne, Switzerland, for the International Congress on World Evangelization, an event one participant called "one of the miracles of contemporary church history." At the conclusion of the 10-day gathering, participants signed the Lausanne Covenant, which was written by British churchman John Stott and boldly declared, "The dominant role of western missions is fast disappearing."

Billy Graham, the event's driving force and honorary chairman, would later say that "Lausanne burst upon us with unexpected significance and power." And in the decades after this historic event, there would be significant changes in the shape, direction, and color of world missions.

A Covenant of Cooperation

Reading the Lausanne Covenant today, one can only imagine how radical certain portions of the document must have seemed at the time. For while sections of the Covenant reaffirmed key evangelical doctrines about God, the authority of the Bible, the uniqueness of Christ, and the power of the Holy Spirit, other sections of the document ventured into areas that were new and troubling to many, including:

- **Dialogue.** Lausanne affirmed the necessity of "the proclamation of the historical, biblical Christ as Saviour and Lord" but added an endorsement of "that kind of dialogue whose purpose is to listen sensitively in order to understand."

- **Social responsibility.** Affirming that "God is both the Creator and the Judge of all men," the statement said Christians "should share his concern for justice and reconciliation throughout human society and for the liberation of men and women from every kind of oppression." Westerners admitted they hadn't always given this issue the attention it deserved:

  > Here too we express penitence both for our neglect and for having sometimes regarded evangelism and social concern as mutually exclusive. Although reconciliation with other people is not reconciliation with God, nor is social action evangelism, nor is political liberation salvation, nevertheless we affirm that evangelism and socio-political involvement are both part of our Christian duty. For both are necessary expressions of our doctrines of God and man, our love for our neighbour and our obedience to Jesus Christ.

  The signers also called on national leaders "to guarantee freedom of thought and conscience, and freedom to practise and propagate religion."
- **Evangelism.** Just as the Father sent his Son to seek and save the lost, Christians should penetrate the world: "We need to break out of our ecclesiastical ghettos and permeate non-Christian society."
- **Cooperation.** Admitting that Christian disunity was a sinful blemish on the cause of Christ, the signers said, "We confess that our testimony has sometimes been marred by a sinful individualism and needless duplication."
- **Culture.** Calling for "imaginative pioneering methods," the *Covenant* criticized earlier approaches that confused the universals of Christianity with the particulars of human society:

  > Missions have all too frequently exported with the gospel an alien culture and churches have sometimes been in bondage to culture rather than to Scripture. Christ's evangelists must humbly seek to empty themselves of all but their personal authenticity in order to become the servants of others . . . .

- **Superficiality.** The signers confessed "that we have sometimes pursued church growth at the expense of church depth, and divorced evangelism from Christian nurture," and committed themselves anew to training national leaders.
- **Spiritual warfare.** Acknowledging that spiritual warfare was a daily reality of the Christian life, the signers said, "We detect the activity of our enemy, not only in false ideologies outside the Church, but also

International Conference for Itinerant Evangelists

At the Lausanne 1974 International Conference in World Evangelism, "Let the Earth Hear His Voice," was the rallying cry for 4,051 participants, observers, and guests from 150 countries. Using seven official languages, and convened by the BGEA in cooperation with other Christian organizations, Lausanne called for fresh approaches to missionary work, national strategies for evangelism, and greater maturity in the Christian community of every nation. Billy Graham, shown here speaking at the 1983 Amsterdam International Conference for Itinerant Evangelists, was the driving force and honorary chairman for the Lausanne event.

inside it in false gospels which twist Scripture and put people in the place of God."

Evangelicalism has produced more than its share of lofty-sounding documents that are forgotten as soon as their ink is dry, but the Lausanne Covenant was different. Many believers heeded its challenge, and a variety of working committees helped Christians cooperate in practical ways with their brothers and sisters around the globe.

In addition, Graham sponsored additional international conferences. Two for itinerant evangelists were held in Amsterdam in 1983 and 1986. These practical training schools gave knowledge and encouragement to more than 13,000 frontline missionary messengers. In 1989 Manila hosted the Second International Congress on World Evangelization, which was attended by 3,000 people from 170 countries. And more than 10,000 Christian leaders around the world attended Amsterdam 2000. An ailing Graham couldn't be there in person but sent his blessings in a videotaped message from the Mayo Clinic.

Reaching the Unreached

The 1989 conference produced the Manila Manifesto, an update of the Lausanne Covenant of 1974. Some of the believers attending the 1974 gathering expressed optimism that the world could be evangelized by the end of the century, but those gathering in 1989 were far less certain. One section of the Manila Manifesto addressed "The Challenge of AD2000 & Beyond," paying special attention to "the unreached," those 2 billion people "who may never have heard of Jesus as Savior, and are not within reach of Christians of their own people or nationalities in which there is not yet a vital, indigenous church movement." In the final decade of the century, a diverse group of evangelicals would try a variety of new methods to reach these unreached people groups.

The AD2000 & Beyond Movement was a loose network of representatives from international evangelical organizations who cooperated in Bible translation, church planting, and Christian broadcasting. At their meetings, members of the movement regularly talked about the "10/40 Window," a rectangular-shaped section of the world map located between the 10-degree and 40-degree parallels above the equator and stretching from West Africa to East Asia. The window includes the heavily populated and largely unreached countries of China, India, Egypt, Japan, and Thailand, and increasingly, local churches are "adopting" unreached people groups in the window, praying for the people who live there and sending their members out on visits and prayer walks to these areas.

Other developments in the rapidly changing world of missions are regularly reported in *Mission Frontiers,* published six times a year by the U.S. Center for World Mission in Pasadena, California. "These stirring new horizons are piling up on us," said center director Ralph D. Winter in an issue entitled "New Horizons in Mission." "The global success of the gospel has forced major changes in the landscape."

Resources

J. D. Douglas, ed., *Let the Earth Hear His Voice* (1975).

Stanley J. Grenz and Roger E. Olson, *20th-Century Theology: God and the World in a Transitional Age* (1992).

The Amsterdam 2000 Declaration is available online (at www.christianity online.com/ct/2000/132/13.0.html).

34. Consumer Christianity: Willow Creek and the Megachurch Marketing Movement, 1975

Strangers viewing the massive Willow Creek Community Church in South Barrington, Illinois, might initially suspect it's an office complex or a shopping center, and that's OK with pastor Bill Hybels, whose $34 million church is nestled among 155 acres of professionally landscaped grounds and is intentionally devoid of crosses, stained glass windows, or any other traditional religious symbols.

Every weekend more than 17,000 people attend Willow Creek's six "seeker-sensitive" services. Among the people filling the comfortable auditorium-style seats are visiting pastors wanting to incorporate the pioneering congregation's philosophy and methods at their own churches. Over the years, tens of thousands of pastors from around the globe have made pilgrimages here for weekend services, teaching conferences, and other events, making Willow Creek the most influential church in the last quarter of the 20th century.

Hybels first attracted attention in the early 1970s, when his Son City youth ministry drew 1,000 young people to its evening meetings. Then, as now, Hybels was known for both his passion to introduce Christianity to nonbelievers and his willingness to do so in new and sometimes controversial ways, including contemporary music, evocative dramas, and sermons that communicate Christian concepts in a simple and direct style thoroughly lacking in religious jargon, or "Christianese."

Willow Creek was born in a rented movie theater in Palatine, Illinois, in October 12, 1975. A 23-year-old Hybels preached on "New Beginnings" to an audience of 125 people. Utilizing secular business techniques like consumer research, niche marketing, and communications and management theory, Hybels had built a congregation of 2,000 people by 1978. The church held its first service at its present facility in 1981, and for the last two decades Hybels has promoted Willow Creek as "a safe place for you to check out the claims of Christianity."

While many churches tailor their programs for believers, Willow Creek's seeker-sensitive services are designed to entertain, relax, and ultimately persuade the prototypical well-educated, upscale, white, male baby-boomer Hybels calls "unchurched Harry." As he explained to a group of pastors:

> What does the seeker walk into in ninety-nine out of one hundred churches across this land? He walks into a service that has been designed from stem to stern for the already convinced. It's a worship service.

Aiming to reform contemporary Christianity, Hybels created the Willow Creek Association (WCA) in 1992 to promote his ecclesiastical agenda. In 1999, more than 65,000 pastors, church leaders, and laypeople attended WCA conferences and training events held in Illinois and at regional locations throughout the globe. Many emerging Christian leaders say they favor these conferences over traditional seminary training. WCA also publishes books, Bible studies, programming materials, videos, musical recordings, and other products. And in 2000, Mesquite Bible Church of Dallas became the 5,000th church to join the WCA. Today, from Sarasota to Seoul, thousands of congregations in hundreds of denominations have been remaking church in Willow Creek's image.

Jesus, Our CEO

The growing popularity of megachurches—the term generally applied to churches with weekly attendance of more than 2,000 people—has come at a time when America is undergoing profound changes. Religious pluralism now exists on an unprecedented scale, and denominational loyalty is—for many—a thing of the past. Many evangelicals now search for churches that meet their felt needs. Those

Bill Hybels is the senior pastor of the Willow Creek Community Church, located in South Barrington, Illinois, a Chicago suburb. Wanting to see why people don't go to church, Hybels formed a three-man survey team that went into the community. The survey revealed that people: "(1) didn't like being bugged for money; (2) found church boring, predictable, and routine; (3) didn't think that the church was relevant to their lives; and (4) always left church feeling guilty (the Christian message was too negative with 'sin,' etc.)." In order to counteract these attitudes, Hybels developed a type of program so that newcomers would feel welcome, unthreatened, and entertained.

who aren't married, for example, look for singles ministries, while parents place top priority on effective youth programs.

Willow Creek didn't launch these trends. In fact, evangelicals have been getting increasingly pragmatic about church growth techniques since at least 1959, when former missionary Donald McGavran released his groundbreaking book *How Churches Grow*. During 30 years in India with the Disciples of Christ, McGavran observed that most mission stations were seeing little or no growth, and he developed methods foreign missionaries could use to evaluate and improve their effectiveness. McGavran's Institute of Church Growth merged with Fuller Theological Seminary's School of World Mission in 1965.

During the 1970s and 1980s, evangelicals in the U.S. increasingly applied church growth techniques to their congregations. In 1988 pollster George Barna's book *Marketing the Church* boldly declared: "My contention, based on careful study of data and the activities of American churches, is that the major problem plaguing the Church is its failure to embrace a marketing orientation in what has become a marketing-driven environment."

Barna urges his readers to "suspend any attachments to traditional thinking about church growth," adding: "Think of your church not as a religious meeting place, but as a service agency—an entity that exists to satisfy people's needs."

Barna described his views as "a perspective you won't get in seminary," and that was certainly the case. He radically reinterpreted the New Testament in the rhetoric of free enterprise, saying the church is "a business . . .involved in the business of ministry," "The Bible is one of the world's great marketing texts," Jesus is a master "of the data gathering and analysis process," Paul's "entire public ministry was based on a continual environmental assessment," and the disciples were "an informed, capable distribution system." As for Jesus' parable of the sower and the seed, it: "portrays marketing the faith as a process in which there are hot prospects and not-so-hot prospects and shows how we should gear our efforts toward the greatest productivity."

Mixed Messages

By the 1990s, tens of thousands of churches had adopted at least portions of the Willow Creek model, some of them blending this approach with the popular "purpose-driven church" model of Rick Warren, pastor of Saddleback Community Church in Southern California.

At the same time, others voiced concern about this historic ecclesiastical shift. Evangelical scholar Greg Pritchard's book-length examination of Willow Creek argued that the church failed to deliver on some of its promises. For example, Pritchard said 80 to 90 percent of the people attending

Willow Creek's seeker services weren't non-Christian seekers but were born-again believers, many of whom had migrated to Willow Creek for its upbeat services. Pritchard also says most Willow Creek regulars don't participate in the church's 2,000-plus small group discipleship programs. Many get lost in the crowd and fail to experience the "authentic relationships" Hybels promises. Pritchard interviewed a man named Steve, who had been attending Willow Creek regularly for nine years:

> Steve's longest conversation, and best personal contact with a fellow church attender during this nine-year period, was the one hour-long interview that I had with him.

George Barna, author of *Marketing the Church,* received two M.A.s from Rutgers University, in political science and city and regional planning. He interprets the New Testament in the jargon of free enterprise, saying the church is "a business involved in the business of ministry" and that "the Bible is one of the world's great marketing texts."

Pritchard also questions the effort to marry marketing and ministry. "The gospel is not a Big Mac," he writes, "and Jesus did not die as the first step in a marketing plan."

Selling Our Souls?

Marketing has been part of American culture for centuries, and it has long been used in mass evangelism campaigns (see chapter 25). But its growing presence in U.S. congregations has some Christian thinkers wondering whether efforts to market the church may short-change believers and cheapen the gospel.

As church historian Bruce Shelley and *Leadership* journal editor (and son) Marshall Shelley wrote:

> In recent years, Americans have chosen churches not so much to meet God and surrender to his revealed ways as to satisfy some personal need. Unlike the rich young ruler in the Gospels, church attenders seldom ask, "What must I do?" They are far more likely to ask, "What do I get out of this?"

Christian thinker Os Guinness credits the church growth movement with having "an immensely positive spiritual, cultural, and historical significance for the church of Christ," but he is also worried that some in

Marketing's Pervasive Power

In 1996 more than 100 Christian thinkers who shared a deep commitment to the principles of the Protestant Reformation traveled to Cambridge, England, where they gathered under the banner of "the Alliance of Confessing Evangelicals." The group's "Cambridge Declaration" said: "Therapeutic technique, marketing strategies, and the beat of the entertainment world often have far more to say about what the church wants, how it functions, and what it offers, than does the Word of God."

But one of the declaration's signers observed that marketing concerns may have influenced the group's choice for a meeting site. "We could have met, at less cost, in Kokomo, Indiana. But we all know that a 'Kokomo Declaration' doesn't have quite the same ring to it."

— *World* magazine,
May 11/18, 1996.

the movement are trying to hot-wire revival by human means and are emphasizing numerical growth over spiritual depth.

Randall Balmer's assessment is even more damning:

> Because of (its) focus on maintaining large popular followings, evangelicalism in America tends not to demand very much of its adherents for fear of alienating them. . . . American religion has effectively "baptized" American consumerism and middle-class values. . . .
>
> Because of its relentlessly populist cast, then, religion in America generally offers very little prophetic challenge to American cultural norms and assumptions but instead endorses these norms. To do otherwise would, of course, be unpopular.

Such criticisms have had little impact on the success of Willow Creek's marketing-oriented ecclesiastical model, which continued gaining new converts—or customers—at a rapid pace.

Resources

Bill and Lynne Hybels, *Rediscovering Church: The Story and Vision of Willow Creek Community Church* (1995).

George Barna, *Marketing the Church* (1988).

G. A. Pritchard, *Willow Creek Seeker Services* (1996).

Bruce Shelley and Marshall Shelley, *The Consumer Church* (1992).

Os Guinness, *Dining with the Devil: The Megachurch Movement Flirts with Modernity* (1993).

Kimon Sargeant, *Seeker Churches: Promoting Traditional Religion in a Nontraditional Way* (2000).

Randall Balmer, *Blessed Assurance: A History of Evangelicalism in America* (1999).

35. Aliens No More:
Carter, Colson, and "The Year of the Evangelical," 1976

The early 1970s had been good to American evangelicals. The charismatic movement had revitalized thousands of churches; the Jesus movement had received glowing press coverage; books by Hal Lindsey and Marabel Morgan had sold millions of copies; Christian broadcasting had become a major media force; and Bill Bright's "I Found It!" campaign had introduced thousands to Jesus. Still, many Americans remained uncertain about who evangelicals were, what they believed, or what they really wanted.

Some of these questions were answered by a peanut farmer and Sunday school teacher from Plains, Georgia, named Jimmy Carter, the Democratic nominee for the 1976 presidential race. Carter's homespun religiosity might have bothered some strict church-state separationists, but in the post-Watergate 1970s, many Americans were hungry for traditional values like faith and honesty. Carter's candid confessions about his own born-again convictions and his call for national healing helped him defeat incumbent Gerald Ford in a close election. In the process, Carter became a poster boy for the mainstreaming of evangelicalism.

Read All About It!

"Born Again!" shouted the headline in the October 25, 1976, issue of *Newsweek*

Former President Jimmy Carter, shown here with wife, Rosalyn, and daughter, Amy, defeated incumbent President Gerald Ford in the 1976 presidential race. Carter had been a peanut farmer and Sunday school teacher in Plains, Georgia.

magazine. A Gallup survey reported that "half of all Protestants—and a third of all Americans—say that they have been 'born again,'" leading both Gallup and *Newsweek* to declare 1976 "The Year of the Evangelical." As the article explained:

> In two weeks, Jimmy Carter, the best-known Baptist deacon in America, may be elected President of the United States. Even if he loses, Carter's dramatic capture of the Presidential nomination has already focused national attention on the most significant—and overlooked—religious phenomenon of the 70s: the emergence of evangelical Christianity into a position of respect and power.

Christianity Today trumpeted the evangelical movement's unprecedented mainstream acceptance:

> Evangelicals suddenly find themselves number one on the North American religious scene. . . . After being ignored by much of the rest of society for decades, they are now coming into prominence. Indeed, 1976 seems to be the year of the evangelical.

Many factors played a role in evangelicals' growing visibility. Celebrations of the nation's bicentennial caused some Americans to reexamine the nation's religious roots, which stood in dramatic contrast to its present-day secularity. The media even covered Gerald Ford's speech to a joint gathering of the National Association of Evangelicals and the National Religious Broadcasters. (Even though Carter was outspoken about his faith, most evangelicals considered him too liberal, preferring conservative Republicans like Ford and Reagan.)

David F. Wells and John D. Woodbridge explained things in their book *The Evangelicals,* saying the movement "now can no longer be regarded as simply reactionary, but is vigorously and sometimes creatively speaking to the needs of the contemporary world."

The mid-1970s also saw many celebrities converting to Christianity and speaking openly about their faith. Graham Kerr, TV's "Galloping Gourmet," U.S. Senator Mark Hatfield, and former Black Panther leader Eldridge Cleaver had all offered public testimonies. Cleaver said he had experienced salvation while looking toward heaven:

> . . . I saw the man in the moon and it was my face . . . . Then I saw the face was not mine but some of my old heroes. There was Fidel Castro, then there was Mao Tse-tung . . . . While I watched the face turned to Jesus Christ, and I was very much surprised . . . . I don't know when I had last cried, but I began to cry and didn't stop. I was still crying and I got on my knees and said the Lord's Prayer.

From Power to Prison

Some people inside the Washington, D.C., beltway were understandably skeptical about the conversion testimony of Charles Colson, the man *TIME* magazine had called "the toughest of the Nixon tough guys." But following the publication of his autobiographical book, *Born Again*, Colson played a starring role in the Year of the Evangelical.

Colson had always led something of a charmed life, as he told journalist Hugh Hewitt in the 1996 PBS series, "Searching for God in America":

Charles Colson, former U.S. Marine and the man *TIME* magazine called the "toughest of the Nixon tough guys," took center stage in the Year of the Evangelical. Colson serves as chairman of the board of Prison Fellowship, one of the largest volunteer organizations in the world. In the last 20 years, Colson has visited more than 600 prisons in 40 countries and, with the help of nearly 50,000 volunteers, has built Prison Fellowship into the world's largest prison outreach, serving the spiritual and practical needs of prisoners in 83 countries, including the U.S.

> I mean, my story was the American dream fulfilled: poor kid grows up in the Depression years, scholarship to Brown University, academic honors, youngest company officer in the Marines, youngest administrative assistant in the United States Senate. I'd succeeded at everything I'd ever done, and I ended up in an office next to the President of the United States.

Named special counsel to the White House in 1969, Colson was better known as Nixon's "hatchet man." He came to faith in 1973 after reading C. S. Lewis's *Mere Christianity*, and left the White House for a private law practice. But he was ensnared by the expanding Watergate investigation and indicted for obstruction of justice for his role in disseminating derogatory information about Daniel Ellsberg, who had released the controversial Pentagon papers to the press. During his eight months in an Alabama prison camp, Colson shared his faith with fellow prisoners and began writing *Born Again*. Freed in 1975, Colson founded Prison Fellowship in 1976. By the mid-1990s, the ministry was working in 800 U.S. prisons and 40 foreign countries, winning kudos for Colson and continued credibility for the evangelical cause.

As *Christianity Today* said in a July 2001 cover story: "Twenty-six years after leaving prison, Charles Colson has become one of America's most significant social reformers."

Charles Colson sat in a prison cell and watched on TV as Richard Nixon resigned as President of the United States. That day he began jotting down notes of the event that had brought about the fall of a president and the rebirth of his "hatchet man." From these notes, *Born Again* had its own birth.

Would American evangelicals ever again experience the massive celebrity, mainstream credibility, and swaggering triumphalism they enjoyed in the 1970s? Marty and others didn't think so. "A period has ended," he wrote. "The evangelical renewal did not lead to general revival, and harder times may be coming."

Resources

Kenneth L. Woodward, "Born Again! The Year of the Evangelical," *Newsweek* (October 25, 1976).

Charles Colson, *Born Again* (1976).

Martin Marty, "The Years of the Evangelicals," *The Christian Century* (February 15, 1989).

Out of the Spotlight

The image of American evangelicalism didn't shine as brightly during the 1980s and 1990s as it had during its mid-1970s glory years. The movement couldn't translate its transient celebrity into real and lasting social influence, even though members of the emerging religious right certainly tried.

Distinguished church historian Martin Marty evaluated the movement's plight in a 1989 piece in *The Christian Century* entitled "The Years of the Evangelicals":

> . . . increasingly, especially after some punishing public encounters, they are aware that, while their power is to be reckoned with, they will not run the show.

During President Carter's term, conservative forces sought to limit the official definition of "family" to people related by blood, adoption, or marriage.

36. Battling Baptists: Theology and Politics Divide a Denomination, 1979

Colorful contradictions have long been a distinguishing characteristic of the Southern Baptist Convention (SBC), from its tumultuous beginnings in the 1840s to its rise to power and prominence in the 1980s. Recently, a pastor stood behind a Plexiglas pulpit to pray at one of the SBC's annual meetings, saying, "We are the largest Protestant denomination—and we say that with all humility."

Baptists in the South originally broke from northern brethren over the issue of whether or not missionaries could be slaveholders. (Some Southerners saw slavery as a necessary evil, while others defended it as a social good; but none of them found an unambiguous prohibition of the practice in the Bible. In the 1990s, the SBC formally repented of the sin of racism.)

Historically committed to freedom of conscience for its individual members (who now number more than 16 million in the U.S.) and freedom from external control for its congregations (currently numbering more than 40,000), the SBC twice wound up in the national spotlight when its own members were elected to the nation's highest office. But the denomination snubbed Democrats Jimmy Carter and Bill Clinton, and instead asked Republican Presidents Ronald Reagan, a Presbyterian, and George Bush, an Episcopalian, to address its annual convention. Clinton and fellow Southern Baptist Vice President Al Gore were attacked for their positions on abortion and homosexuality and admonished to "stand for Biblical morality."

Long recognized for their unparalleled zeal for evangelism and world missions, the denomination's leaders made a commitment at their 1978 convention to share the gospel with every person in the world by the year 2000. But intense infighting, which surfaced that same year, would divert precious energy from evangelism and threaten to permanently divide the denomination.

The Battles Begin

Jean Caffey Lyles, who occasionally covered the SBC for the mainline Protestant magazine *The Christian Century*, once marveled at the fact that:

> . . . one pastor says "the Bible is the authoritative and trust-worthy word of God" and another pastor says "the Bible is the inerrant and infallible word of God," and that means the two of them are on opposite sides of the theological and political fence.

That's pretty much the way things were after Harold Lindsell, a former editor of *Christianity Today*, brought his crusade for biblical inerrancy to the SBC after already having won over leaders of the Lutheran Church-Missouri Synod. In his 1976 book *The Battle for the Bible*, Lindsell argued that the Scriptures were without error in their original autographs—an assertion that seemed curious to some, since no one had ever seen any of the original biblical manuscripts, and all anyone had were a series of imperfect copies. Lindsell was denied permission to hold a press conference on the matter in denomination-controlled facilities at its 1978 convention in Atlanta, but the issue would not be ignored.

Dr. Harold Lindsell, a former editor of *Christianity Today*, wrote *The Battle for the Bible* in which he argued that the Scriptures were without error in their original manuscripts. He won over leaders of the Lutheran Church-Missouri Synod, then brought the battle to the Southern Baptists.

In 1979 SBC delegates met in Houston, where they narrowly elected Memphis pastor Adrian Rogers, an inerrancy advocate, as their president amidst charges of election irregularities. This was the first time in memory that a conservative was the SBC's leader—marking a change in the denomination's direction—but it certainly wouldn't be the last.

Oklahoman Bailey Smith, who would gain unwanted international renown for his comment that "almighty God does not hear the prayer of a Jew," was named president at the SBC's 1980 and 1981 meetings, signifying the conservatives' growing hold on power. Delegates at these conventions were unusually combative, and it was becoming increasingly clear that conservatives cared about more than inerrancy.

Battles would rage on many fronts throughout the next decade. Conservatives were concerned that the SBC's six seminaries, which enrolled one quarter of the nation's divinity students, were "infected with the liberal virus," and they sought to require professors to sign narrow doctrinal statements. There were also problems at the denomination's Broadman Press publishing house, which had released "liberal" books. Over at the Baptist Press news service, mass firings sought to root out moderates and improve "balance" in news coverage of the denomination.

Southern Baptists have always placed a premium on preaching, making it a centerpiece of both their Sunday services and their annual conventions. Bailey Smith was happy to defend the inerrant position with powerful prose. "I believe that Jonah was a literal man who was eaten by a literal fish and vomited up out of a literal stomach. And he was a literal mess," he said on one occasion. He also charged moderates with subscribing to a "Dalmation theology—the theory that the Bible is inspired in spots, and that it's up to the theologians to decide where those spots are."

Caught in the Crossfire

Moderates complained, and some fought back. In 1981 Houston pastor Kenneth Chafin said the inerrancy crusade was nothing more "than a naked, ruthless reach for personal power"; and in 1984, moderate Roy Honeycutt, president of the Southern Baptist Theological Seminary in Louisville, Kentucky, declared "holy war" on "ungodly forces which, if left unchecked, will destroy essential qualities of both our Convention and this seminary." But by this time, the battle was effectively over. Conservatives were already entrenched in key positions in SBC boards, commissions, seminaries, and colleges, where they would make major appointments to ensure the institutionalization of their ideals over the next decade and more.

Not giving up, Baptist moderates founded the Cooperative Baptist Fellowship, which had 1,800 supporting congregations by 2000 and was organizing its own seminary, publishing, and missions programs. That same year, the annual Baptist General Convention of Texas voted to withhold $5 million in support from the SBC.

Critics said denominational conservatives had turned their backs on key aspects of SBC tradition. A denomination that had long refused to be bound by creeds was said to be embracing a "creeping credalism." Even the SBC's long-standing support for strict separation between church and state was giving way as conservatives applauded Ronald Reagan's school prayer amendment. Increasingly, as one journalist noted,

> . . . the annual sessions of the Southern Baptist Convention have resembled a family quarrel inside a large plantation house . . . . The neighbors have begun to wonder how folks who quarrel so much can live under one roof. And many of the cousins and aunts and uncles *inside* the family are wondering the same thing.

Carter Severs Ties with SBC

In 2000, former President Jimmy Carter announced he was severing his ties with the denomination that had been his home for 65 of his 76 years. In a statement, he explained his reasons:

"Over the years leaders of the Convention have adopted an increasingly rigid creed, called a Baptist Faith and Message, including some provisions that violate the basic tenets of my Christian faith. These premises have become mandatory criteria that must be accepted by employees, by members of committees who control the Convention's affairs, and by professors who teach in the SBC-owned seminaries. Obviously, this can have a far-reaching and permanent effect. . . .

"Most disturbing has been the Convention's recent decision to remove Jesus Christ, through his words, deeds, and personal inspiration, as the ultimate interpreter of the Holy Scriptures. This leaves open making the pastors or executives of the SBC the ultimate interpreters.

"We are quite concerned by the effort of SBC leaders to impose their newly adopted creed on state conventions and individual believers. . . .

"My hope is that church congregations and individuals will consider the serious consequences of this proposed departure from our traditional beliefs."

Paige Patterson, a former SBC president and now president of the SBC's Southeastern Theological Seminary, dismissed Carter's complaints, saying, "President Carter has not in fact been much of a Southern Baptist for a long time."

Patterson also predicted Carter's defection would have no negative impact on the denomination: "I would imagine it will enhance our ministry overall and probably be the cause for not a few people who have questions about Baptists becoming Baptists."

—Religion News Service and the *Los Angeles Times*, October 20, 2000

The Baptist battles illustrated long-running tensions, not only within the SBC, but between fundamentalist, liberal, and moderate evangelicals in all denominations.

"What the rift also shows," said *New York Times* religion writer Gustav Niebuhr, "is how difficult it can be, at a time when many Protestant church members' loyalties to denominations have weakened, to hold together big church bodies amid divisive issues."

Resources

Bill J. Leonard, *God's Last & Only Hope: The Fragmentation of the Southern Baptist Convention* (1990).

Nancy Ammerman, *Baptist Battles: Social Change and Religious Conflict in the Southern Baptist Convention* (1990).

Jesse C. Fletcher, *The Southern Baptist Convention: A Sesquicentennial History* (1994).

37. Bibles and Ballots: The Rise and Fall of the Religious Right, 1979

Jerry Falwell, the fundamentalist pastor of Thomas Road Baptist Church in Lynchburg, Virginia, stood in his pulpit in March of 1965 to deliver the sermon "Ministers and Marches," which condemned pastors who used their pulpits to talk about politics:

> . . . our only purpose on this earth is to know Christ and make him known. Believing the Bible as I do, I would find it impossible to stop preaching the pure saving gospel of Jesus Christ and begin doing anything else—including the fighting of Communism or participating in the civil rights reform . . . . Preachers are not called to be politicians, but to be soul winners.

Falwell later repented of his opposition to political activism, calling his own isolationist views a "false prophecy." "I have misled you on that issue," he said. "Our lack of involvement is probably one of the reasons why the country's in the mess it's in."

In June 1979 Falwell, Tim LaHaye, and Charles Stanley founded the Moral Majority, a "pro-life, pro-family, pro-moral, and pro-American" activist group that opposed abortion, homosexuality, feminism, and perceived government hostility toward religion. The group dedicated itself to educating and motivating conservative Christians who were as politically inactive and separatist as Falwell himself had once been. Barnstorming the country and talking to groups of ministers, Falwell said their responsibilities were: "Getting people saved, baptized, and registered to vote."

Christians Come Out of the Closet

The Moral Majority was just one of the many grassroots groups that wedded theological and political conservatism during the 1970s and 1980s and became known, collectively, as the religious right. Beverly LaHaye's Concerned Women for America was founded in the D.C. area in 1979. The

Family Research Council was established as a division of Focus on the Family in 1980 but was made an independent organization in 1992. Focus launched its Public Policy Division in 1986 after organization founder James Dobson finished work on a government commission on pornography. And the Christian Coalition was founded in 1989 following Pat Robertson's unsuccessful 1988 bid for President.

For better or worse, though, the Moral Majority was the most visible religious-right group until Falwell dissolved it in June 1989, saying it had achieved its goal of establishing conservative Christians in the public arena. With chapters in all 50 states and a colorful leader, the organization had received more media coverage during the 1980s than all the other groups combined.

Many liberals were surprised by the sudden rise of Christian conservatism, and their shock often led to overreaction. Groups like Hollywood producer Norman Lear's People for the American Way hysterically condemned the religious right as a threat to American liberties. Liberal critics also characterized the various conservative Christian groups as part of a vast and monolithic fascist conspiracy. It's true that many of these groups did agree on core issues, but they were often fiercely independent and frequently competed with one another for publicity and funding.

Jerry Falwell founded the Moral Majority with fellow board members Tim LaHaye and Charles Stanley in June 1979. In talks to groups of ministers, Falwell said their responsibilities were: "Getting people saved, baptized, and registered to vote."

Nor did the religious right escape the slings and arrows of fellow evangelicals, who criticized the movement's loose hodgepodge of biblical and extra-biblical notions and the bare-knuckled tactics that were used to promote this mixed agenda.

For example, the Moral Majority claimed it was defending the Bible when it spoke out on abortion, homosexuality, and women's rights. But Falwell's organization was equally vehement on issues the Bible didn't mention, including its opposition to the SALT II arms-limitation treaty and the U.S. decision to relinquish control of the Panama Canal.

"Evangelical left" groups like Jim Wallis's Sojourners fellowship and Ron Sider's Evangelicals for Social Action frequently pointed out that such positions came not from the Bible but from the game plan of the secular conservative movement. Wallis and Sider criticized the religious right for baptizing secular causes and ignoring more fundamental biblical issues like justice and the poor, but these two leaders failed to create an alternative movement of any major size or significance.

The Moral Majority's tactics also came under fire. After a group of gays was given permission to lay a wreath at the Tomb of the Unknown Soldier in Arlington Cemetery, Falwell's direct-mail operation went into attack mode, claiming that "we are losing the war against homosexuals," and warning that the gays were turning the site into "The Tomb of the Unknown Sodomite!" At his public rallies, Falwell used a controversial audiovisual presentation to frighten his hearers into righteous indignation. According to historian William Martin, the presentation included images of Charles Manson, Times Square "adult" theaters, aborted fetuses, nuclear explosions, and other evils, all of which were blamed on secular humanists and their operatives in the U.S. government, otherwise known as Democrats.

Pat Robertson, son of a U.S. Senator, graduated from Yale University Law School and New York Theological Seminary. His message is carried on the *700 Club* talk/news program. In 1997 he relinquished day-to-day operations of his eight-year-old grassroots political organization, the Christian Coalition, but he has become board chair, a new position. He unsuccessfully ran for President of the United States in 1988.

Dashed Hopes

At first, the religious right seemed successful. Political leaders listened to what the groups said, conservatives welcomed an influx of inspired activists, and Ronald Reagan expertly exploited their policy concerns and theological code words. Authors of the GOP platform even removed the document's commitment to the Equal Rights Amendment and added a pledge to support a constitutional amendment outlawing abortion. "Had we not been Baptists, we would have danced in the streets," said Ed Dobson, a top Falwell associate in those heady, early days.

But things didn't turn out as planned. The family values revolution never took place. The religious right never attracted broad-based support outside fundamentalist and evangelical circles. And the movement never achieved any of its major legislative goals, including its top objective—outlawing abortion.

> ### Seeking the Upper Hand
>
> Why have the leaders of the Religious Right, many of them Baptists, turned their backs on the principle of the separation of church and state? My only guess is that they no longer believe they can compete in a free marketplace of religion in America. That is, they feel so overwhelmed by the successive waves of multiculturalism the United States has seen in the twentieth century that they seek some kind of advantage.
>
> — Randall Balmer, *Blessed Assurance: A History of Evangelicalism in America* (1999).

Evangelicals also became increasingly frustrated with politicians who courted their support at election time but ignored their views once in office. Mark Hatfield, a Republican senator from Oregon, had earlier predicted such problems: "Most politicians have typically utilized religion much like a woman uses makeup; a little, used discreetly, can improve one's appearance, but too much, used lavishly, can make one look like a clown."

During the 1990s, evangelicals evaluated the lessons they had learned duking it out in the public square. "I believe that people, myself included, were well-intentioned, and our goals were noble, but we got caught up in the illusion that politicians really cared for us, and that political change would bring moral change," says Ed Dobson.

Cal Thomas was even more blunt. "We failed," he says. Today Thomas is best known as a newspaper columnist. But for years he was the Moral Majority's media spokesperson. He teamed up with Dobson to write *Blinded by Might*, a Christian critique of the religious right, published in 1999. "Very little that we set out to do has gotten done," said Thomas. "In fact, the moral landscape of America has become worse."

Falwell claimed he hadn't read *Blinded by Might*, but in a press statement he charged its authors with advocating "the withdrawal of American churches and people of faith from the cultural conflict of the day." Thomas and Dobson, though, said they weren't withdrawing but merely seeking ways to transform culture that didn't rely primarily on power and politics.

Resources

William Martin, *With God on Our Side* (companion book to a 1996 PBS documentary on the religious right).

James Davison Hunter, *Culture Wars: The Struggle to Define America* (1991).

Cal Thomas and Ed Dobson, *Blinded by Might* (1999).

Dean Merrill, *Sinners in the Hands of an Angry Church: Finding a Better Way to Influence Our Culture* (1997).

Robert Booth Fowler, *A New Engagement: Evangelical Political Thought, 1966–1976* (1982).

Richard John Neuhaus, *The Naked Public Square: Religion and Democracy in America* (1986).

38. The Lure of Liturgy:
The Migration to Orthodox, Episcopal, and Catholic Churches, 1979

Many churches call their Sunday morning gatherings "worship services," but only about a third of church-goers feel they regularly experience the presence of God at these gatherings, according to a Barna Research Group study released in 2001.

"I too have been troubled by the increasing vacuity of much Protestant preaching and worship," wrote theologian Donald G. Bloesch in *Christianity Today*. "The atmosphere in most of our services is clubby and convivial rather than adoring and expectant. What is missing is the fear of God, the experience of God as the Wholly Other."

Problems like these help explain why increasing numbers of evangelicals have been looking to Episcopal, Catholic, or Orthodox traditions for a greater sense of mystery, transcendence, and worship.

As children of the Reformation, heirs of the Enlightenment, and orphans from centuries' worth of tradition on Christian spirituality, mysticism, and contemplation, evangelicals have long dismissed robes and readings, incense and icons, and ancient traditions of monastic and contemplative spirituality as so much high-church window dressing. And in the 20th century, fundamentalists and evangelicals spent more time hammering out the intellectual content of their faith than they did cultivating transformative religious experiences. As a result, many evangelical churches host Sunday services that are contemporary, entertaining, seeker-sensitive but devoid of the divine. A former Vineyard pastor by the name of Charles Bell once described the shallowness and superficiality of such services:

> I found them to be barren and lacking . . . . It was as if we had been eating one single item from a ten-course meal, never tasting any of the other entrees and never experiencing the fullness of the banquet that God had prepared for us.

In June 1993 Pastor Charles Bell became Father Charles Bell, and his San Jose Vineyard congregation became St. Stephen's Orthodox Church. Earlier, evangelical thinker Thomas Howard and pioneering Protestant musician John Michael Talbot had discovered the depth and mystery they were seeking in the Catholic Church; Wheaton College theology professor Robert Webber and many others discovered sacramentality and holistic spirituality in the Anglican communion; and authors like Richard Foster and Dallas Willard found food for famished souls in the ancient but often neglected Christian disciplines of meditation and contemplation.

By the end of the century, evangelicals had grown accustomed to seeing their brothers and sisters seek renewal through ritual, but back in 1979 such practices were far less common.

Pilgrimage to the Past

For Peter Gilquist, a graduate of Oral Roberts University who worked for Campus Crusade for Christ, the journey toward something more ancient and more complete began in 1966. At that time he and other evangelicals who were "unsatisfied with the status quo of what we perceived as dull, denominational American Christianity" started meeting to study the New Testament church. In time, they were devouring the works of the early Christian fathers, but the more they studied, the less they liked what they saw in their churches. So in 1975 they formed their own fellowship called the New Covenant Apostolic Order. In 1979 the group renamed itself the Evangelical Orthodox Church, and in 1987, it and other like-minded congregations were brought into full communion with the worldwide Orthodox Church. Gilquist asked the rhetorical question:

John Michael Talbot, formerly a Protestant, is Catholic music's number-one recording artist with sales of nearly 4 million records worldwide. With more than 40 albums, 14 books, and numerous video teachings on ministry to the poor, simple living, Franciscan and community living, Talbot has set himself apart as a true servant of God.

What on earth would motivate a body of two thousand North American Christians to move from a very upbeat form of evangelical Protestantism to arguably the oldest form of apostolic faith?

An answer was offered by Frank Schaeffer, the son of evangelical thinker Francis. "The Protestant experiment has failed," said Frank, who converted to Orthodoxy in 1990. "The deeper I dug, I was more convinced that Protestant leadership is mostly based on a series of self-proclaimed charismatic leaders who are not apostolically based but who happen to be popular."

Gilquist, Schaeffer, and writer Frederica Mathewes-Green are part of a growing body of evangelicals the magazine *U.S. News & World Report* says are "discovering Byzantium." They were attracted to Orthodoxy not only by its "smells and bells," but also by its historic claim to being Christendom's original church. "Orthodoxy has maintained the New Testament tradition," says Gilquist, who works as director of missions and evangelism for the Antiochian Orthodox Archdiocese, "whereas Rome has often added to it and Protestantism subtracted from it."

Majesty and Mystery

Wheaton's Robert Webber was on a search for "the sense of mystery that rationalistic Christianity of either the liberal or evangelical sort seems to deny." Raised in an evangelical culture that placed more emphasis on the mind than the spirit, Webber hungered for more. "What we need is not answers about God, but God himself," said Webber, who found what he was seeking in the liturgy of the Episcopal church. "Sacrament is a way of encountering the mystery."

Founder of the Institute for Worship Studies, Webber travels the country leading workshops on "blended worship," which combines elements from different traditions, such as the austere liturgies of the Episcopal tradition with the spiritual intensity of the charismatic movement. Some of Webber's most avid students are pastors of emerging Generation-X congregations. These passionate young leaders are distressed by the blandness of worship at many baby boomer megachurches—where people are passive spectators rather than active participants—and are determined to change things in their own congregations.

Rediscovering an Ancient Faith

In 1993 Richard Foster spoke at Glen Eyrie Conference Center in Colorado Springs on "Celebrating the Spiritual Disciplines," the subject of his best-selling 1978 book *Celebration of Discipline*. The Navigators, who own Glen Eyrie, received criticisms from some who said Foster was using Glen Eyrie as a "Trojan horse" to smuggle non-Christian practices into the church. At a local Christian bookstore, an announcement about the event featured this penciled-in warning: "Very close to New Age. BEWARE!" Foster had heard such criticisms before:

Richard J. Foster is the executive director of the Milton Center at Newman University and professor of theology and writer in residence at Friends University, both in Wichita, Kansas. He is best known as author of *Celebration of Discipline, Freedom of Simplicity* and *Money, Sex & Power: The Challenge of the Disciplined Life.*

The kinds of things I am stressing are about as far from a New Age emphasis as it is possible to get. I stress the God of Abraham, Isaac and Jacob. There is a God to be in touch with, and that God is in charge of the universe. And that stands in very stark contradistinction to the New Age notion that I am God, that I can make my own reality, and that I can empower myself.

For some evangelicals, the very mention of words like "meditation" still suggests Eastern gurus sitting in the lotus position, not Psalm 1, which describes the man who meditates on God's law day and night. "We've lost touch with our historical roots," says Foster. And during the 1980s and 1990s, increasing numbers of evangelicals searched for these roots in the teachings and traditions of older lines of the Christian family.

Resources

Thomas Howard, *Evangelical Is Not Enough* (1984).

Robert Webber, *Evangelicals on the Canterbury Trail: Why Evangelicals Are Attracted to the Liturgical Church* (1985).

Peter Gilquist, *Becoming Orthodox: A Journey to the Ancient Christian Faith* (1989).

Doug LeBlanc, "Westerners on the Eastern Orthodox Trail," *Christian Research Journal*, Summer 1995.

39. The Parachurch Explosion: Growth, Diversity, and the Need for Accountability, 1979

In the 1940s and 1950s, evangelicals founded major missionary organizations and relief and development efforts, but the real boom years for Christian organizations came during the 1960s and 1970s, when thousands of new parachurch ministries were created.

"Para" comes from the Greek word "alongside," and parachurch organizations are intended to work alongside or assist the church, much like a paramedic works with a doctor. Unlike churches, which employ ordained clergy, adhere to well-defined doctrines, and serve broad-based memberships, parachurch organizations are nonprofit corporations set up along secular lines. They are typically led and staffed by laypeople, operate independently of any outside control or accountability, and focus on narrowly defined needs, such as fighting media immorality (Donald Wildmon's well-publicized American Family Association) or providing fellowship for like-minded believers (the lesser-known Christian Bowhunters Association).

Unfortunately, the profusion of parachurch organizations and other religious nonprofits during the 1970s opened the door for greed, fraud, and intense public criticism in the U.S., where there were no industry standards or government regulations concerning fundraising or financial management and disclosure.

In the years after the Watergate scandal rocked the public's confidence in government, major philanthropic institutions were accused of financial misdeeds. For example, less than 5 percent of the $20 million a Catholic group called the Pallatine Fathers raised was actually spent on the group's missionary efforts, with the bulk paying for big salaries and fund-raising fees. A 1978 headline in *U.S. News & World Report* said: "For Many, There Are Big Profits in 'Nonprofits,'" and U.S Senator Mark Hatfield, an outspoken evangelical, threatened government action unless nonprofits cleaned house. As World Vision executive Ted Engstrom said: "Much of

Ted Engstrom, a former president of World Vision, helped found the Evangelical Council for Financial Accountability, a voluntary organization that monitors the financial practices of its 900-plus members who have combined budgets of $6.5 billion.

the 1970s can be described by such words as 'cover up,' 'twisting the truth,' 'mistrust,' and . . . 'crisis of confidence.'"

In 1979 Engstrom helped found the Evangelical Council for Financial Accountability (ECFA), a voluntary organization that monitors the financial practices of its 900-plus members, which have combined budgets of $6.5 billion. ECFA didn't eradicate wrongdoing, as the televangelist scandals of the 1980s amply demonstrated. "People are people," says Paul Nelson, ECFA's president. "The American public is very generous, and the Christian public is particularly generous. That is going to attract some counterfeits."

However, ECFA did instill confidence by helping donors find out what ministries do with their money, and that confidence has fueled a continuing parachurch boom. Still, important questions about the nature of the impact nonprofits have on the church remain unanswered.

Two Centuries of Growth

Historian Bruce Shelley says the father of the contemporary parachurch movement was English evangelist William Carey, who in 1792 used private donations to establish the Baptist Missionary Society, which was patterned after the British East India Company. In the 19th century, American Christians organized private "voluntary associations" to campaign for the abolition of slavery, the prohibition of alcohol, and other reforms. It wasn't until the 20th century that parachurch organizations blossomed. Experts estimate there may be as many as 50,000 parachurch groups in the U.S. today.

American evangelicalism has provided a fertile environment for these groups' rapid growth, thanks to its freewheeling individualism, its entrepreneurial spirit, and its utter fascination with anything new. In addition, U.S tax laws make it relatively easy for anyone to start a nonprofit organization.

What has been most amazing is to see the powerful impact these groups have had on American life. In many nations, church and denominational organizations exert the greatest influence in believers' lives, but in the U.S. parachurch groups have greater influence than the churches. As authors Nathan Hatch and Michael Hamilton argue:

> The organizational structures that house the throbbing heart of evangelicalism are not denominations at all, but the special-purpose parachurch agencies that sometimes seem as numberless as the stars in the sky.

During the 1980s and 1990s, dozens of these groups relocated to Colorado Springs, Colorado, making it—and not Wheaton, Illinois—America's parachurch capitol. Groups headquartered there represent every major ministry type, including international evangelism and discipleship (The Navigators), youth ministry (Young Life), relief and development (Compassion International), Scripture translating and publishing (International Bible Society), broadcasting (HCJB World Radio), missions and church planting (OC International), industry trade groups (Association of Christian Schools International, Christian Booksellers Association, and Christian Camping International/USA), and other specialized ministries, such as Missionary Internship (which trains missionaries), and Global Mapping International (which provides computer mapping and population analysis for mission groups).

Focus on the Family, the city's biggest ministry with an annual budget exceeding $130 million, is in a category all its own. Often described as a mass media ministry, Focus exists primarily to disseminate the values of its founder, James Dobson, which it does internationally through a wide range of radio broadcasts, books, periodicals, videos, events, and other activities.

Church and Parachurch

Part of the reason parachurch organizations are so numerous and so big is because they are accomplishing things churches can't. Their structure, which is more like that of secular corporations than religious denominations, gives them greater flexibility, efficiency, and openness to innovation, allowing them to quickly recognize and respond to problems or issues

Philanthropy at a Glance

Evangelical parachurch organizations are part of a much larger philanthropic industry. According to Independent Sector 2001, a report on tax-exempt charitable, religious, educational, scientific, and literary organizations in the U.S.:

— There are 1.6 million such organizations, an increase of 74 percent in a decade (the number includes 354,000 religious groups and congregations);

— The organizations employ 10.9 million people;

— Their total annual revenue is $664.8 billion.

churches may not be addressing. Their expertise at fund-raising helps them find individuals and foundations willing to finance their work. Their reliance on layleaders and employees has unleashed a torrent of talent. And their ecumenical spirit often allows them to transcend narrow denominational distinctives, a fact that has led some observers to conclude that parachurch organizations, not churches, best illustrate the universality of the body of Christ.

But in some cases, ministries' greatest strengths can also be their biggest weaknesses. Visionary leaders can become dictatorial tyrants who run roughshod over their workers. Dependence on fund-raising can lead ministries to overstate the impact they're having or exploit hot-button issues like homosexuality. And the absence of any real spiritual accountability can make them self-centered and unbalanced.

Another concern is that parachurch organizations can create an all-encompassing evangelical subculture that isolates believers from the world. Historian Joel Carpenter described this danger as it may have existed decades ago:

> A fundamentalist layperson in Chicago in the 1930s, for example, could attend special meetings at the Moody Memorial Church, support the China Inland Mission, listen to station WMBI, do volunteer work at the Pacific Garden Mission, read the *Sunday School Times*, take the interurban train down to the Winona Lake Bible Conference, and enroll her son in Wheaton College . . . .

The growth and increasing prominence of parachurch organizations has been one of the major stories of the 20th century and promises to be a powerful force in the future. As Jerry White, president of The Navigators, wrote in 1983:

> Twenty years ago, many pastors viewed the parachurch as a temporary phenomenon or a small irritant needed to spur the church to renewal. Today the exploding number and power of parachurch

groups appear to be a permanent and growing fixture in the evangelical community as it approaches the 21st century.

Resources

Jerry White, *The Church & the Parachurch: An Uneasy Marriage* (1983).

Wesley K. Wilmer and J. David Schmidt with Martyn Smith, *The Prospering Parachurch: Enlarging the Boundaries of God's Kingdom* (1998).

Robert Wuthnow, *The Restructuring of American Religion* (1988).

Nathan O. Hatch and Michael S. Hamilton, "Can Evangelicalism Survive Its Success?" *Christianity Today* (October 5, 1992).

40. Crossover Controversy: Amy Grant Cracks the Top 40, 1985

Long before it became a half-billion-dollar industry, contemporary Christian music was a little-known offshoot of the Jesus movement of the late 1960s and early 1970s. Condemned by many in the church as too worldly and dismissed by many mainstream music consumers as too holy or too hokey, Christian music faced a double-edged dilemma. As the late musician Mark Heard, who drew his inspiration from Larry Norman and Francis Schaeffer, put it in his song "Stuck in the Middle":

I'm too sacred for the sinners
And the saints wish I would leave.

Christian recording artists like Keith Green, who died in a 1982 plane crash, believed they were called to minister to believers, but others had always talked about "crossing over" and making their music available to mainstream music consumers. By the 1990s, Christian music was enjoying growing respect and sales in both religious bookstores and mainstream music outlets.

Amy Grant, whose recordings have sold more than 20 million copies, has done more to encourage these changes than anyone else. As a result, she has been both lionized and demonized throughout her controversial and precedent-setting career. Her experiences provide insight into the Christian music industry and illuminate important issues about pop culture that have divided evangelicals for decades.

A Sweet Superstar

Grant grew up in a loving Christian family, spending her teen years listening to the music of popular singer/songwriters like James Taylor, John Denver, and Carole King before writing songs of her own. She was 17 when she recorded her self-titled debut album for Word Records' contemporary Myrrh division, but she was so shy she asked that the studio lights be turned down.

Blessed with top-notch management, personal charisma, girl-next-door attractiveness, and an innate understanding of pop songcraft, Grant rapidly became a Christian music superstar, selling more than 1 million copies of her *Age to Age* (1982) and *Straight Ahead* (1984) albums.

In 1985 Myrrh linked up with A&M Records to ensure that Grant's new *Unguarded* album—which was given a then unprecedented $200,000 recording budget and a costly publicity and marketing campaign—would be sold in mainstream stores. In addition, the catchy song "Find a Way," which Grant wrote with Michael W. Smith, was released as a single and promoted to mainstream radio stations. The song broke into *Billboard* magazine's coveted Top 40 ranking that fall, the first single by a contemporary Christian artist to do so.

Throughout the 1980s and 1990s, Grant blazed trails through pop-music territory previously unexplored by Christian-label artists. Some fans raised a ruckus when Grant sang barefoot on a Grammy Awards telecast. Others complained when she performed in venues where concertgoers consumed alcohol. Operation Rescue picketed Grant to protest her promotional partnership with the Target retail chain. (Target's parent company, the Dayton Hudson Corp., supported Planned Parenthood, and protesters objected to Grant's "compromise" on abortion, even though she was a major supporter of the Crisis Pregnancy Support Center in her hometown of Nashville.) And her 1999 divorce from husband Gary Chapman and later remarriage to country star Vince Gill were even more disappointing to many.

By 1994 Amy Grant had won five Grammy Awards and 17 Dove Awards. Her recordings have sold more than 20 million copies, and she has done more than any Christian singer to help Christian music enjoy growing respect and sales in both religious bookstores and mainstream music outlets.

Crossing Over

During the 1980s, contemporary Christian musicians were enjoying both increased sales and growing creative freedom. Bands like Petra (which is Greek for "rock") argued that God could use modern music to evangelize the lost and encourage believers, and Stryper took that argument to spectacular extremes. A Los Angeles-based hard rock quartet whose members dressed in yellow-and-black spandex outfits, they threw Bibles into their rabid crowds and released albums like *To Hell with the Devil*. Stryper recorded for a secular label and appeared in concert with unsavory rock bands like Ratt and Motley Crue. A mid-1980s article about the band in *Christianity Today* drew dozens of angry letters and numerous subscription cancellations, but most readers of *CCM*, a Christian music magazine founded in 1978, believed the gospel message could be expressed in any conceivable musical form so long as its lyrics remained Christ-centered.

Grant, who had cracked the Top 40 in 1985, achieved a second major musical milestone in March 1991, when her catchy ditty "Baby, Baby" became the nation's number-one single, an achievement *CCM* described as "the most significant event in the history of contemporary Christian music."

Grant has never had a number-one album. That honor went to Bob Carlisle for 1997's *Butterfly Kisses*. Still, her historic status remains secure. In 1998, *CCM* magazine asked critics to chosoe the best 100 contemporary Christian songs and albums of all time. Grant had seven albums on the list (including 1988's *Lead Me On*, which was the top pick, and *Age to Age* at number three) and seven songs (including "El Shaddai" at number two on the song ranking).

The Lyrical Litmus Test

In 1996 Grant challenged Christian music conventions once again with an album some hailed as theologically profound but others condemned for its failure to mention Jesus. "The complete absence of explicitly Christian lyrical content on *Behind the Eyes* has renewed a debate in the CCM industry about what constitutes Christian music," wrote Calvin College professor and author William Romanowski. Some Christian retailers refused to stock the album, while religious broadcasters debated whether to play it.

The Gospel Music Association joined the lyric debate in 1997 after GMA director Frank Breeden said an increase in lyrically ambiguous songs was making it more difficult for the association to select its Dove Awards. In 1998 the GMA adopted a new lyric-content criteria. The new criteria required that any song nominated for a Dove Award in 1999 or after would be required to contain explicitly Christian content.

Defining "Christian" Music

Gospel music is music in any style whose lyric is substantially based upon historically orthodox Christian truth contained in or derived from the Holy Bible; and/or an expression of worship of God or praise for His works; and/or testimony of relationship with God through Christ; and/or obviously prompted and informed by a Christian worldview.

—The Gospel Music Association

Some artists and industry insiders complained that the new rules smacked of censorship or Phariseeism. April Hefner, editor of *CCM*, dismissed the new criteria, saying they would merely lead to an increase in "JPMs," or "Jesuses Per Minute." But Breeden remained convinced that the industry required clear standards. "If you want to stand by the seashore, you can paint what you want for yourself and for God to witness," said Breeden, "but the day you want to sell it, you have involved some more forces in the discussion."

Such issues had perplexed musicians for years. In a 1984 interview with Bill Flanagan of *Musician* magazine, T Bone Burnett, an acclaimed and iconoclastic musician and producer who is perhaps best known for producing the soundtrack for the movie *O Brother, Where Art Thou?* articulated one of the central issues separating Christian-label recording artists from their brothers and sisters working in mainstream markets:

> I learned early on that if you believe Jesus is the Light of the World there are two kinds of songs you can write—you can write songs about the Light, or about what you see by the Light.

Today, Christian artists like Point of Grace and 4Him continue to provide loyal Christian consumers with a steady stream of industry-approved material, while Grant and artists like Kirk Franklin and Sixpence None the Richer seem willing to risk alienating some believers in order to make music for the masses.

Regardless of which side of the line they're on, Christian musicians continue to generate healthy sales. A July 2001 cover story in *Newsweek* magazine declared: "Contemporary Christian music is now the hottest genre in the entire music industry."

Resources

"Special Anniversary Issue," *CCM* (July 1998).

Charlie Peacock, *At the Crossroads* (1999).

Jay R. Howard and John M. Streck, *Apostles of Rock: The Splintered World of Contemporary Christian Music* (1999).

William Romanowski, "Where's the Gospel?" *Christianity Today* (December 8, 1997).

Steve Rabey, "What Makes Music Christian?" *CCM* (May 1999).

41. A Novel Idea:
Evangelical Fiction and the Growth of
Christian Publishing, 1986

For earlier generations of Puritan and fundamentalist Christians, novel reading, like other worldly amusements such as dancing, card playing, and attending the theater, was considered suspect or sinful. Didn't the Bible warn against "vain imaginings"? Weren't there more important things to do, like reading the Bible or saving the lost? And who could imagine Jesus whiling away valuable hours reading a novel when he could be out feeding the multitudes?

But during the 1980s and 1990s, amusements were no longer forbidden, so long as they were properly sanitized. During these decades, Christian fiction became the fastest-growing segment of the $3 billion Christian retailing industry, making it, in one writer's words, "the 500-pound gorilla of the Christian publishing industry." In 1993 alone, Christian publishers released nearly 200 new fiction titles, inspiring the Christian Booksellers Association to start publishing a fiction best-seller list in January 1994. Before long, celebrated nonfiction authors like Charles Colson, Pat Robertson, and Larry Burkett were trying their hand at evangelical novels.

Of course, there were precedents for combining faith and fiction. England's

Janette Oke published her first book in 1979, *Love Comes Softly.* When Bethany House Publishers published the book, fiction was an unknown genre in the Christian publishing marketplace. The book was so successful that she has since published 36 romance novels. With their focus on the lives of early prairie settlers, her books have sold over 20 million copies. In 1992 she received the President's Award from the Evangelical Christian Publishers Association.

C. S. Lewis had written his science fiction trilogy during the 1930s and 1940s before launching his best-selling *Chronicles of Narnia* during the 1950s (see chapter 23). Lewis was a primary inspiration for writers like Frederick Buechner, Walter Wangerin, Madeleine L'Engle, Larry Woiwode, and Stephen Lawhead, all of whom sought to write literary fiction about Christian themes for both churched and unchurched readers.

But most of the novels that began flying off Christian bookstore shelves in the 1980s weren't so highfalutin'. Rather, early evangelical fiction was an often saccharine blend of romance and inspiration written by pioneers like Grace Livingston Hill, Catherine Marshall, and Marjorie Holmes. In 1979, Bethany House Publishers released *Love Come Softly*, a "prairie romance" by an unknown writer named Janette Oke. More than two decades later, Oke's three dozen novels had combined sales of more than 20 million copies, and Bethany House was proclaiming itself *"The* Source for Inspirational Fiction."

Former Assemblies of God pastor Frank E. Peretti helped turn Christian fiction into a popular and lucrative genre with his 1985 novel *This Present Darkness*. It landed at the top of the Christian Booksellers Association best-seller list. By the turn of the century more than 8 million copies of Peretti's novels had been sold.

This Present Darkness, a fast-paced, high-energy, page-turner of a yarn about an all-out battle between angels and demons in a once-peaceful small town, finally made it okay for evangelical men to read fiction.

Written by a former Assemblies of God pastor named Frank Peretti and published in 1986, the novel sold 4,000 copies in its first six months, which is better than some at Crossway Books had hoped. Then things got interesting: it sold 10,000 during the next six months and 20,000 in the six months after that. Spurred by enthusiastic word-of-mouth and endorsements from Christian music celebrities like Amy Grant, the book sold 70,000 copies during the first half of 1988, landing atop CBA's paperback best-seller list. Americans would buy more than 8 million copies of Peretti's books by 1999, when his latest novel, *The Visitation*, would enjoy a first printing of 600,000-plus copies and a marketing budget of $500,000.

"When I first started out, I was pretty lucky to get my book in the neighborhood mom-and-pop Christian bookstore," says Peretti. "Now, Word and Thomas Nelson have the ability to make things happen in a wider

In *This Present Darkness,* a newspaper editor and a pastor find themselves fighting a plot to subjugate the human race; in *Piercing the Darkness,* the 1989 sequel, a woman is the victim of relentless pursuit in a colossal spiritual struggle.

marketplace, so my new book is in Barnes & Noble, B. Dalton, and Wal-Mart." Peretti is thankful the modern Christian publishing and retailing colossus he calls "the machine" exists but does everything he can to keep from getting "caught in the gears."

Along the way, Peretti demonstrated how novels could influence evangelicals' theology. As *Christianity Today* put it, *This Present Darkness* "revived a long-dormant evangelical interest in spiritual warfare."

Humble Beginnings

In the 1940s, Christian publishing and retailing were in "a sorry state," says Ken Taylor, creator of the best-selling *Living Bible* and founder of Tyndale House Publishers. "Christian bookstores were quite small and dilapidated."

Taylor thought a trade association could help, so in 1949 he helped found the Christian Booksellers Association. CBA's 50th anniversary convention in 1999 opened with record-high numbers of retailers and suppliers (more than 14,000 from around the world) and displays (489 publishers and other vendors occupying six acres of booth space).

Doug Ross, CEO of the Evangelical Christian Publishers Association, has been amazed at the industry's growth:

> The industry has dramatically changed from privately held single stores operated by largely inexperienced mom-and-pop owners to a highly professional, highly visible chain-driven industry. Publishing companies that started on someone's kitchen table are today multi-million-dollar entities.

A major factor in the growth of the CBA industry is that publishers began producing fewer high-brow theological works and instead focused on giving consumers more of what they wanted, especially fiction. Some decried this transformation, but Jan Dennis, vice president of Crossway Books, defended Christian fiction against its critics in the church:

> The imagination is an authentic part of the human that needs to be fed, and if it's not fed by things that are morally and aesthetically edifying, it will be fed by things that are not.

Most CBA fiction featured comforting and faith-affirming stories devoid of the sex, substance abuse, gratuitous violence, or dirty language found in mainstream novels. Robin Hardy, author of *Streiker's Bride,* had to replace her "rich bitch" with a "rich witch" in the second edition of her book, while Stephen Lawhead, who had a character in one of his novel's say, "Damn you, Simon," was the subject of an open letter in a CBA magazine. A disappointed Christian bookseller wrote, "Profanity is around us every day. My question is, why is it necessary in Christian fiction?"

Equally unnecessary, say some, are humor, real-life characters, and challenging story lines. "Too often the phrase 'Christian fiction' doesn't mean fiction; it means propaganda," says author Richard Foster. Or as writer Lauren Winner put it, "There has always been great Christian fiction" by authors like Walker Percy, Flannery O'Connor, or Tolstoy. "What one is hard-pressed to find is great fiction published by evangelical houses."

Unhappy Endings

The 1990s brought a shift in the content and tone of Christian novels as literary novels by writers like Jan Karon and Vinita Hampton Wright shared shelf space with more escapist historical or romance novels.

At the same time, other Christian writers confronted the problems of the real world. Charles Colson's antiabortion sermon *Gideon's Torch* and Pat Robertson's millennial thriller *The End of the Age* took a long, hard look at the world, declaring it both horrifying and—except for supernatural help from God—utterly hopeless.

The *Left Behind* novels written by Tim LaHaye and Jerry Jenkins were the best-known novels in this new woe-is-us genre. In fact, this end-times series was the most popular evangelical fiction ever published (see chapter 29).

According to Gustav Niebuhr of the *New York Times,* these books "tap deep into the current stream of American anxieties, telling stories of righteous individuals confronted by corrupt institutions like the government, the news media, or law enforcement." *Christianity Today* summarized the mood of these best-selling nay-saying novels: "The world is a bad place and getting worse."

Resources

Frank Peretti, *This Present Darkness* (1986).
Elizabeth Cody Newenhuyse, "Our Novels, Our Selves," *Christianity Today* (April 25, 1994).
Michael G. Maudlin, "The Bible Study at the End of the World," *Christianity Today* (September 1, 1997).

42. How the Mighty Are Fallen: The Televangelist Scandals, 1987

Before it all came crumbling down around him, the evangelical empire Jim Bakker built was big, gaudy, and unbelievably lucrative. The PTL television show (the initials stood for "Praise the Lord," or as critics suggested, "Pass the Loot") was reaching more than 13 million viewers, and the Heritage USA theme park was drawing 6 million guests a year, a number surpassed only by the two Disney parks. All told, Bakker's empire took in as much as $170 million a year and employed 3,000 people.

The Bakkers enjoyed regal splendor in their six sumptuous homes, complete with garages full of luxury cars, closets full of clothes and shoes, cabinets full of jewelry, and yes, an air-conditioned dog house. In one of their better years, the couple took in more than $1.6 million in salaries and self-approved bonuses.

On their show, Jim and his excitable wife, Tammy, were all happiness, hokiness and "hallelujahs." As humor columnist Dave Barry, a self-confessed fan of the show, put it: "There would be Jim, smiling with all the sincerity of a man selling time-share condos in Zaire; or there would be Tammy Faye, her eyeballs gushing liquefied mascara and looking like two holes in the side of the *Exxon Valdez*."

Off-screen, though, the Bakker's marriage was turbulent. Jim had a tryst with a young secretary named Jessica Hahn at a Clearwater, Florida, resort in 1980, and later used PTL funds to buy her silence. The affair, which was ignored by the evangelical press, became front-page news across the nation in March 1987, forcing Bakker's resignation.

Investigations revealed that Bakker had drastically oversold $1,000 lifetime 'partnerships' good for lodging at Heritage USA. For this and other financial indiscretions, he was convicted on 24 counts of mail fraud, wire fraud, and conspiracy to commit fraud. Bakker, 49, was sentenced to 45 years in prison. His nervous breakdown was televised internationally, as was his release after being paroled in 1994.

Ironically, time behind bars may have been the best thing that ever happened to Bakker, an ordained Assemblies of God minister who got his start in broadcasting cohosting a puppet show for children on Pat Robertson's Christian Broadcasting Network. In *I Was Wrong*, Bakker's 1996 memoir, the fallen televangelist confessed to having proclaimed heretical views (while steadfastly denying any legal wrongdoing). He said his days in prison had consisted of cleaning toilets, reading the Bible, praying, and reflecting on the errors of his ways. "What I learned in prison (was) that my previous philosophy of ministry and life was fundamentally flawed," he wrote.

"I Have Sinned"

Although few thought it possible, things were about to get even weirder for the high-gloss world of Christian broadcasting. Bakker turned his empire over to Jerry Falwell but later claimed Falwell had deceived him and was "trying to take over the ministry." About the same time, fellow Assemblies of God televangelist Jimmy Swaggart called Bakker "a cancer that needs to be excised from the Body of Christ."

Swaggart, who had dropped out of high school to become an evangelist, preached a raw and rugged message of righteousness and belted out old-timey gospel songs, accompanying himself with a boogie-woogie piano style that came straight from his cousin, the rockabilly rebel Jerry Lee Lewis.

Swaggart took his message from tent crusades to radio in 1969 and started preaching on TV in 1973. By 1986 he had his own $140 million empire in Baton Rouge, Louisiana, complete with a 7,000-seat worship center and the Jimmy Swaggart Bible College.

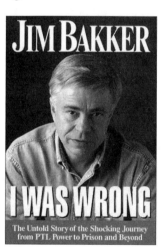

It's not clear why Swaggart attacked Bakker, but his venom came back to haunt him when it was revealed that Swaggart had spent time with a prostitute. In his televised, tear-stained 1988 confession, Swaggart said:

> I have sinned against you, my Lord, and I would ask that your precious blood would wash and cleanse every stain until it is in the seas of God's forgetfulness, never to be remembered against me.

Jim Bakker, shown here on the cover of his book *I Was Wrong*, said, in a 1997 interview, that he was changed in prison most of all by "the words of Christ. For two solid years in prison, I read and reread everything He said. I wrote it all out countless times and studied it, even going back to the Greek."

The Assemblies of God imposed a two-year period of discipline on Swaggart, but that was more repentance than he had bargained for. He began preaching three months later, a move that led the denomination to defrock him. Crowds at Swaggart's church never again reached pre-scandal levels, and things got worse in 1991, when the preacher was pulled over by a California policeman. Sitting next to him in the car was another prostitute.

Rotten Apples

Overnight, Christian hypocrisy became fodder for shocking headlines and late-night comedians. Just as suddenly, donations plummeted to ministries that did all or most of their fund-raising through broadcast channels. The National Religious Broadcasters (NRB) tried to develop a financial integrity arm similar to—but not as stringent as—the Evangelical Council for Financial Accountability, but the effort failed. Now, all NRB members must be in good standing with ECFA.

But Bakker and Swaggart weren't the only televangelists in the spotlight. Pentecostal evangelist Oral Roberts was one of the medium's pioneers, doing TV broadcasts of his healing crusades as early as 1954. When Roberts's City of Faith hospital and medical research complex ran low on

---

Catching Up with the Bakkers

Once the first family of televangelism, the Bakkers had gone their separate ways by 2000:

— After being paroled from prison, Jim wrote *I Was Wrong,* a 630-page autobiography published in 1996. Relocating to Los Angeles, he served at an inner-city ministry called The Dream Center, where he met his second wife, Lori Graham. By decade's end, they divided their time between L.A. and Charlotte, where they operated New Covenant Ministries.

— Tammy Faye was the subject of a 2000 film entitled *The Eyes of Tammy Faye.* Produced by two gay filmmakers, the movie portrayed her as both a compassionate Christian and a flamboyant queer icon. Now living quietly with second husband Roe Messner, a former Heritage USA contractor, in Palm Desert, California, Tammy Faye sells cosmetics over the Internet and directs the choir and plays the organ at her local church.

— Son Jay was disillusioned by his parents' divorce and the way Christians turned on the family. He went through a period of rebellion and substance abuse before getting married and establishing Revolution, an Atlanta ministry ministering to members of the "Goth" youth subculture. His book *Son of a Preacher Man* was published in 2000.

— Daughter Tammy Sue, the most publicity-shy Bakker, is content to be a homemaker. But she did join the family for a stunning May 2000 edition of CNN's *Larry King Live.*

dough, the preacher resorted to high-pressure appeals, at one point saying that a 900-foot-tall Jesus appeared to him, spoke about the urgent need for more funds, and said Oral would be taken home to glory if the money didn't come in soon.

In 1986 evangelist Peter Popoff was taking in $6 million a year through broadcasts and healing crusades. Audience members were particularly impressed by the evangelist's ability to deliver "words of knowledge" about their personal problems, but hoax-buster James "the Amazing" Randi used electronic surveillance equipment to pick up one of Popoff's assistants transmitting information about audience members to the evangelist, who had a hidden earpiece. Tapes of the scam were broadcast on Johnny Carson's *Tonight Show,* forcing Popoff to declare bankruptcy and lay low before resurfacing years later. His high-tech methodology to conning the faithful was featured in the 1992 film *Leap of Faith,* which starred Steve Martin as unethical evangelist Jonas Nightengale.

And Dallas evangelist Robert Tilton was just one of three major preachers who came under fire in a 1991 broadcast of ABC TV's *PrimeTime Live.* The show alleged that Tilton lied when he said he prayed over donors' letters (thousands of discarded letters were found in dumpsters outside the Tulsa firm that processed donor checks), and that his lavish lifestyle would have made a pre-prison Jim Bakker jealous.

These varied scandals brought shame and ridicule upon the church and revealed the many ways Christianity had been infected with the spirit of the age. "Televangelism largely reflects the values, sensibilities, and attitudes of contemporary culture," said author Quentin Schultze.

Perhaps Dave Barry summarized things best when he said televangelists like the Bakkers "were successful because they personified a very appealing, very convenient moral philosophy that flourished in the 1980s, a philosophy that can be summarized as follows: You can't do good unto others unless you feel good about yourself, and you can't feel good about yourself unless you have a lot of neat stuff."

Resources

Charles Shephard, *Forgiven: The Rise and Fall of Jim Bakker and the PTL Ministry* (1989).
Jim Bakker, *I Was Wrong* (1996).
Quentin J. Schultze, *Televangelism and American Culture: The Business of Popular Religion* (1991).

43. Film and Faith:
Thumbs Down for *The Last Temptation of Christ*, 1988

Cinema buffs were intrigued when director Martin Scorsese, perhaps the world's most esteemed living moviemaker, said he wanted to make a "deeply religious film." Describing his plans to adapt Nikos Kazantzakis's controversial 1960 novel, *The Last Temptation of Christ,* Scorsese said, "This is a motion picture I have wanted to make for 15 years, both as a filmmaker and as a Christian." The script was written by Calvin College graduate Paul Schrader.

But the complicated circumstances surrounding the film would set the stage for the century's most contentious showdown between evangelicals and the entertainment industry—two parties that have rarely seen eye to eye.

Blasphemy at the Box Office?

Believing evangelicals to be an important market for *Last Temptation,* Universal Pictures hired consultant Tim Penland, who had helped promote films like *Chariots of Fire* (1981) and *The Mission* (1986) to the Christian community. By early 1988, Penland was busy hyping the upcoming film to members of the National Religious Broadcasters and cautioning evangelicals not to speculate about its content. "The desire of Universal and director Martin Scorsese is to make a faith-affirming movie," said Penland. "We're asking Christians not to prejudge the film."

By June, though, Penland was singing a far different tune. Donald Wildmon of the American Family Association had distributed copies of a script for the unfinished film, and Penland found objectionable material on 80 out of its 120 pages. Among other things, Jesus visited a brothel, passionately kissed John the Baptist, and had sex with Mary Magdalene during a dream sequence. "I was a babe in the woods, and I regret my role in recommending the project to the Christian community," said Penland, who quit working for Universal and began helping evangelicals organize protests against the film.

Evangelical leader James Dobson had already expressed reservations about the still-unseen film. "It would appear to be the most blasphemous, evil attack on the Church and the cause of Christ in the history of entertainment," said Dobson, who hosted Penland on his popular *Focus on the Family* radio program and urged listeners to contact Universal. Other Christian leaders held a press conference in Hollywood where they pleaded with Universal "to abandon its plans to release the movie." Campus Crusade's Bill Bright went even further, offering to buy the film for $10 million so he could destroy it. "I would personally be responsible for reimbursing Universal Pictures for the amount already invested in the movie," wrote Bright in a letter he sent to the studio and the *Los Angeles Times*. Universal found Bright's offer offensive and responded with full-page national newspaper ads, which cited constitutional freedoms of speech and religion:

> These freedoms protect all of us.
> They are precious.
> They are not for sale.

Universal capitalized on the free publicity by releasing the movie on August 12, one month earlier than planned. Evangelical, Catholic, Orthodox, and Episcopalian Christians responded with an August 11 rally in Universal City. Thousands of protesters (the Associated Press estimated 7,500, while evangelicals claimed 25,000) surrounded Universal's headquarters, where they listened to speakers and waved placards like "God Is Not Mocked" and "The Lie Costs $6.50; the Truth Is Free." Things got ugly when fundamentalist pastor R. L. Hymers condemned "Jewish money" in Hollywood and staged a mock crucifixion in front of the home of Universal's Jewish president.

Protests continued the next day outside the 9 U.S. and Canadian theaters showing the film. Some protesters were dignified and peaceful, but others taunted moviegoers or splattered theaters with red paint. Many evangelical leaders called for a boycott of Universal. Jerry Falwell challenged believers to make "an all-out effort to cripple Hollywood and make it regret ever releasing this piece of garbage," and bought TV ads that promoted his own "Battle Plan Kit."

Bad Movies

The movies are still bad! Even the best of them are bad. They are made by unchristian, immoral people. They appeal to the basest lusts of men and young people. Their sole aim is to make money. Human art and science are employed to make lust appealing, to make drinking popular, to present the world's ungodly standard of morals as the ideal for the young and unsuspecting youth who sees the film.

— John R. Rice, *What's Wrong with the Movies?* (1938)

The National Association of Evangelicals was more subdued, making no official statements until its representatives actually viewed the film. Having done so, the NAE called the film deeply offensive, urged evangelicals not to patronize it, and suggested that believers give moviegoers tracts or copies of the Gospels; however, they stopped short of endorsing some of the actions of its most vociferous members:

> We concede that Universal Pictures has the right to make and distribute the film. But those who believe in Christ have the right to boycott it.

Praised by many critics, the film did poorly at the box office but not as poorly as it might have without all the hoopla. "The protests probably added some to the box office," said Christian filmmaker Ken Wales ("Christy"), who regretted that the protests had only "perpetuated the confrontational spirit" existing between evangelicals and Hollywood.

Reel Religion

In the 1990s, Hollywood was more open to films about faith. Meanwhile, a growing number of evangelicals turned their backs on unsuccessful "culture war" approaches like attempting to defund the National Endowment of the Arts or boycotting the Walt Disney Company. Instead, a new breed of evangelicals tried using their energy to create entertainment that was more positive and wholesome.

By 1997 Scorsese was back with another film about religion called *Kundun,* which lovingly portrayed the life of Tibetan Buddhist leader the Dalai Lama. The following year, Robert Duvall released *The Apostle,* his critically acclaimed, self-financed film about a flawed but faithful Pentecostal evangelist. "We make great gangster movies, so why not make this kind of movie right, too?" asked Duvall. In fact, the late 1990s brought so many honest portrayals of religion and religious people that *U.S. News & World Report* reported, "Wonder of wonders, Hollywood seems to have gotten religion."

Christians turned their attention to improving the quality of fare on the small screen, where TV viewers were making hits out of faith-affirming shows like *Touched by an Angel* and *7th Heaven*; while PAX TV, the seventh national TV network, was giving its relatively small audience a full slate of "pro-family" programming. Meanwhile, millions of parents bought up copies of the popular "Veggie Tales" videos, which gave their children Christian lessons and cutting-edge computer-generated animation.

Soon, films like *Omega Code* and *Left Behind: The Movie* sought to bring Hollywood-style professionalism to end-times subjects, with mixed results. And by 2001, Christian filmmakers were releasing more broad-based projects like *Extreme Days,* a youth-oriented drama, and *Hometown Legend,* based on a novel by Jerry Jenkins.

What had inspired such a change of heart? Evangelicals who work in and around the entertainment industry say it wasn't high-pressure protests or mass-mailing campaigns orchestrated by conservative Christian organizations.

"There are different types of ministry, but what we're trying to do is build bridges to Hollywood and help people there understand Christians and their concerns," says Ted Baehr, publisher of *Movieguide* magazine and chairman of the Christian Film and Television Commission, which was founded in 1985 after decades of official Protestant absence from Hollywood.

Baehr believes the bridge-building approach pioneered by him and other Hollywood ministries like Mastermedia International and Media Fellowship International is much more effective than demonstrations of force. "There are more films containing a strong Christian worldview now than there were in the 80s," he says.

Resources

Larry W. Poland, *The Last Temptation of Hollywood* (1989).

Michael Medved, "A Declaration of War," in *Hollywood vs. America: Popular Culture and the War on Traditional Values* (1992).

William D. Romanowski, *Pop Culture Wars: Religion & the Role of Entertainment in American Life* (1996).

Donald E. Wildmon with Randall Nulton, *Don Wildmon: The Man the Networks Love to Hate* (1990).

44. Muscular Christianity:
Promise Keepers and the Christian Men's Movement, 1991

The tough-guy truism that religion is for women, girls, and sissies faced a serious challenge during the mid-1990s as hundreds of thousands of men gathered in football stadiums across the country to sing, pray, hug, cry, confess, chant "J-E-S-U-S!" and pledge themselves to being better men, stronger Christians, and more loving husbands and fathers.

"A man's man is a godly man," said Promise Keepers founder Bill McCartney, who demonstrated his own mettle coaching the University of Colorado Buffaloes to a national football championship.

McCartney, who says God gave him a vision for thousands of men worshiping together and confessing their sins to one another, first explained his ideas for ministry at a low-key 1991 event attended by a few dozen men. By 1996 Promise Keepers had skyrocketed to national prominence as its stadium events attracted more than 1 million men and its clergy conference brought 42,000 leaders to Atlanta. "Stand in the Gap," PK's 1997 "sacred assembly of men" gathering, brought hundreds of thousands to the nation's capitol.

In time, the organization's $100 million budget and attendance figures would decline, but not before it had transformed the lives of many men and changed the way churches did men's ministry. "In the past, Christian men repressed a lot of what was really inside," said one Promise Keeper, "but now more men are trying to channel that and figure out what God called them to be instead of just being religious tin figures."

Historian Timothy Weber said the Christian men's movement represents an effort to put the brakes on some of the more destructive consequences of the sexual revolution, like runaway divorce, illegitimacy, and family breakdown. "It's a new way of negotiating all of society's competing tensions," says Weber. "The old equilibrium has been disrupted, and people are trying to find a new one."

Encouraging the Church

McCartney wasn't the first man to baptize masculinity. Nearly a century earlier, Harry W. Arnold founded the Men and Religion Forward movement, which reached an estimated 1.5 million men and boys with the message that Christianity was relevant to males. Earlier, men were drawn to Dwight Moody's businessmen's crusades and England's muscular Christianity movement. "Let me tell you the manliest man is the man who will acknowledge Jesus Christ," said Billy Sunday, a baseball-star-turned-evangelist who died in 1935.

What made Promise Keepers (PK) unique is the way it inspired churches and denominations to change the way they relate to men.

"We're grateful that Promise Keepers has drawn the church's attention to men's ministry," says Lutheran leader Doug Haugen. "Promise Keepers has by and large forced the church to address men's needs, and it has provided a very positive challenge for all of us to determine and develop our own niche in men's ministry."

The Southern Baptist Convention's Brotherhood Commission worked with PK to redesign its men's ministries effort, which now uses large rallies, medium-sized retreats, and smaller accountability groups to help men focus on their duties to God, home, church, and marketplace.

The Assemblies of God also set up new discipleship programs, accountability groups, and other programs. "We are grateful for what Promise Keepers is doing to evangelize men, build strong families and point them to strong Bible believing churches," said Wayde Goodall, national coordinator of ministerial enrichment for the Assemblies of God.

Even the mainline Presbyterian Church (U.S.A.) was inspired to develop new programs and materials, though many of its members differ with McCartney's conservative views on homosexuality (he was a staunch supporter of Colorado's gay rights limitation measure, Amendment 2). "This will be an excellent tool for men who have returned from Promise Keepers events excited about their faith and looking for a good

Bill McCartney, founder of Promise Keepers, was head football coach of the national title-winning University of Colorado Buffaloes. Promise Keepers skyrocketed to national prominence in 1996 when its stadium events attracted more than 1 million men. Lutheran leader Doug Haugen said, "Promise Keepers has by and large forced the church to address men's needs."

way to connect to the local congregation," said a Presbyterian official. Even Catholic groups revised their men's ministries in the 1990s.

Books, Bibles, and Ministries

The rapid growth of Promise Keepers spawned a brief mini-revolution in the once female-dominated Christian publishing and retailing industries, which saw a sudden boom in manly Bibles, books, and musical products.

Publishers like Focus on the Family, NavPress, Zondervan, Tyndale, Moody, Broadman & Holman, Crossway Vision House, HarperSan-Francisco, and Concordia rushed out masculine products. Rolf Zettersten, the publisher at Thomas Nelson, said, "Books for men will play an important and central role in Thomas Nelson's strategic plan." Unfortunately, many men's books failed to sell as well as expected, and most publishers drastically scaled back their plans.

Meanwhile, Cook Communications Ministries, the country's leading publisher of church curriculum products, developed church materials for men. *New Man,* a bimonthly Christian magazine published by Strang Communications, debuted in 1994 and soon had more than 300,000 paid subscribers.

PK also introduced thousands of men to smaller ministries like Christian Men's Network, Dad's University, National Center for Fathering, Career Impact Ministries, Business Life Management, M.A.N., Men Reaching Men, Fathers and Brothers, and Dad, the Family Shepherd.

Giving It All Away

Bill McCartney says he tries to do what he hears God telling him to do. That's why PK made racial reconciliation a top priority, even though the ministry proved more successful at meeting racial diversity goals in its own staffing than it was in the crowds attending its rallies.

During Promise Keepers' boom years, the organization attracted hundreds of thousands of men to football stadiums like Folsom Stadium in Boulder, Colorado.

Along with the growing popularity of the Promise Keepers came controversy. However, the National Organization for Women reached new heights of paranoia with this 1997 announcement:

Whereas, the Promise Keepers is a militaristic, anti-women organization with ties to the extreme religious right which promotes an uncompromising message of biblically mandated male domination; and

Whereas, the Promise Keepers' agenda is to subordinate women and overturn the gains that women have made in the last century; and

Whereas, its agenda is deceptively innocuous so that it has insinuated itself into many mainstream churches and the mainstream media; and . . .

Whereas, it has spawned a number of subordinate reactionary women's organizations, and its ultimate goal is to destroy the Constitutional principle of separation of church and state;

Therefore, be it resolved, that the National Organization for Women monitor the activities of the Promise Keepers . . . and expose (its) misogynist agenda, and actively campaign to defeat that agenda . . . .

McCartney also said God told him to make PK's ministry available to all men, regardless of their ability to pay. That's why he stood up at Stand in the Gap and made the surprise announcement that all future PK rallies would be free. To meet the ministry's budget—72 percent of which had come from admission fees—PK would rely instead on donations. In March 1998, after donations failed to materialize, McCartney laid off all 345 of the ministry's employees, 100 of whom were later rehired.

Attendance at the ministry's 1998 men's gatherings plummeted, and 1999 gatherings, which featured fewer big-name speakers, were underwritten by corporate sponsors who pitched their products and services to men in attendance. In 2000, PK had a budget of around $30 million and its events attracted about 300,000 men. "We believe we still have a very important role to play," said McCartney in 2001.

In less than a decade, Promise Keepers had grown from one man's vision to become one of the nation's largest parachurch organizations before decreasing in size as its founder placed ministry values over conventional financial wisdom. Throughout its cycle of growth and retrenchment, PK illustrated the unique ability of parachurch organizations to respond quickly to widespread needs that are being ignored by many churches. PK responded to the need of U.S. men and challenged the churches to do likewise.

Resources

Ken Abraham, *Who Are the Promise Keepers?* (1997).

Bill McCartney with Dave Diles, *From Ashes to Glory* (1990).

Tony Ladd and James Mathisen, *Muscular Christianity: Evangelical Protestants and the Development of American Sport* (1999).

45. Meeting with the Antichrist?: Evangelicals and Catholics Seek Common Ground, 1994

If the National Association of Evangelicals' June 1999 letter to its members didn't create any shock waves, that only proves how much things had changed since the early years of the century. In those days, conservative Christians claimed that they alone were God's people and shied away from associating with those who disagreed. "We saw the liberals as believing *less* than we did," writes Richard Mouw, "whereas the problem with Catholics was that they believed *more.*"

By the end of the century, though, NAE was trying to build a unified opposition to the sexual trafficking of women and children. As its letter stated:

> NAE initiated a meeting . . . with representatives from the Protestant, Catholic and Jewish communities.

The authors of *The Fundamentals,* a series of booklets that spelled out conservative Christian belief in the early 1900s, would have been shocked to see their theological descendants sitting down with Catholics and Jews, but such meetings had become increasingly common since the 1970s, when evangelicals like John Stott quietly began meeting with Catholics to discuss evangelism and other theological matters.

The rise of the religious right presented more pragmatic reasons for interfaith cooperation. Francis Schaeffer had convinced evangelicals they would accomplish more on social issues like abortion if they cooperated with "cobelligerents" who differed with them theologically but shared their positions on social issues. Schaeffer inspired Jerry Falwell to found the Moral Majority in 1979, and for the next two decades, the religious right sought to bring together conservatives from different faith groups.

But a funny thing happened on the way to the abortion protest. As evangelicals and Catholics stood arm-in-arm on street corners, they began talking to one another about their values and beliefs. Surprisingly, many of them found they weren't all that different after all. "In the best American fashion, activism led to reflection," said historian Mark Noll.

Evangelicals, many of whom deeply respected Pope John Paul II, also came into contact with Catholics through the charismatic movement, and soon, evangelical leaders were meeting with Catholic officials, who had been seeking improved relations with other Christians ever since Vatican II.

"Evangelicals and Catholics Together"

In 1992 Charles Colson, the evangelical who founded Prison Fellowship, teamed up with Richard John Neuhaus, the former Lutheran pastor turned Catholic priest who edited the journal *First Things*. These two Christians invited other key evangelical and Catholic leaders to an unprecedented ecumenical gathering. Over the next year, participants critiqued an evolving document called "Evangelicals and Catholics Together: The Christian Mission in the Third Millennium" (ECT), which was published in 1994. After nearly half a dozen revisions, the document was signed by prominent evangelical leaders like Pat Robertson and Bill Bright.

This historic statement called Catholics and evangelicals "brothers and sisters in Christ" and said their respective traditions represent "authentic forms of discipleship." It also acknowledged that significant theological differences still existed between the two traditions, particularly on the issue of interpreting the Bible, which evangelicals believe can be done by any believer, but which Catholics affirm must be done in the context of Church tradition. Still, ECT affirmed their fundamental agreement on the essentials of the faith. "All who accept Christ as Lord and savior are brothers and sisters in Christ," it said.

The document also expressed regret at the disunity that had plagued Christianity for centuries. "We together, evangelicals

Father Richard John Neuhaus is the author of a number of books, including *The Naked Public Square,* and is editor-in-chief of *First Things,* a monthly publication of the Institute on Religion and Public Life. The institute is an interreligious, nonpartisan research and education organization whose purpose is to advance a religiously informed public philosophy for the ordering of society. Neuhaus was a Lutheran who became Catholic. He and Charles Colson invited evangelical and Catholic leaders to an unprecedented ecumenical gathering in 1992.

and Catholics, confess our sins against the unity that Christ intends for all his disciples." An editorial in *Christianity Today* pointed out that "substantial and persistent differences remain" between the traditions but added, "For faithful evangelicals and believing Roman Catholics, this is a time to sew, not to rend."

Journalist David Briggs asked Colson if he was expecting the document to generate any fallout. Colson, who said some evangelicals grew irate when he mentioned Mother Teresa in his speeches, responded, "I'm putting the storm windows and doors on." Bill Bright received some flack from Campus Crusade supporters but stood his ground. "This is a historic moment," he said.

Two executives of the Southern Baptist Convention were criticized for signing the agreement, which did not claim to officially represent their denomination. They defended their actions. "I feel like evangelicals have a lot more in common today with conservative Catholics than we do with liberal Protestants who deny the cardinal doctrines of our faith like the very deity of Christ and his atoning death and resurrection," said Larry Lewis, president of the SBC's Home Mission Board.

The Southern Baptists went even further in 1995, jointly producing a series of Bible reflection booklets with the U.S. Catholic Conference that were designed to help members of Baptist and Catholic congregations sit down together and discuss ways they could jointly respond to issues like poverty, racism, healing, and life in their local communities.

In 1997 many of the authors of the ECT statement released a follow-up document called "The Gift of Salvation," which affirmed the signers' commitment to the Reformation doctrine of "justification by faith."

Worldwide Cooperation, Not Competition

Baptists may be the largest Protestant group in the U.S., but Pentecostals are the most plentiful non-Catholic Christians in the rest of the world. The Assemblies of God denomination still prohibits its ministers from supporting the "ecumenical movement," but Cecil M. Robeck, an ordained Assemblies pastor and professor at Fuller Theological Seminary, has been engaged in ongoing dialogue with Catholic leaders since 1985.

The discussions between Pentecostals and Catholics grew heated as participants debated a controversial document called "Evangelization, Proselytism, and Common Witness." The talks sought to distinguish between evangelism, which the document called "an essential part of the mission of the church," and proselytism, which was described as "a disrespectful, insensitive, and uncharitable effort to transfer the allegiance of a Christian from one ecclesial body to another." Both sides shared horror stories from Latin America, where the growing presence of Pentecostals is causing increased tensions, angry demonstrations, violence, and church burnings. Or as Robeck stated the matter when he met with Pope John Paul II in 1997, "We believe that Pentecostals and Catholics have far too often sinned against one another, thereby bringing shame upon the Name of the One who died for us."

But not everyone is jumping on the ecumenical bandwagon. Some in the Assemblies of God have called for Robeck to be disciplined, while others charged he was "meeting with the Antichrist." Others were critical of the ECT statement, which pastor and author John MacArthur said "camouflages the lethal errors of the Roman Catholic system." He added, "This may be one of the most hotly contested issues of the decade. The future of evangelicalism may hang in the balance." Cult researcher Dave Hunt even resurrected charges that the Catholic Church was the prostitute depicted in Revelation 17–18, saying the Catholic Church "claims to be Christian . . . but has its roots in Babel and Babylon." And in 2001, Southern Baptists' North American Mission Board, who had participated in dialogue with Catholics for decades, announced the talks would cease in 2002.

Voices of dialogue and demonization would continue to battle it out in the evangelical world, but during much of the 1990s, dialogue seemed to be winning the most converts.

Resources

Charles Colson and Richard John Neuhaus, eds., *Evangelicals and Catholics Together: Toward a Common Mission* (1995).

Thomas P. Rausch, ed., *Catholics and Evangelicals: Do They Share a Common Future?* (2000).

Dave Hunt, *A Woman Rides the Beast: The Roman Catholic Church and the Last Days* (1994).

46. Give Me That Online Religion: The Promise and Peril of the Internet, 1994

Engineers at the University of Pennsylvania made history in 1946 when they assembled 18,000 vacuum tubes and miles of wire into a 30-ton monstrosity called the Electronic Numerical Integrator and Calculator, or ENIAC, the world's first multi-purpose electronic computer. The massive thinking machine consumed so much electrical power that Philadelphia's lights dimmed when it was running.

All of ENIAC's computing power could be squeezed onto a tiny silicon wafer the size of a postage stamp by 1971, and by 1977, an upstart launched the home computer revolution when it introduced the Apple II. Over the next two decades, computers would become ever faster, smaller, and cheaper, invading businesses and homes and making many people wonder how they ever got along without them.

Meanwhile, military experts worked on connecting computers to one another so users could share files and data. Department of Defense engineers first linked computers at four American university campuses in 1969. In 1991, Tim Berners-Lee helped move computer networking out of academia with the publication of the first programming code for the World Wide Web. Within a few years, the Web transformed the way people shopped, studied, and invested. By early 2002, more than half of the U.S. population was cruising the information superhighway, where they could find everything from online prayer groups to sites about pedophilia and bestiality.

The untamed anarchy of the Web worried many conservative evangelicals, some of whom unsuccessfully sought to control its content or limit access to its seedier sites. Others boldly ventured into cyberspace to promote the gospel. As Jason Baker wrote in *Christian Cyberspace Companion:*

> Throughout church history, Christians have witnessed numerous technological advancements. Some of these, such as movable type,

have been well harnessed to produce great benefits for the church. In the last decade, the explosion of personal computers brought irrevocable changes to the way people work and play. Fortunately, pioneering Christians sought ways to employ this technology on the personal and corporate levels.

Finding God Online

In 1994 Greg Darby founded the Christian Interactive Network (CIN), a "Christ-centered ministry dedicated to reaching out into the technology marketplace and providing the Good News of Jesus Christ to a lost 'new' world." CIN was available only to members of the CompuServe online service. Over on the competing America Online service, members could visit the Christianity Online site developed by Christianity Today, Inc. (now a stand-alone site available at www.christianitytoday.com).

The Gospel Communications Network (GCN) was the first major Christian site available to surfers who went straight to the Web without going through commercial services like CompuServe or AOL. Launched in 1995 by Gospel Films, Inc., GCN hosted numerous organizations like InterVarsity Christian Fellowship, International Bible Society, Youth for Christ, and The Navigators. Calvin College professor Quentin Schultze, an early evangelist for the online revolution and a consultant to GCN, wrote about the Web's allure for evangelicals in his book *Internet for Christians:*

> Not surprisingly, parachurch ministries have been among the leaders in getting on the new computer networks. For one thing, they often have the freedom to adopt new media without all of the denominational bureaucracy. For another, they frequently are looking for new ministry opportunities to expand their mission and to build their constituencies.

Other Christian "portals" like iBelieve.com, Lightsource.com, and Crosswalk.com struggled to survive.

By the late 1990s, many major evangelical churches and groups were spending hundreds of thousands of dollars a year developing and maintaining their own Internet sites, which they used to keep in touch with their donors, provide updated information about their activities and programs, and—thanks to a new Internal Revenue Service mandate—post their financial information.

Parachurch organizations beat churches to the Web. Some groups used it to evangelize. Harvest Crusades, the ministry of Greg Laurie, used its site to broadcast live ministry events and tell people how to know Christ, claiming that nearly 50 people a week accepted Christ through the site. Other groups experimented with online fund-raising. Campus Crusade for

Souls for Sale

By the 1990s, everyone from the Vatican to the sci-fi doomsday cult Heaven's Gate was using the Internet for spiritual purposes. In 2001 a University of Washington student tried to use the Web to sell his own soul.

The listing on online auction site eBay was short and simple: "20 yr-old Seattle boy's SOUL, hardly used." In a disclaimer, soul vendor Adam Burtle, a self-proclaimed atheist, added, "Please realize, I make no warranties as to the condition of the soul."

Bidding began at five cents before culminating in a sale for $400. But delivery proved to be a problem, and Burtle was suspended from the site.

Christ raised $2.5 million online in 2000, up from $750,000 in 1999.

By 1999 Christian companies were flocking to cyberspace, where they were setting up hundreds of Web sites to sell books, Bibles, music, and videos. Evangelical consumers could usually get better prices and a wider range of products through mainstream online "e-tailers" like amazon.com, but Christian online retailers promised not to offend evangelical sensibilities. One e-tailer said its wares were designed to "equip the saints for their walk with the Lord and to help them share their faith with others."

Bill Anderson, president of CBA, said, "Internet sales are increasing, but the Internet can't begin to duplicate brick-and-mortar stores' greatest advantage, which is live interaction with people." Still, online retailers were becoming an increasingly significant part of the business, and in 1999 CBA first allowed e-tailers to be CBA members.

Soon, increasing numbers of congregations were flocking to the Internet, according to a study funded by the Pew Charitable Trust. "Churches and synagogues may have concerns about pornography, privacy and rampant commercialism on the Internet, but that isn't stopping them from leaping online themselves," said a *USA Today* article about the study.

One pastor even claimed the Web was superior to his space-time church. "I love the church. The church is great. But in a church, my message only goes about a hundred feet. On the Net, it goes to a hundred countries."

Virtual Spirituality

Christian thinker Douglas Groothuis's book *The Soul in Cyberspace* sounded a warning about the implicit gnosticism of the Internet and "the danger of the technological replacement of the personal." As he says:

An artificial and impersonal means of communication replaces human interaction in ways that are not immediately obvious. In so doing, it debases the personal dimension God values so highly.

Throughout the 1990s, Groothuis and other Christian thinkers debated the impact of the computer revolution on the church: Could meaningful fellowship ever really happen in cyberspace chat rooms? And did the disembodied nature of online communication promote social cohesion or lead to social fragmentation?

Meanwhile, it didn't take a computer scientist to realize that the Internet had given millions of people access to a spiritual cornucopia, as many alternative religious movements set up sites in cyberspace. According to Jeff Zaleski, a former editor of *Parabola* magazine and author of *The Soul of Cyberspace*, Christianity may be the dominant faith in "meatspace," but in cyberspace, all faiths are equal:

> How will this ease of access to the universal store of sacred knowledge reshape the spiritual life of our species? Will religions keep their belief systems and their body of believers intact in a virtual world where it takes only a click of a mouse to jump from one temple, one mosque, one church to the next?

Questions like these promised to keep Christians surfing for answers well into the 21st century.

Resources

Erik Davis, *Techgnosis: Myth, Magic and Mysticism in the Age of Information* (2000).
Doug Groothuis, *The Soul in Cyberspace* (1997).
Jeff Zaleski, *The Soul of Cyberspace* (1998).
Brenda Brasher, *Give Me That Online Religion* (2001).

47. Revive Us Again: Renewal Movements Awaken the Church, 1994

It used to be that revival was the term a church used for a week-long series of evangelistic meetings featuring a preacher from out of town. During the 1990s, though, revival of a much different kind was something millions of evangelicals were discussing, praying for, and even fasting to bring about. The shelves at Christian bookstores weighed heavily with books on the subject. Churches and conference centers offered workshops on how to pray and prepare for God to awaken his people. And untold numbers of individuals, churches, parachurch organizations, and high-profile leaders were devoting regular prayer times to local and global spiritual renewal.

Of course, not everyone agreed about what revival was, and there were even heated debates about whether celebrated congregational revivals in places like Toronto and Pensacola, Florida, were real or "counterfeit" revivals. Still, as the millennium approached, unprecedented numbers of American evangelicals were asking God to renew and reinvigorate their churches.

Praying and Fasting for Renewal

Bill Bright, founder of Campus Crusade for Christ, says it was 1994 when he first became aware that God was preparing the American church for revival. God also impressed upon him the importance of prayer and fasting, inspiring Bright to send a letter on the subject to a large list of U.S. church leaders. More than 600 accepted his invitation to Orlando for his first three-day Fasting and Prayer conference, which would become a growing annual event. Fasting and Prayer '99 attracted more than 3,000 people from 40 countries to Houston's Astroarena, and another 2 million participated via satellite, radio, and the Internet.

"God blesses or judges countries and cultures according to the obedience or disobedience of His children," says Bright, whose 1995 book, *The*

Coming Revival, was an urgent plea for believers to get serious about God's desire to stir his followers. "There has never been a greater need in all of history for Christians to fast, pray, repent, and seek the face of God. We're asking God to send revival to our nation and the world to enable us to help fulfill the Great Commission."

In October 1997 hundreds of thousands of men gathered in Washington, D.C., for Stand in the Gap: A Sacred Assembly of Men, a one-time event organized by Promise Keepers. PK founder Bill McCartney said the goal of the event was "to gather a diverse multitude of men to confess personal and collective sin," but the PK executive who organized the event said there was a deeper purpose to the national rally. "In both the Old Testament and the New Testament, we see cycles of revival," said Dale Schlafer, who was PK's vice president for revival and spiritual awakening. "We're in a pre-revival state with little pockets springing up, but it's not full-blown revival yet. If we would confess our sin and repent, perhaps God would ignite the church to be what He wants it to be."

By 1999 thousands of evangelical churches were joining the growing prayer and fasting movement. "Called by My Name," an outreach of the Evangelism and Home Mission Association (EHMA) of the National Association of Evangelicals, was designed to encourage NAE-member churches to pray and fast from September 21 to October 31, 1999. The EHMA produced sermon resources, drama sketches, prayer calendars, posters, and other products to help churches practice an ancient spiritual discipline. "This is an opportunity for Christians to lead the way in personal growth, church renewal, national revival and social transformation," said Marlin Mull, who organized the campaign.

Churches on Fire

Revival is an antidote to the spiritual cooling that has accompanied moves of God for the past 20 centuries. It didn't take long for the Pentecostal fires described in the book of Acts to cool, leading Jesus to chastise seven churches in the book of Revelation, specifically telling the church of Ephesus, "You have left your first love." Christian congregations have been seeking the fires of revival and renewal ever since.

American revivalism began with the Great Awakening of 1725 to 1760, which was initiated by the preaching of George Whitefield. Some dignified Easterners disliked the revival's unbridled emotionalism and populist appeal, but things only got wilder during the Second Great Awakening, which swept through America between the 1780s and the 1820s. At backwoods camp meetings, people shook, jerked, fell to the ground, and barked like dogs, claiming they were responding to the touch of a loving God.

Ten Characteristics of Revival

The following elements have been present in many of history's major revivals:

1. Saints are revived as revival transforms once-lethargic laypeople into zealous servants of God.

2. Sinners are saved as classic sinners such as prostitutes and drunks join society's beautiful people at the altar to confess their evil ways and seek God's forgiveness.

3. Sermons hit home. Revival sermons shy away from complex theology to focus the basic gospel message of sin and salvation in all its staggering simplicity, often upping the ante with descriptive pictures of the sufferings of hell.

4. Music moves the masses. From the days of the Wesley brothers through Dwight L. Moody's collaboration with song leader Ira Sankey, musicians have augmented the impact of revival sermons by stirring people's emotions and helping them sing their praises to God.

5. Churches work together. When revival hits, workers seize the opportunity without worrying about preserving strict denominational purity.

6. People do strange things. Evangelical etiquette usually dictates that believers keep a lid on their emotions, but during revival, people overcome with a sense of the closeness of God lose control and often begin weeping, wailing, falling, jerking, screaming "Hallelujah," or experiencing an outpouring of spiritual gifts.

7. Believers battle sin. Billy Sunday attacked demon rum. Charles Finney went after Christians who smoked. Sexual sins have always been seen as a Satanic stronghold, including the contemporary temptation of online pornography.

8. Society is influenced. Revived believers have founded schools, universities, and Bible colleges; fought evils like slavery and child labor; and campaigned to elect godly leaders to office. Revival may begin as an individual awakening, but it impacts culture beyond the doors of the church.

9. Missions and evangelism flourish. Revival-transformed William Booth went on to found the Salvation Army, now one of the world's largest Christian organizations. Likewise, revival sparked many of the world's biggest and best-known missionary groups, evangelism efforts, parachurch organizations, and Christian denominations.

10. Controversy causes clashes. Brownsville isn't the first revival to stir up arguments. Christians look back with dewy-eyed nostalgia at the First Great Awakening, but at the time, minister Charles Chauncy ascribed the whole affair to mental illness. Revival has always been a divisive force.

—Adapted from *Revival in Brownsville*

Charles Finney deemed such manifestations "spurious" and developed a series of "New Measures" designed to help streamline the process of revival. His efforts to rationalize revival may have been designed to domesticate revival, but messy and chaotic outbreaks of spiritual renewal continue to be a regular feature of the American religious scene.

On Father's Day 1995, members of the Brownsville Assembly of God in Pensacola, Florida, first experienced the manifestations of something they would call the Brownsville Revival. Rick Bragg, an award-winning *New York Times* writer, said, "What started as a typical, temporary revival . . . has snowballed into what is apparently the largest and longest-running Pentecostal revival in America in almost a century."

Over the next few years, nearly 3 million people from around the world would visit Brownsville, and a quarter million would claim that God had met them there in powerful and unusual ways. Many of those who visited Brownsville shook, jerked, and fell to the ground, including many pastors. Soon, revival fire was spreading through other Assemblies congregations, ending a stagnant period for the 2.5-million-member denomination. "This is really a sovereign move of God, and the impact has been powerful," said Thomas Trask, the denomination's general superintendent.

But not everybody was so sure. In April 1997, Hank Hanegraaff of the cult-watching Christian Research Institute appeared on CNN's *Larry King Live* to discuss the recent suicides of 39 members of the Heaven's Gate UFO cult. According to Hanegraaff, author of the best-selling 1997 book *Counterfeit Revival,* cultish practices like "psychosocial manipulation" and "altered states of consciousness" weren't the sole property of non-Christian cults but could be found in Christian churches like the Brownsville Assembly of God.

Disagreements about revival have been a recurring feature of American religious life for nearly three centuries, and their continuation today indicates that the unity Christians have been praying and fasting for has yet to arrive.

What remains unclear is whether the movements of the 1990s represented a true revival or merely the latest version of something historian Joel Carpenter calls "a revival of revivalism."

Resources

Bill Bright, *The Coming Revival* (1995).
Joel Carpenter, "Will Revival Come?" Chapter 6 in *Revive Us Again* (1997).
Steve Rabey, *Revival in Brownsville: Pensacola, Pentecostalism, and the Power of American Revivalism* (1998).
Christine J. Gardner, "Hungry for God," *Christianity Today* (April 5, 1999).

48. From Boomers to Busters: Generation X and Postmodern Ministry, 1996

The stately, castlelike building at The Navigators' Glen Eyrie conference center in Colorado Springs had stood for more than a century, but when a high-decibel praise band and around 200 people involved in "Ministering to Generation X" descended on the facility in March 1996, the windows were quaking.

These young leaders were involved in evangelizing and discipling "baby busters," a group that fiction writer Douglas Coupland, who coined the term Generation X, described as "the first generation raised without religion." Those trying to minister to this post-baby-boom, post-Christian, and sometimes post-hope generation are calling for a reappraisal of Christian mission every bit as radical as that demanded by members of the Jesus movement a quarter century earlier.

"For many of the nearly 40 million young people between the ages of 18 and 34, preachers are like used-car salesmen, or politicians," said Ken Baugh, the director of Frontline, a ministry to baby busters at McLean Bible Church in McLean, Virginia.

Author George Barna also spoke at the gathering, which was convened by Dallas-based Leadership Network, and was the first major national meeting of some of this generation's most influential and passionate emerging evangelical leaders. Barna and others discussed the power of stories to communicate with baby busters and other postmodern listeners.

"This is our first post-modern, post-Christian generation," said Barna. "They've been immersed in the philosophy of existentialism, and the view that there's no objective reality. They're very non-linear, very comfortable with contradictions and inclined to view all religions as equally valid. So the nice thing about telling stories is that no one can say your story isn't true."

Kevin Ford, an evangelism consultant (and nephew of Billy Graham) agreed. "Find the stories behind the [biblical] passages," he told the group.

"Don't destroy a good narrative by breaking it up with points. Just tell a story. And don't explain it. That's condescending."

New Wineskins

With his short-cropped hair, goatee-style beard, and Sunday-NOT-go-to-meetin' wardrobe of sneakers, baggy jeans, and a plain cotton shirt, 24-year-old Chris Seay looked more like the lead singer in an alternative rock band than one of the most successful new pastors in Texas, but that's just fine for the young people attending University Baptist Church in Waco, Texas, one of the hundreds of new Gen-X congregations launched by an emerging generation of Christian leaders.

Seay is a third-generation Baptist minister who says the thought of being a pastor once looked "pretty revolting" but who senses a calling to take the gospel to members of his generation.

"They're open to the God thing," says Seay (pronounced "see"), "but they're not into the church thing."

Nor are they into the typical hymn-and-sermon thing, as one could tell from a visit to Waco's downtown Hippodrome Theater, where the church meets. Instead of hymns or even laid-back praise choruses, a seven-piece band belts out aggressive Christian rock while young congregants sing and sway. Unable to find relevant songs in the contemporary Christian praise repertoire, the band writes its own, like "There's No Chain," which captures the congregation's hunger for authentic spirituality in a world of processed foods, spin-controlled politicians, and prepackaged religion:

> There's no heart too wounded
> No heart so broken that he can't mend
> No life so hopeless
> No life so empty
> Jesus can't fill.

After the musicians lay down their instruments and take their seats, Seay strides to a simple stool in the middle of the pulpit-free stage, sits down, props his feet on a nearby speaker, takes a drink from a bottle of Snapple, and launches into a meandering monologue about the R-rated Richard Gere movie *Primal Fear*.

Before long, Seay has used the movie's plot of dishonesty and intrigue to bring his audience around to a Socratic inquiry on the nature of truth: whether it can be known, how it can be understood, and where it can be found. "We can spout Sunday school answers," he says, "but when it comes to reality, it doesn't really flesh out in our lives."

Delivering his talk in a conversational, self-deprecating style, Seay tells his congregation not to base their lives on pop culture icons like talk show

---

Jesus and the New Generation

Jesus was in his early thirties when he began his public work; he had no career path and no place he could call home. His greatest battles were against the dogmas of his day, and he showed little faith in institutions and rules and regulations. Rather, his message was of a Father full of grace, and the context of his work was his personal relationships. He built community, first with his small group of 12 and then across class, gender, racial, and lifestyle lines. He liked a good party, even turning water into wine to keep one from ending prematurely. He spoke against injustice and did not have the stomach for inauthentic people. He thought globally but acted locally.

As we confront the growing irrelevance of the church among many Xers, we must wrestle with the idea that Jesus would have felt very much at home with the MTV generation.

— Andres Tapia, "Reaching the First Post-Christian
Generation," *Christianity Today,* September 12, 1994.

---

host Oprah Winfrey, fitness guru Susan Powter, or motivational speaker Tony Robbins, but to trust "this really cool gift from God, the Word of God."

It's an approach that connects with the church's youthful members. "When he gives his messages, it's like he's talking right to you," says Brandy, a marketing major at nearby Baylor University, who attended church only infrequently before coming to University Baptist. "He's the same age as us, he has the same concerns as us, and he has the same hurts as us."

Living and Learning

In 1999 Seay left University Baptist in the care of an associate and set off for Houston to start a new Gen-X church called Ecclesia. Although he was still revising his ecclesiology, he was sure of one thing: he was doing everything he could to distance his congregation from the "seeker-sensitive" megachurch model pioneered by baby-boomers like Bill Hybels at Willow Creek Community Church near Chicago and Rick Warren at Saddleback Valley Community Church in Orange County, California. Seay thinks the boomer model works fine with older folks but repels members of his generation. "When you coordinate the color of your shirts with the color of your lights, people don't see that as authentic," says Seay.

Authenticity was just one of the subjects Gen-X leaders were debating at the end of the decade, others being worship, creativity, religious experience, ecumenism, and pluralism. Many of the debates were happening online, while others were taking place in the pages of magazines like *re:generation quarterly, FaithWorks, Echo,* and *Beyond.*

While many of the debaters were members of Generation X, the discussion was being joined by increasing numbers of their elders, many of whom were coming to believe that postmodernism might be bringing the church a new reformation in ministry and methods—a reformation that looked to both the past and the future for its inspiration.

Resources

Tom Beaudoin, *Virtual Faith: The Irreverent Spiritual Quest of Generation X* (1998).

Jimmy Long, *Generating Hope: A Strategy for Reaching the Postmodern Generation* (1997).

Douglas Coupland, *Life after God* (1994).

Steve Rabey, *In Search of Authentic Faith: How Emerging Generations are Transforming the Church* (2000).

49. Feeling Their Pain:
Waking Up to the Worldwide
Persecution of Christians, 1996

Graham Staines was a dedicated missionary. The 58-year-old had spent more than 30 years of his life working in the East Indian state of Orissa for the Brisbane, Australia-based Evangelical Missionary Society. He was a familiar face in Orissa, and he was generally well liked, both by local Christians and members of the Hindu majority.

So it came as a shock to locals when a mob of up to 100 Hindu militants brutally killed Staines and his two sons, aged ten and six, in January 1999.

As he had done for years, Staines attended an annual meeting of a local Christian church. After the meeting was over, the father and his two sons slept in their van before starting the long drive home the next morning. During the night, a mob surrounded the van and set it on fire. Local villagers who came upon the scene said they heard men in the mob shouting, "Long live Hunuman," who is a Hindu monkey god revered by many in the area.

Immediately, Indian officials condemned the atrocity and arrested 47 people suspected of participating in the killing, many of them affiliated with a Hindu nationalist group that has been increasing its attacks on Indian Christians in recent years.

The killing of Graham Staines received widespread media coverage and gave greater visibility to the worldwide persecution of Christians, a tragedy that a U.S. State Department report said was routine in more than 70 countries around the world. During the 1990s, evangelicals were among those who began devoting more time, prayer, and attention to this issue.

A Distant Tragedy

Roman emperor Nero persecuted Christians in the decades after Christ's death, and believers have faced various forms of harassment ever since. The reasons for persecution have been as varied as its methods and instigators.

Nero considered it politically expedient to blame Christians for the burning of Rome. In the 20th century, it has been totalitarian states and Islamic regimes that have been at the forefront of efforts to curtail the activities and freedoms of believers.

The Voice of the Martyrs, an organization based in Bartlesville, Oklahoma, has been sounding the alarm about the plight of the persecuted since 1967, but it wasn't until the mid-1990s that the issue began to appear on the radar screens of significant numbers of American evangelicals.

In the fall of 1996, nearly 5,000 U.S. churches observed the first annual International Day of Prayer for the Persecuted Church. The following year, 50,000 churches participated. In 1998, reports claimed more than 150,000 churches in 130 countries set aside the same Sunday to pray for their brothers and sisters facing pressure around the world.

About the same time, persecution was becoming an increasingly important political issue. According to journalist Mark O'Keefe of the Portland *Oregonian,* it was a Jew who helped rouse evangelicals to fighting persecution through political means. Michael Horowitz, an attorney and former Reagan administration official, became aware of the issue in 1994 and wrote letters to more than 100 evangelical missions groups, saying he was "pained and puzzled" about their failure to confront the problem. In 1996 Horowitz wrote "A Statement of Conscience," a document that was adopted by the National Association of Evangelicals and other groups. The statement helped inspire American believers to pressure the U.S. government into action.

On October 27, 1998, President Bill Clinton signed into law the "International Religious Freedom Act of 1998," which spelled out a number of economic and political measures the U.S. could initiate against countries that restricted the religious freedom of their citizens. The following

Robert Seiple, shown here when he was president of World Vision, with survivors of the 1993 earthquake that devastated Killari, India. In March 1999 Seiple was named Special Representative of the Secretary of State for International Religious Freedom by President Clinton.

March, Clinton named Robert Seiple, formerly president of World Vision, to the impressive-sounding position of Special Representative of the Secretary of State for International Religious Freedom. But there are serious doubts about whether America has the political will to enforce the act, which might hurt American businesses. There are even deeper questions about how much politics alone can achieve. For example, could the imposition of economic sanctions on a country that allows Christians to be persecuted cause retaliation against believers and generate even more persecution?

Suffering for the Faith

Conservative Christian activists have frequently used the term *persecution* to describe the restrictions endured by Christians in the U.S. who are unable to pray publicly in schools, or who are the victims of poor coverage in the mainstream news and entertainment media. During the 1990s, though, increasing numbers of American evangelicals have come to see that the inconveniences they face pale in comparison to the ordeals believers in other countries endure, such as harassment, barriers to employment or schooling, interrogation, abduction, rape, mutilation, forced conversion, forced labor, forced resettlement, enslavement, murder, and execution.

Journalist Mark O'Keefe spent nine months of 1998 visiting five countries that are the most notorious for persecuting Christians and other religious minorities. In the Islamic Republic of Pakistan, Rev. Noor Alam was killed and the simple brick church he was building was destroyed, while other Christians were arrested and charged with blasphemy against Islam. In Burma, combatants in a decades-old civil war use religion as a weapon. In Sudan, believers endure famine and an Islamic holy war. In Egypt, where memories of medieval Crusades remain potent, Christians who make their faith public are tortured and killed. And in China, where religion was once totally banned, the government now exercises control over many congregations. Meanwhile, members of an underground evangelical church movement face harassment and horrors on a daily basis.

In years past, evangelicals believed their sole duty to the rest of the world was to evangelize it, and missionary groups and cooperative

Helping the Helpless

The following groups specialize in helping Christian martyrs:
— Christian Solidarity International (202/785-5266).
— Freedom House (202/295-5101).
— Institute on Religion and Democracy (202/986-1440).
— International Christian Concern (301/989-1708).
— Open Doors (714/531-6000).
— Voice of the Martyrs (918/337-8015).

ventures like The CoMission have done an admirable job of proclaiming the gospel around the globe. During the 1990s, though, evangelicals' increasing awareness of the persecution suffered by their brothers and sisters around the world has prompted a greater sense of Christian solidarity, sending many to their knees in prayer and inspiring others to intercede with governments around the world to let their brothers and sisters worship God in freedom.

Resources

Kim A. Lawton, "The Suffering Church," *Christianity Today,* July 15, 1996.

Mark O'Keefe, "Christians Under Siege," The (Portland) *Oregonian* (October 25–29, 1998, available online at: www.oregonlive.com/series/christians/html).

Paul Marshall, *Their Blood Cries Out: The Worldwide Tragedy of Christians Persecuted for Their Faith* (1997).

The New Encyclopedia of Christian Martyrs (2001).

50. Apocalypse Now:
Facts, Fears, and Y2K, 2000

Few people heeded computer expert Peter de Jager's 1993 article for *Computerworld* magazine entitled "Doomsday 2000." The article was one of the first to warn people about a persistent software problem that, depending on who you talked to, would either cause minor inconveniences or hasten the end of the world. By 1998, people were paying attention, as the *New York Times* reported:

> For many . . . people the Y2K problem plays on a sense of unease that society is growing dependent on a lattice of technology that is now so far-reaching, interconnected and complex that no one completely understands it, not even the priesthood that writes its digital code.

Missing Information

Long, long ago during the computer Dark Ages (that would be the 1960s and 1970s), programmers working on primitive machines with little internal memory decided to conserve precious disk space by shortening dates like 1972 to "72." That may have worked fine back then, but as de Jager pointed out, computers wouldn't be able to distinguish between the years 2000 and 1900.

After America's government and corporate leaders finally realized how many problems the Y2K glitch could cause, they spent an estimated $100 billion on repairs, or about $365 for each man, woman, and child in the country. "It's very hard to tell how bad the situation will be," wrote a concerned Microsoft executive in *Fortune* magazine.

Soon, Y2K began appearing on advertisements for everything from automobiles to coffeemakers, all guaranteed to keep running after January 1. "Don't Let Y2K leave You Out in the Cold!" read one ad for wood stoves. Even candymakers got on board. One campaign proclaimed: "M&M's are the candy of the new millennium."

End-Times Scenarios

While America's government and businesses sought to battle the Y2K bug, in conservative evangelical circles, fears about Y2K were combined with centuries-old traditions of world-weariness and biblical prophecies about end times and the return of Christ. The result was pockets of apocalyptic anxiety that some doomsayers were more than happy to inflame and exploit.

Both Hal Lindsey and Jack Van Impe, who have made surprisingly successful careers out of promoting a never-ending, ever-changing stream of errant predictions and end-times scenarios, created videos about the Y2K crisis. Lindsey's, called *Facing Millennial Midnight: The Y2K Crisis Confronting America and the World,* promised to provide details about the unfolding crisis. Jerry Falwell's pitch was even more urgent. "Y2K may be God's instrument to shake this nation," he said in his $28 video, *A Christian's Guide to the Millennium Bug.* "He may be preparing to confound our language, to jam our communications, scatter our efforts, and judge us for our sin and rebellion against his lordship," warned Falwell, who said his own preparations included stocking up on food, gasoline, and ammunition. A column on the Christian Coalition's Web site predicted widespread "looting, robbery, [and] gang warfare," and suggested President Bill Clinton might use the crisis to become America's "first dictator," and urged everyone to gather food, water, and bullets.

Christian publishers churned out dozens of ominous-sounding titles like Grant Jeffrey's *The Millennium Meltdown*; Steve Farrar's *Spiritual Survival*

Hanegraaff Assails Y2K Conspiracy Theories

Hank Hanegraaff of the Christian Research Institute was one of the most outspoken critics of evangelicals' Y2K hysteria. In his 1999 book, *The Millennium Bug Debugged,* he explained his concerns:

"It became abundantly clear that I needed to launch a primary source research project [on Y2K]. I proceeded, fully aware that I would pay a significant personal price for speaking out against the selling and sensationalism surrounding this issue . . . . It is my firm conviction, however, that the ministry is not a place to strive for popularity or political correctness . . . people are being significantly frightened by what they are hearing from Christian leaders regarding Y2K. I am deeply grieved over the spiritual, emotional, and financial havoc that so many have already suffered.

" . . . unsubstantiated stories circulated by spiritual leaders inevitably give Christianity a black eye. It is becoming all too common for those who take the sacred name of Christ upon their lips to spread stories that have little basis in fact."

During the Y2K Crisis; and Donald McAlvany's *The Y2K Tidal Wave: Year 2000 Economic Survival*. Michael Hyatt, vice president of Thomas Nelson Publishers, wrote circles around the competition, authoring three separate books: the best-selling *The Millennium Bug: How to Survive the Coming Chaos*; *The Y2K Personal Survival Guide*; and the fictional *Y2K: The Day the World Shut Down*, which provided an imaginative descriptive of how things would unwind. Meanwhile, Shaunti Feldhahn, founder of a group called The Joseph Project 2000, said believers were overreacting, and wrote *Y2K The Millennium Bug: A Balanced Christian Approach*.

But Gary North, a reconstructionist theologian and eternal pessimist who had been predicting the imminent destruction of the world for decades, continued to sow hysteria. He described the impending cataclysm in a newsletter topped with the bold headline "The Day the World Shuts Down":

This visually oriented book serves as a popular guide to the issues, people, and movements relevant to the coming millennium. The authors combine church history, theology, and cultural analysis to place our contemporary setting in both biblical and historical perspective. Readers will be informed and assured by this helpful guide's balanced and user-friendly contents. This book's visual appeal is enhanced by plentiful sidebars and over 75 illustrations.

In a nutshell, the Y2K problem is the trigger that is about to cause a massive, date-sensitive worldwide computer crash—a crash of such gargantuan proportions that it will literally bring down governments. It may even bring down ours.

Things were so bad, said North, that concerned Christians should flee their homes, rush to the nearest bank, withdraw $299, and send it off to North for his "full 6-part Y2K Preparation, Protection and Survival Kit."

A Topeka, Kansas, group called The Prophecy Club offered videos and emergency dehydrated food. In an ad published in the February issue of *Charisma* magazine, the group offered the *Y2K Chaos* video (which "briefly explains the Y2K problem, and why it WON'T be corrected in time") and three different food packages. The top-of-the-line Plan A promised "Food for 4 people for 1 year" for $4,100. Other suppliers hawked everything from human waste disposal systems, tooth extraction videotapes, an amazingly overpriced gold coin (the $20 coin was offered for $599), and magazines (*American Survival Guide* boasted it had a circulation of 60,000, and *Preparedness Journal* even sponsored a series of Preparedness Expos.)

Not everyone was willing to go that far, but a July 1999 Associated Press article reported that one-third of Americans told pollsters they were going to stock up on essentials like food and water, and one-quarter planned on taking extra money out of the bank. The news brought a response from Federal Reserve Chairman Alan Greenspan, who predicted that fear-induced stockpiling would hurt the American economy more than the Y2K glitch itself.

A Lasting Legacy

The world didn't end as some had predicted it would. Even before 1999 became 2000, some Christian thinkers were arguing that the more extreme predictions about Y2K had been wildly off course.

As Richard V. Pierard, one of the coauthors of a book on millennium predictions, told *Christianity Today:* "I see this as just a bunch of nonsense and hysteria to sell books, get money, and alarm people."

The Assemblies of God exhorted its members to "fear not," saying, "Needless fear and alarmist tactics over the Y2K issue and the approaching turn of the millennium are directly in conflict with the teaching of our Lord."

The same could be said about many of the other fears and phobias that afflicted evangelicals during the 20th century, some of which left them unable to reach out to the world with the incarnational and redemptive love Jesus had demonstrated 2KY before.

Resources

Mark A. Kellner, "Y2K: A Secular Apocalypse?," *Christianity Today* (January 11, 1999).

Robert G. Clouse, Robert N. Hosack, and Richard V. Pierard, *The New Millennium Manual: A Once and Future Guide* (1999).

Acknowledgments

There are a few people we would like to thank, for without them, this book never would have happened.

Greg Johnson of the Alive Communications Literary Agency brought this project our way and made it happen. Len Goss saw the light and persuaded Broadman & Holman to publish it.

Our wives, family members, and friends put up with our lengthy absences, both physical and mental; looked the other way while we turned our once-comfortable homes into crowded research libraries; forgave our numerous references to arcane historical topics; and didn't institutionalize us when we were glassy-eyed and noncommunicative.

Larry Eskeridge of the Institute for the Study of American Evangelicals at Wheaton College was a godsend. When we were struggling to complete our list of the 50 events we would include in this book, he provided us with careful and thoughtful critiques without once referring to us as dolts or nincompoops. He also thoroughly read and corrected our draft manuscript, helping us avoid many potential errors of fact and interpretation that we were too blind to see.

Bruce Shelley of Denver Seminary also gave us helpful input on our early topic lists. Both Dr. Shelley and Tim Weber were Steve's church history professors at Denver Seminary, so they're at least partly responsible for this book.

We would also like to express our sincere appreciation to the many scholars whose important work on the topics covered in this book made our task manageable. We have attempted to cite the works that we found most helpful in the "Resource" sections that conclude each chapter.

Four particular historians come immediately to mind: George Marsden, Mark Noll, Joel Carpenter, and William Martin. It is our hope that people who have read and enjoyed our overview of the last century will be encouraged to sink their teeth into some of the many more substantial works that treat these subjects in the greater detail they deserve. If so, we can heartily recommend Marsden's *Reforming Fundamentalism: Fuller Seminary and the New Evangelicalism* (Eerdmans, 1995), Noll's *A History of Christianity in the United States and Canada* (Eerdmans, 1992), Carpenter's *Revive Us Again* (Oxford, 1997), and Martin's *With God on Our Side: The Rise of the Religious Right in America* (Broadway, 1996), for starters.

Two other sources were our constant companions during all stages of this project: IVP's *Dictionary of Christianity in America* (1990) and *Christianity Today*'s Web site (www.christianityonline.com).

Index